ANARCHY AND AUTHORITY

ANGELA BYRNE

PRAISE FOR *ANARCHY AND AUTHORITY*

'A kaleidoscope of life stories told by a fine historian, Anarchy and Authority vividly illuminates Irish encounters with Russia from the time of Peter the Great through the revolutionary upheavals of the early twentieth century. An absorbing read.' – Breandán Mac Suibhne

'Anarchy and Authority draws on a wealth of research to uncover the incredible stories of Irish women and men in Romanov Russia. Written with skill and sensitivity, this is an important and timely book.' – Dr Liam Chambers

'a fascinating account of a colourful cast of Irish men and women who travelled around or settled in the Russian Empire during a period of profound change and upheaval. Through a cast of extraordinary characters – many of them intrepid Irish women seeking new lives outside the strictures of 18th and 19th century life in their homeland – the book underlines how Irish identity has never been one-dimensional but is constantly in a state of redefinition. [...] This meticulously researched book paints an illuminating and entertaining picture of an often overlooked branch of the Irish Diaspora. It is a timely reminder that the Irish business of forging links and finding cultural commonalities in far-flung places has long been how this small nation makes its way in the world.' – Lise Hand

'this book offers a much-needed insight into the relations, cultural and personal interactions, and perceptions between the geo-political behemoth that was and is Russia and a small nation and its individual people.' – Dr Paul Huddie

'The history of the Irish connections with Russia is not an oversubscribed field of study and this is a very welcome addition to the existing literature, such as it is. It offers an intriguing insight into a pattern of connection, developed over two centuries. It offers us an opportunity not only to reconsider Russia during this period and also to re-evaluate how Irish people saw themselves, Ireland and the wider world. As cutting edge research goes, this new volume on Irish-Russian connections represents the tip of the spear.' – Dr David Murphy

Anarchy and Authority

Irish Encounters with Romanov Russia

Angela Byrne

THE LILLIPUT PRESS
DUBLIN

First published 2024 by
THE LILLIPUT PRESS

62–63 Sitric Road,
Arbour Hill,
Dublin 7,
Ireland
www.lilliputpress.ie

Copyright © Angela Byrne, 2024

10 9 8 7 6 5 4 3 2 1

All rights reserved. No part of this publication may be reproduced in any form or by any means without the prior permission of the publisher.

A CIP record for this title is available from The British Library.

Paperback ISBN 978 1 84351 893 8

eBook ISBN 978 1 84351 907 2

The Lilliput Press gratefully acknowledges the financial support of the Arts Council/An Chomhairle Ealaíon

Set in 12pt on 16pt Adobe Jenson Pro by Compuscript
Index by Jane Rogers
Printed and bound in Sweden by ScandBook

For Donnchadh

Fool, nothing is impossible in Russia but reform.

Oscar Wilde, *Vera; or, The Nihilists* (1902).

There are two phases of enjoyment in journeying through an unknown country – the eager phase of wondering interest in every detail, and the relaxed phase when one feels no longer an observer of the exotic, but a participator in the rhythm of daily life.

Dervla Murphy, *In Ethiopia with a Mule* (1968).

CONTENTS

Preface	xi
Acknowledgments	xiv
List of Maps and Illustrations	xvi
Abbreviations	xvii
Note on Terminology and Usage	xix

INTRODUCTION	xxi

I MERCENARIES AND AMBASSADORS: IRISH CAREERS IN EIGHTEENTH-CENTURY RUSSIA	1
1. Early Contacts: Irish Soldiers in Russian Service	4
2. Anthony O'Hara's Constructed Irishness	13
3. John O'Rourke, International Mercenary	18
4. Irish-Born Diplomats in Eighteenth-Century Russia	22

II TO RUSSIA WITH LOVE	35
5. The Mysterious Identities of Jenny O'Reilly or Evgeniya Ivanovna Vyazemskaya	39
6. The Wilmot Sisters and Princess Dashkova: Friendship across Generations	46
7. A View from Downstairs: Eleanor Cavanagh, a Lady's Maid in Russia	56

III JAUNTS TO INTER-WAR RUSSIA	62
8. An Irish Gentleman Experiences Russian Poverty	66
9. Arthur and Thomas MacMurrough Kavanagh's Eastern Expedition	72
10. Blight and Cholera in Tipperary and St Petersburg	83
11. Imperial Prison Systems and the Murder of Lord Mayo	89

Contents

IV ADVENTURERS AND INNOVATORS AFTER CRIMEA	97
12. A 'Chilling Effect': Selina Bunbury Reports on Russia after Crimea	101
13. James Bryce, the Mountaineering Viscount	111
14. Scientists and Innovators	119
15. Adventures by Land, Sea and Rail	128

V PRELUDE TO REVOLUTION	142
16. A Fright with the Bear: Lady Dufferin and the Assassination of Alexander II	147
17. 'Our Englishwoman': Ethel Lilian Boole Voynich's Underground Activism	155
18. An Occupation without Borders: Margaretta Eagar, Nanny to OTMA	168
19. Irish Nationalists and Russian Imperialism	177

| CONCLUSIONS: IMAGINING RUSSIA, IMAGINING IRELAND, FROM PETER THE GREAT TO NICHOLAS II | 187 |

Appendix: Chronology of Accounts of Romanov Russia by Irish Authors	194
Notes	199
Index	235

Preface

When I was eight years old, my favourite television programme – RTÉ's *The Den* – recorded a special episode in Moscow. It showed exactly the Russia one might have expected to see in a children's programme in 1991 – snow, fur hats, Red Square with St Basil's and the Lenin Mausoleum, accordion-playing buskers. But I was enchanted, and my fascination with Russia's complex history and rich cultural heritage was born. The presenters poked fun at popular stereotypes, joking about the coldness of the temperature and planning to tell Irish audiences that they were the first Western Europeans to ever go inside the walls of the Moscow Kremlin. They must have known, too, that Irish viewers would have been familiar with news reports showing people queuing for food in the new, post-Soviet Russia. But looking back today on a recording of the episode, I suspect the Muscovites caught on camera were not impressed by the Irish presenters' antics.

I had the chance to start studying the Russian language as a teenager, when my family hosted Belarusian children through the Chernobyl Children's Project. One of the first of these children to stay with us was extremely confident and clever for her seven years and was delighted to teach me the Russian alphabet and some basic phrases. I later continued my studies through night classes in Trinity College Dublin and seasonal courses at Moscow State University.

Preface

I visited Russia and Belarus for the first time in 2004. The day my bus from Helsinki rolled into St Petersburg, news of the Beslan school siege was breaking. Those terrible events overshadowed my ten days in western Russia. My first sight of Red Square was from behind a security cordon manned by armed military personnel. I have returned to Russia many times since then, travelling the length and breadth of the west of the country, from St Petersburg to Elbrus near the Georgian border. One of the highlights of my long student career was the semester I spent at Voronezh State University, where I made lifelong friends.

This project was born in 2003, when I had just started work as a researcher in the Royal Irish Academy. In a casual conversation during my first week there, the librarian told me about one of her favourite items in the collection – the Wilmot papers, letters and diaries by Cork sisters who lived in Russia during the Napoleonic Wars. I had been forming ideas for a postgraduate research project on women's travel writing, and I still remember the first day I began reading the sisters' 200-year-old notebooks and letter books. I was captured by Martha's and Katherine's personalities – respectively empathetic and irreverent – and as I immersed myself in their lives and experiences, they became as friends to me. But I could not stop with the Wilmots, and over time the project expanded to cover all Irish residents, travellers and migrants to Russia during the two long centuries from the reign of Peter the Great until the end of Romanov rule. I could never have foreseen in summer 2003, when the seeds of this book were sown, the variety of personalities, stories and connections that would emerge.

As I write, Russia's brutal and illegal invasion of Ukraine continues. It is impossible not to view these terrible events in the light of the Russian state's long history of aggressive expansionism, annexation of neighbouring territories and subjugation of the peoples living there. The interactions studied in this book almost entirely took place against the backdrop of war, imperial expansion, violence and oppression: the Great Northern War of 1700–21, Napoleonic Wars, Crimean War, Russo-Japanese War, World War I and wars with Turkey and Persia; Russia's serial attacks on

Preface

and annexations of Finland, Ukraine, Poland, Georgia and other nations of the Caucasus and Central Asia; the persecution of the Bashkirs and Circassians; and state-sanctioned anti-Semitism and pogroms. That is to say nothing of the violence inherent in everyday life for serfs, servants, religious minorities and women. It is my hope that this study of Irish encounters with the Russian Empire will contribute to understandings of how people related to one another in the past through such questions as how international diplomatic, commercial and scientific relationships were formed, maintained and conducted; and how Irish observers bore witness to the horrors of serfdom, Russia's many wars against the peoples forcibly drawn over the centuries into its vast empire, and the oppression of dissenting voices through such means as exile, imprisonment without trial and forced labour in Siberia. It is also vital to acknowledge that Irish people were implicated in Russian imperial aggression through their service in the Russian army and navy, with some rising to the highest levels of the imperial administration and benefiting from their positions for generations. Some Irish people had proximity to political, military, social and economic power in Imperial Russia, while Irish activists participated in international radical networks, bearing witness to abuses of power.

Inishowen, December 2023

Acknowledgments

I have run up many debts in the two decades since I first started this project. I owe special thanks to Michael Lavelle, Susan Grant, Georgina Laragy, David Murphy and Jessica Traynor. Ulster University has provided invaluable access to resources by granting me honorary research associate status since 2018; I am particularly grateful to Prof. Ian Thatcher for his ongoing support.

Part of this book had its first iteration as my PhD thesis, focusing on the period 1690–1815, and under the supervision of Dr David Lederer at NUI Maynooth. Professor Vincent Comerford and the History Department provided practical assistance and mentorship in those early stages of the research. I was the grateful recipient of a National University of Ireland Travelling Studentship in 2006–9. During research trips to Russia, I received generous hospitality and assistance from Irish Embassy staff in Moscow, particularly former ambassador His Excellency Justin Harman, and Elizabeth Keogh and Niall Keogh. The faculty and students of the Irish Centre at Voronezh State University made me welcome for a semester in 2006. Research on Jenny O'Reilly/Evgeniya Ivanovna Vyazemskaya was completed during a short residency at the All-Russia State Library for Foreign Literatures in 2013.

Thanks to the archivists, librarians and staff at the following repositories: Bodleian Library, Oxford; Boole Library, Cork; British Library; Historical Library of the Religious Society of Friends in Ireland; National Archives

Acknowledgments

of Ireland; National Library of Ireland; Public Records Office of Northern Ireland; Royal Irish Academy; Russian State Archive of Literature and Art; Russian State Library, Moscow; State Archive of Voronezh Region; and the university libraries of Cambridge, Maynooth and Ulster. I also wish to note the excellent services provided by Irish public libraries, with a particular note of thanks to the branches in Buncrana and Carndonagh.

Bridget Farrell at Lilliput Press has had a formative influence on the final shape of this book. Since 2020, she has been a midwife to this project; Bridget, I owe you a great deal of thanks. In later stages, the book benefited hugely from Larissa Silva McDonnell's editorial eye, and from the guidance of Stephen Reid at Lilliput Press. I am also grateful to Professor Emeritus David Dickson for his generous and considered advice.

This book followed me through full-time and part-time academic jobs in Ireland, Canada and the UK. I worked on it in my spare time while freelancing as an editor and, more recently, alongside a full-time non-academic job. But the final pieces fell into place in 2021 while my baby son nursed or slept in the crook of one arm, the fingers of the other hand pecking out words on a laptop balanced on the arm of a sofa. I dedicate this book to him.

List of Maps and Illustrations

(Figs. 1.1–1.4) Sketches of Russian people drawn by Martha Wilmot, 1803–8, Royal Irish Academy MS 12 L 20 (i, ii, iii, iv)

(Fig. 2) Portrait of Yekaterina Vorontsova-Dashkova by Dmitry Grigoryevich Levitsky, 1784. Oil on canvas, Hillwood Estate, Museum & Gardens, Washington

(Fig. 3) John Ladeveze Adlercron's Russian passport, 1807. National Library of Ireland.

(Fig. 4) Nikolskaya Tower, Moscow, by Sir John Fiennes Twisleton Crampton, c. 1858–1860. National Library of Ireland

(Fig. 5) 'Prisoners for Siberia, Moscow' by Bayard Taylor, 1862/3. Library of Congress

(Fig. 6) Ethel Lilian Boole Voynich, 1955. Planeta Press

(Fig. 7) Hariot Georgina (née Rowan-Hamilton), Marchioness of Dufferin and Ava by H. Walter Barnett, 1900–1910. National Portrait Gallery

(Fig. 8) Depiction of the assassination of Tsar Alexander II in January 1881 published in the *Illustrated London News*, 2 April 1881. Mary Evans Picture Library

(Fig. 9) Margaretta Eagar with the eldest four Romanov children (l–r): Tatiana, Anastasiia, Olga, and Maria. C.E. de Hahn & Co.

(Fig. 10) Constance Markievicz, Woman of Zywotowka, 1902. By kind permission of the Lissadell Collection

(Fig. 11) Constance Markievicz in Ukrainian dress, 1902. The Deputy Keeper of the Records, Public Record Office of Northern Ireland and Sir Josslyn Gore-Booth, PRONI D 4131/K/4/1/32

(Fig. 12.1–12.2) Maps of places mentioned in the text. Matthew Stout

Abbreviations

BL	British Library, London
DIB	*Dictionary of Irish Biography*, online edition
FJ	*Freeman's Journal*
NAI	National Archives of Ireland, Dublin
NLI	National Library of Ireland, Dublin
ODNB	*Oxford Dictionary of National Biography*, online edition
OS	Old Style
PRONI	Public Records Office of Northern Ireland, Belfast
RGALI	Rossiiskii gosudarstvennyi arkhiv literaturi i iskusstva [Russian State Archive of Literature and Arts], Moscow
RIA	Royal Irish Academy, Dublin
SEER	*Slavonic and East European Review*
SIRIO	*Sbornik imperatorskogo russkogo istoricheskogo obshchestva* [Collection of the Imperial Russian Historical Society] (148 vols, St Petersburg: Academy of Sciences, 1867–1916)

Abbreviations

ABBREVIATIONS RELATING TO RUSSIAN ARCHIVAL MATERIAL

F.   *fond* [collection]

op.   *opis* [inventory]

d.   *delo* [file]

l. / ll.   *list / listy* [leaf / leaves]

Note on Terminology and Usage

Until 1918 the Julian calendar was used in Russia, meaning the date was eleven days (in the eighteenth century) or twelve days (in the nineteenth century) behind the 'New Style' Gregorian calendar in use in Western Europe. All dates in this book are given in New Style, unless otherwise noted as Old Style (OS).

Transliterations from Cyrillic follow the British Standard 2979 (1958), omitting diacritics and using -y to represent *-й*, *-uй* and *-ый* at the end of personal names. However, the common English-language usage of well-known names is adhered to, such as the names of rulers and writers.

In relation to the early modern period, 'Russia' and 'Muscovy' are used interchangeably, as was common at the time. Throughout this book, 'Russia' includes the territories annexed by the imperial state at any given time. It is not my intention to erase the identities or distinct histories of those subsumed into the empire, but to underline the long and brutal history of Russian expansionism. It also serves to reflect the understanding of the Irish people studied in this book, who saw and experienced Russia as an absolutist empire peopled by many ethnicities.

Throughout this book, I use the word 'Irish' to refer to any person born on the island of Ireland, born abroad of Irish parentage or who self-identified as Irish. It is not my intention to gloss over the complex identities of people formerly generally referred to as Anglo-Irish, but instead to emphasize the fluidity and malleability of identities that worked within and above national frameworks. I consider these people simply as being *of Ireland*.

Note on Terminology and Usage

Note on Sources

Direct quotations from contemporary sources are presented here as is, unless otherwise stated, including italicization and capitalization, with the exception of the replacement of ampersands with the word 'and' or 'et' as appropriate. Due to the common occurrence of spelling errors in those sources, the distracting '*sic*' is not used.

INTRODUCTION

Wild Irish are as civil as the Russies in their kind; hard choice which is best of both, each bloody, rude, and blind

George Turberville, 1568

The English first made direct contact with Muscovy in 1553, when navigator Richard Chancellor rounded the northern tip of Scandinavia and sailed to the port of Arkhangelsk. English poet George Turberville wrote the above lines just fifteen years later, during his time as secretary to Sir Thomas Randolph, the first English royal envoy to Russia, in 1568–9. It did not take long for the idea of a kinship between the Irish and the Russians to gain a foothold among the English. Thirty years later Edmund Spenser wrote in *A View of the Present State of Ireland* that the Irish were descended from the Scythians, 'barbarians' from the grassy expanse of the Russian Steppe.[1] It had been widely accepted since the medieval period that the Irish were descended from the Milesians of Iberia, who were themselves understood to have descended from the wandering Scythians.

The comparisons drawn by Turberville and Spenser had enduring power and appeal, continuing into the twentieth century and deployed to portray both Ireland and Russia as culturally 'backward' and marginal to the 'civilized' European world. Ever since England's first direct contact with Russia in 1553, writers have focused on the harshness of the Russian winter

Introduction

and the seemingly barbaric and childish winter games and pastimes that even the highest nobles would join in, like sledding, or sprinting from a steaming *banya* to plunge into a nearby icy lake. Early observers were also disturbed by the paganism and suspected cannibalism of the indigenous Samoyed, Nenets and Saami peoples subjected to Muscovite rule.[2]

English writers had looked at Ireland through a colonial lens for centuries. The picture of rude incivility and barbarism painted by Gerald of Wales in the thirteenth century lingered into eighteenth-century accounts that portrayed an economically underdeveloped island blanketed by bogland, where a Catholic underclass laboured under the twin yokes of Rome and poverty.[3] Ireland was at once a kingdom and a colony, both at the heart of the British Empire and a place apart. Dogged by poverty and emigration, Ireland was easily marginalized, as were the Irish networks that stretched across the Continent, influencing European cultural life since the early Christian era.

The Irish upper class, differentiating themselves from the largely Catholic, labouring and poor Irish, borrowed from the narrative traditionally applied to Ireland when they visited and wrote about Russia. In the late eighteenth century Irish Protestant clergyman Thomas Campbell recorded in his *Philosophical Survey of the South of Ireland* that Peter the Great had a great love of potato-based spirits (*poitín*) or 'Irish wine'.[4] This apocryphal story played on established stereotypes of both nations and was part of a wider set of negative perceptions that overshadowed Irish reporting on Russia for centuries.

Irish connections with Russia can be traced to the tenth century, with fragments of Central Russian silver found in Viking archaeological remains in County Dublin.[5] These were not direct contacts, however, but exchanges mediated by Scandinavian traders. The Vikings established trading relationships and settlements in medieval Russia, most significantly at Novgorod, an important point on the north–south trading axis between Scandinavia and Greece. Today, Novgorod is a popular tourist destination, but in the Middle Ages it was a thriving trading centre where Scandinavian merchants exchanged Northern and Western European goods with dealers

Introduction

from Persia and Central Asia. In *c.* 1100, an Irish monk named Mauritius travelled to Kyiv, where he collected donations of valuable furs towards the building of a new monastery in Regensburg; a short-lived Irish monastery or *Schottenklöster* would be established in Kyiv itself in the first half of the thirteenth century.[6] Evidence for direct Irish contact with Russia then quiets until the early seventeenth century, when Irish soldiers began seeking employment in Russia.[7]

The Irish people who travelled to, worked in and lived in Russia were relatively small in number, but were not isolated cases of individual eccentrics. Over the two centuries studied in this book definite patterns can be clearly seen, even in the absence of formal census or migration data – Russian officialdom did not distinguish between Irish and British.[8] From the late seventeenth century Irish soldiers were recruited into the army and navy of Peter the Great, and the formalization of diplomatic relations between Britain and Russia saw several Irish-born diplomats represent British interests in St Petersburg. Peter I's, Elizabeth's and Catherine II's ambitious cultural programmes gave St Petersburg a thriving arts scene, attracting Irish pianist John Field to spend his entire career entertaining and teaching Russian nobles and their children. The late eighteenth century also brought the first waves of Western European visitors to Russia, particularly during the Napoleonic Wars, when the traditional grand tour of France and Italy became too risky. Among them were Cork sisters Martha and Katherine Wilmot, whose letters and diaries are still considered some of the most important English-language accounts of early nineteenth-century Russian life. Katherine Wilmot's maid, Eleanor Cavanagh, also left two letters giving her impressions – a unique record of travel from 'below stairs'. These interactions took place against the backdrop of Anglo-Russian diplomacy and trade, one of Britain's most important official relationships in the period.

After 1815 and the reshaping of post-Napoleonic Europe Russia had a new status among the European nations. It became more common for thrill-seeking, landed and titled young gentlemen like William Hartigan Barrington and Arthur MacMurrough Kavanagh to travel in search

Introduction

of good hunting grounds, or sexually liberating experiences. The wealthy landowner Richard White, Lord Berehaven (1800–1868), visited Russia during one of his annual overseas tours, collecting works of art and exotic plants to adorn Bantry House (regrettably, his handwritten journals did not survive a fire in the estate office). Mid-nineteenth century advances in communications, a booming newspaper trade and improving literacy rates in Britain and Ireland were reflected in a growing public appetite for journalism and quality travel writing, as any possible warming of relations between Britain and Russia was troubled by Russian imperial expansion in Central Asia. Crimean War journalists like William Howard Russell and professional travel writers like Selina Bunbury responded to this demand. The Crimean War brought unprecedented numbers of Irish soldiers and nurses to Russia's south-western frontier, and the returned soldiers were feted at a massive banquet in one of Dublin's largest buildings. The war generated an unprecedented level of reporting on matters relating to Russia, invigorating Irish interest in the region and bringing a wave of adventurers and writers to the empire's southern reaches. Simultaneously, Irish engineers and scientists played a role in modernization and industrialization in Russia, employed in the expansion of the rail and canal networks.

Finally, at the close of the nineteenth century – and in the wake of a brief reconciliation between Britain and Russia on the 1874 marriage of Queen Victoria's son Alfred to Alexander II's daughter Grand Duchess Maria Alexandrovna, after which the tsar visited Britain – the complexity of an increasingly globalized and industrialized world is reflected in new kinds of Irish migration and contacts with Russia. Ethel Lilian Boole Voynich became enmeshed in the dangerous intrigue of international radical politics, drawing on her experiences to write *The Gadfly*, one of twentieth-century Russia's best-loved novels. Meanwhile, Margaretta Eagar, like so many unmarried Irish women of her generation, emigrated alone in search of better prospects and a little adventure, becoming nanny to the children of the last tsar. The 'new woman' of the late nineteenth and early twentieth centuries is embodied in the figure of adventurer, author and mountaineer Lizzie le Blond, whose daring life on the peaks of Norway and the Alps

Introduction

contrasted sharply with her rather pedestrian visit to Moscow and St Petersburg. The story, as I tell it, closes on the eve of the establishment of a new set of relationships as Irish radicals looked with critical appreciation to the Soviet Union's experimental society.[9]

None of this is to say that the Irish were in any way exceptional in their global reach, or in their ability to forge international networks. Eighteenth-century Russia was home to a significant German diaspora and thriving English and Scottish merchant communities.[10] British connections with Russia have been studied in-depth by Anthony Cross,[11] while Irish connections with Russia, particularly the military diaspora, invite comparisons with the Scottish case. Scottish scholars have examined historic connections with Russia, from David Dobson and Jacqueline Cromarty's collective biographies to Steve Murdoch and Rebecca Wills' detailed work on the Scottish military diaspora there.[12] Academic conferences dedicated to Russo-Scottish connections have taken place in Russia (2000) and in Scotland (2016), and their proceedings have been published.[13] A special issue of the *Journal of Irish and Scottish Studies* (2014) was dedicated to the diary of Patrick Gordon, a Scottish general and rear-admiral who became a trusted advisor of Peter the Great.[14]

Histories of Ireland's connections with the wider world have flourished in recent decades, broadening and deepening understandings of diaspora, nationalism and networks, as well as the ways in which the Irish were implicated in the British Empire and its global wars, especially in the nineteenth century. Although a rich body of scholarship exists on the Irish diaspora in Britain, North America and Australia, little attention was paid to the Irish in Europe until relatively recently.[15] The study of Irish religious, educational and mercantile links with Continental Europe in the medieval and early modern period has also developed over the past twenty years or so, but Ireland's lively connections with pre-Revolutionary Russia have been relatively forgotten.[16] During the 1950s John Jordan and others published research on the Irish in imperial Russian military service in *The Irish Sword*. This burst of interest in Irish–Russian links was short-lived, however, and only resurfaced in a smattering of articles in *Irish Slavonic Studies* in

xxv

Introduction

the 1980s.[17] Biographical works dedicated to high-profile individual Irish travellers to and residents in Russia have also appeared sporadically.[18] Since then, studies of Ireland's historic connections with Russia have focused on two main themes: the Crimean War and radical political links in the early decades of the Soviet Union. Excellent, detailed studies of Irish participation in the Crimean War and the war's impacts on Ireland have been published by David Murphy (*Ireland and the Crimean War*, 2002) and Paul Huddie (*The Crimean War and Irish Society*, 2015). The Irish Easter Rising of 1916 and the Russian Revolutions of 1917 ushered in a new era of covert connections between the two countries, examined in detail by Emmet O'Connor (*Reds and the Green: Ireland, Russia and the Communist Internationals, 1919–43*, 2004). Barry McLoughlin's *Left to the Wolves: Irish Victims of Stalinist Terror* (2007) brought to light the tragic consequences of totalitarianism for some Irish in the USSR. Polish–Irish contacts enlivened following EU enlargement in 2004 and the establishment of a significant Polish diaspora in Ireland. Róisín Healy leads scholarship on the historic contexts of Irish contacts with Poland and a shared narrative and experience of subjugation and religious persecution, while Thomas McLean has studied Irish and British literary representations of Poland.[19] These themes are extended into the twentieth century in Tim Wilson's comparative study of the experiences of minority groups in Ireland and Poland.[20] Sabine Egger and John McDonagh's collection *Polish–Irish Encounters in the Old and New Europe* (2011) reviews those connections over the long term and in international comparative contexts.

This book examines connections and exchanges between Ireland and Russia between pivotal dates in the histories of both countries: from the ascent of Peter the Great to the Russian throne (1682) and the Battle of the Boyne that sounded the final death-knell to Gaelic Ireland (1690), up to the eve of World War I, the Irish 1916 Rising and the 1917 Russian Revolutions. The reverberations of those events are still felt in both countries today, and in between were two fascinating centuries of war, diplomacy, advances in travel and communications and international radical political movements.

xxvi

Introduction

IMAGES OF RUSSIA IN IRELAND

Aside from the experiences of individual migrants and visitors, what do we know of ideas about Russia in eighteenth- and nineteenth-century Ireland? In the 1780s Elizabeth Tighe of Woodstock, Co. Wicklow, received a light-hearted letter from William Tighe in London, in which he mulled over his options for an overseas tour. The future MP played on negative stereotypes of all parts of Europe, but Poland and Russia fared worst of all:

> Was I to go to Ireland [...] I should be tempted not to leave the potatoes and whiskey, which I prefer greatly to the stewed dirt of France or the oil and garlic of Italy. But travellers must never consider eating. I used to reckon an old sausage stuffed with guts and garlic no bad meal in Italy. Lord Darnley says that the travelling is excellent in Poland and Russia, if you can go without inn and victuals.[21]

William knew that employing stereotypes about different parts of Europe would entertain Elizabeth because they were established and recognizable – she would get the joke. Eastern Europe was not perceived as a destination for the faint-hearted. William did go on a grand tour shortly after writing this letter, and then promptly went into a career in politics. What were the origins of Irish people's poor opinions of Russia, as expressed in this simple piece of family correspondence?

Because Russia remained a relatively unusual destination for Western Europeans until the nineteenth century, for a long time there was a shortage of up-to-date, reliable travel accounts of the country. A number of well-known English accounts were written in the mid-sixteenth century, when formal Anglo-Russian relations were first established. These included Stephen Burrough's foray into Siberia and Anthony Jenkinson's voyage down the Volga to the Silk Road. Records of these expeditions were included in Richard Hakluyt's important anthology, *The Principal Navigations, Voyages, Traffiques and Discoveries of the English Nation*. First published in 1589 and expanded considerably in a second edition of 1598–1600, Hakluyt's work was, in historian Marshall Poe's words, 'the largest early modern collection of Moscovitica ever issued'.[22] The second

xxvii

Introduction

edition included previously unpublished texts relating to 'the North and Northeast quarters', many of which were quite negative about Muscovite life and customs but recognized the potential for the development of an eastern maritime trade route or Northeast Passage. Hakluyt's collection was hugely influential in early modern trade policy, exploration and navigation, and in the establishment of diplomatic relationships. *The Principal Navigations* was of enduring interest and was still read in the early nineteenth century. Katherine Wilmot, one of the most important Irish observers of imperial Russian life and culture, included it in her reading list alongside other important English- and French-language texts about Russia. She was so keen to learn and record all that she could that she transcribed a full chapter from an original French edition of Pierre Charles Levesque's *Histoire de Russie* – at thirty-four manuscript pages, it was a task that must have taken many hours. She read some of the most famous and influential books about Russia that were available at the time, and her reading list gives us an idea of the titles that an Irish person interested in Russia might have reached for.[23]

Mountaineer and politician James Bryce published a weighty, almost 600-page account of his 1877 journey south along the Volga and into the Caucasus in which he revealed the influence childhood reading had on his perceptions of the region. Crossing the steppe en route from Voronezh to Rostov-on-Don, he allowed his imagination to engage with his historical knowledge, 'to understand the kind of impression that Scythia made on the imagination of the Greeks: how all sorts of wonders and horrors, like those Herodotus relates, were credible about the peoples that roamed over these wilds'. He was delighted with what he saw as the Oriental flavour of life in Georgia and Armenia – then under Russian rule – recalling how his 'childish imagination [was] fed by the Bible and the *Arabian Nights*' and how, 'with the sacred mountain of the Ark looking down upon all, this seems like a delightful dream from far-off years'.[24]

The records of Marsh's Library in Dublin and Armagh's Public Library (now known as the Robinson Library) also indicate the kinds

xxviii

Introduction

of information Irish people had access to about Russia. These were Ireland's first public libraries, established in 1707 and 1771 respectively. Marsh's Library held a copy of Hakluyt's *Principal Navigations*, as well as a number of Russian religious texts and late seventeenth-century travel accounts. These included *An Account of a Voyage from Archangel in Russia in the Year 1697* (1699) by Russia Company trader Thomas Allison, who found himself stranded on the shore of the White Sea in winter 1697–8; *Voyage en divers états d'Europe et d'Asie* (1693) by the Jesuit Philip Avril; and *The Present State of Russia* (1671) by Samuel Collins, physician to the tsar and resident in Russia for much of the 1660s. Marsh's Library also held the Oriental manuscript collection of Narcissus Marsh (1638–1713), which included Cyrillic texts.[25] It seems that Armagh Public Library only held one early printed book relating to Russia, *Purchas his Pilgrimes* (1625 edition).[26] While not a public library, the library of Trinity College Dublin had catalogued over 350 titles relating to Russia by 1872, but the majority of these were nineteenth-century publications.[27] The small minority who had access to these libraries would not have learned a great deal about Russia, given the limitations of the collections.

Those who could afford to buy books might have opted for one of the relatively inexpensive counterfeit travel books produced by Dublin's printers who, in the eighteenth century, had something of a reputation for publishing unauthorized editions. The earliest books directly relating to Russia that were published in Ireland —not necessarily by Irish authors — included *Memoirs of the Life of Prince Menzikoff* (1727); John Mottley, *The History of the Life of Peter I Emperor of Russia* (1740); and *Memoirs of the Life of John-Daniel Mentzel* (1744). Later in the century Byrne and Company published William Coxe's important three-volume *Travels into Poland, Russia, Sweden, and Denmark* (1784) and *Memoirs of Peter Henry Bruce ... in the Services of Prussia, Russia, and Great Britain* (1783).[28] It is interesting to note that only one of these titles was a travelogue, and that the majority of the Irish-published titles related to the lively political and military affairs of Eastern and Northern Europe. In 1826 Dublin printers

xxix

Introduction

Bentham and Hardy published the anonymous *Travels in European Russia*, a low-quality publication compiled from various sources and illustrated with simple plates showing aspects of Russian life and architecture.

The first comprehensive English-language account of Poland, Bernard Connor's *History of Poland* (1698), contains tantalizing glimpses into early-modern Irish views on Muscovy.[29] The author, an Irish Catholic anatomist, physician and historian, served as royal physician to Jan III Sobieski in 1694–5 before moving to London, where he befriended fellow Irish naturalist and physician Sir Hans Sloane and impressed the members of the Royal Society with the plant and mineral specimens he had collected in Poland.[30] Presented as a series of letters to eminent English gentlemen, Connor's book reaches back to the earliest history of Poland–Lithuania, with its ever-changing borders, and includes snippets of information on neighbouring Muscovy. Russia and Sarmatia (partly present-day Ukraine) were, for Connor, 'desolate countries' where 'Peasants Children, especially in Russia, go Naked till they are four or five years Old' and are bathed in cold water so that 'it need not be wonder'd that they afterwards become so exceeding hardy'.[31] Notably, the second volume of the book – the portion relating to Russia – was compiled not by Connor, but by his friend John Savage. We do not know what other sources Connor used, but if any of his information about Muscovy was obtained from Polish sources, his observations must be considered in light of negative Polish perspectives on Russia at the time.[32] Connor found much to praise in Polish life and government, portraying a modernizing state that was, in his view, at a much better advantage than its neighbours in Muscovy or Scandinavia. He was at pains to separate Russia and Poland in his readers' minds by correcting unfair and out-dated perceptions of Poland, writing that the Polish nobility were 'not so barbarous nor so unpolish'd, as they are generally represented'.[33] His generally positive representation of the Eastern European kingdom is significant, given the negative tone of almost all English-language writing on the region at the time.

Irish-authored book-length eyewitness accounts of Russia were slow to appear in print. The first, *Recollections of a Tour in the North of Europe*

Introduction

in 1836–1837 (1838), was by soldier and diplomat Charles William Vane, Marquess of Londonderry. Irish-born diplomat George, Earl Macartney, privately published an account of Russia in 1767 for a very limited circulation – it was not publicly available, but selected extracts were published in John Barrow's account of Macartney's life and career in 1807. Irish journalist Robert Bell published a three-volume *History of Russia* in 1836–8, but it was compiled entirely from other sources, and it is unlikely that he ever visited the country. On the title page, he acknowledges that he was 'assisted by eminent literary and scientific men' in compiling the work. Even though it seems that he had never been to Russia, he still claimed that his work was original, stating in the opening lines, 'The geography and statistics of Russia have never been satisfactorily recorded. Except, perhaps, some of the estimates collected at great pains within our own time, there are no available documents of that description extant that can safely be relied upon.'[34] His history ends with the 1807 Treaty of Tilsit, which made foes of Britain and Russia against the backdrop of the global conflict of the Napoleonic Wars.

Many other Irish visitors to Russia kept important and detailed records of their journeys but did not publish them. Unpublished manuscripts may not appear to be broadly influential, but travellers' letters and diaries are an important record of lived experience, and in the eighteenth and nineteenth centuries it was commonplace for letters and diaries to be shared with family and friends. In this respect, unpublished records did go some way towards informing Irish opinions of Russia. Historian Sara Dickinson finds that although the majority of eighteenth-century Russian travel accounts remained unpublished, this did not mean that they were not circulated – many travel writers and their readers were used to reading each other's personal letters and diaries, did not see it as out of the ordinary and did not think them any less valuable for remaining unpublished.[35] This book gives primacy to the voices, experiences, motivations and intentions of Irish visitors and residents in the Russian Empire as recorded in both published and unpublished records.

Introduction

MARGINAL STATES?

In her landmark study of Poland's place in nineteenth-century Irish nationalism, Róisín Healy writes that by the late eighteenth century, the relative lack of direct contact and the geographical distance between Ireland and Poland came to matter less and less because 'one did not have to leave one's seat to become knowledgeable about foreign places'.[36] Travel writing dominated the literary marketplace, and the booming newspaper trade made knowledge of life overseas more accessible than ever before to an increasingly literate public. The same could be said of Irish knowledge of Russia, but unlike connections between Irish and Polish nationalists, Irish–Russian contacts were not founded on mutual sympathy. As is so often the case with travel writing, though, the records of Irish encounters with Russia tell us as much, if not more, about Ireland and Irish people than they do about Russia. They hold a clearer mirror to the face of the observer than the observed.

In Enlightenment European thought, geography and climate were understood to influence the moral fibre of a nation and the extent to which a people were 'civilized'. Racial stereotypes emerged from this theory, as extremes of weather were thought detrimental to advancement. For example, Southern Europeans were thought to have been made lazy and amorous by the heat and humidity; Northern Europeans were thought to have been made more hardworking and temperate by the cooler weather. This racist theory was perhaps best summed up in the words of Irish travel writer John Ross Browne when he assessed the prospects of civilizing Russia:

> No human power can successfully contend against the depressing influences of a climate scarcely paralleled for its rigor. Where there are four months of a summer, to which the scorching heats of Africa can scarcely bear a comparison, and from six to eight months of a polar winter, it is utterly impossible that the moral and intellectual faculties of man can be brought to the highest degree of perfection.[37]

xxxii

Introduction

Feudal, despotic Russia and poor, Catholic Ireland, with their vast stretches of seemingly useless tundra and bog emanating harmful vapours, were not thought conducive to attaining the highest forms of civilization. Observers found the problems of under-industrialization and unsophisticated agricultural methods in both countries, as well as similarities between Catholicism and Russian Orthodoxy, the Irish rural labourer and the Russian serf, and their folk traditions. Meanwhile, the tradition of seeking assistance for Irish independence from Britain's foes runs throughout the period studied in this book, from eighteenth-century Jacobite attempts at alliances with Peter the Great (see Chapter 1), to attempts by Young Ireland to secure Russian Arms during the Crimean War and further Fenian attempts at a Russian alliance during the Russo-Turkish war of 1877.[38]

The Russian Empire as declared by Peter the Great was a transcontinental, contiguous landmass, but the Ural Mountains formed a geographic and cultural divide between the Europeanized west and the conquered territories of Siberia. (That said, in 1767 Catherine the Great wrote to Voltaire from Kazan, west of the Urals, declaring, 'I am in Asia'.[39]) Until at least the 1820s Siberia functioned as a reassuring barometer of western Russia's 'civility'. The Caucasus was another focal point for Russian empire-building in the eighteenth and nineteenth centuries, prompting Orientalist literary responses from major writers like Pushkin and Lermontov.[40] Russia itself fulfilled the same role for Western European and Irish observers, who could point eastward and be assured of their own, presumed, relative superiority.

Irish pro-imperialists seized on Russia as an example of unenlightened empire, particularly for its continuation of feudal serfdom until 1861, which on the surface of things compared poorly with Britain's ban on the slave trade from 1807. Russia's imperial ambitions and incursions into neighbouring territories generated negative commentary; Walpole was moved to refer to Catherine II as 'the imperial vulture of Russia'.[41] Irish nationalist leaders from Wolfe Tone to William Smith O'Brien compared

xxxiii

Introduction

Russia's annexation of Poland to Ireland's relationship with Britain.[42] The politician and diplomat Sir Thomas Wyse made Russia's treatment of Poland the topic of his maiden speech in parliament in 1832.[43] The partition of Poland even prompted some to call on Britain to take military action in defence of Polish freedom, positioning Britain as the more modern, enlightened power.[44] Russia's ruling elite recognized the need for social reform after the humiliation of the Crimean War. Russia, like Britain, was a multi-ethnic empire that oppressed indigenous people in the territories to which it laid claim, but the British Empire was portrayed as a civilizing force while the Russian Empire was seen as despotic. This is the process described in Larry Wolff's classic study *Inventing Eastern Europe*, whereby travel writers created an image of Eastern Europe as unmodern by contrasting it with Britain and France.[45]

Some slightly more reliable accounts of the Russian Empire appeared on the market in the late eighteenth century, and the Napoleonic Wars sparked new interest in Russia as a travel destination – a fresh alternative to the well-trodden paths of the grand tour. The quality of information on Russia gradually improved, but problems persisted. Until the mid-nineteenth century few visitors strayed far beyond St Petersburg and Moscow, and observers stubbornly continued to focus on the apparent strangeness of Russian life and the barbarity of its government, perpetuating an image that was both commercially profitable for booksellers and pleasing to the reading public's imagination. Irish visitors relished brushes with the Russian police, from Meath barrister John Ladeveze Adlercron's arrest for brutally beating a postillion in Belarus in 1806, to Dublin publisher Joseph Maunsell Hone's and mountaineer Page Lawrence Dickinson's being charged with spying in Baku for photographing a mounted unit of Cossacks, and mountaineer Lizzie le Blond's being interviewed by police for photographing Peterhof palace in 1913.[46] The wealth of Russia's ethno-religious diversity went unnoticed by most observers. Western Russia's Jewish population and the Circassians and Muslims to the south and east were usually only seen as symbolic of the empire's perceived Oriental barbarism – not because these people laboured under the Russian yoke,

xxxiv

Introduction

but because their customs, religion and ethnicity were judged inferior to those of Western Europe.

More astute observers found a disparity between the images peddled in travel accounts and the realities on the ground. Katherine Wilmot, for example, wrote that she had expected her visit 'to be a fairy tale', but found that she needed to do some 'rummaging for Russia' to peel away the layers of French and English influence on noble Russian life.[47] Ironically, many Irish–Russian contacts were facilitated by the French language, which was a pillar of Russian polite society in the eighteenth and nineteenth centuries.[48] German had formerly been the language of the Russian court and military – the latter populated at its highest ranks by the nobility's compulsory service until the mid-eighteenth century – but was replaced by French when Peter and Catherine the Great imposed their 'civilizing mission' on Russian society. French was the universal language of diplomacy and international relations – Irish-born diplomats James Jefferies and George Forbes communicated with their London superiors in French.[49] Cork-born Martha Wilmot wrote in 1803: 'For language, it is a Tower of Babel as you may suppose [...] 'tis quite common to hear four or five at one dinner table – French is universal.'[50]

IRISH CULTURE IN RUSSIA, RUSSIAN CULTURE IN IRELAND

Military and diplomatic connections existed between Ireland and Russia from the seventeenth century, but ties were also strong in culture and the arts. Irish and Russian culture and traditions were reinterpreted for audiences on both sides of Europe, on the page and on the stage. From the late eighteenth century literature and music in the Irish tradition permeated Russian high culture, while Dublin theatre audiences were treated to performances of Russian song and dance. Irish craftspeople contributed to the of Russian life and culture. Catherine II brought foreign craftspeople to St Petersburg, making the city an international centre for jewellery production.[51] In 1781–5, Scottish-born cameo maker James Tassie received substantial orders (worth thousands of pounds) from

xxxv

Introduction

Catherine II. He wrote to his friend, Dr Henry Quin in Dublin to share the news and to suggest that he received the business thanks to Quin's having presented Princess Dashkova with a collection of his pastes during her visit to Ireland. Tassie had lived in Dublin in 1763–6, during which time he and Quin experimented with imitating ancient Roman pastes and cameos. These techniques made Tassie famous and established him as a leading cameo-maker of the age. His time in Dublin and his connections with the Irish doctor Quin endure in the impressive cabinet collection held by the Hermitage Museum in St Petersburg.[52]

John Field (1782–1837) was the most prominent Irish figure in nineteenth-century Russia. Born into a musical family at Golden Lane, Dublin, he migrated to London with his family at the age of eleven. In 1802 he embarked on a Continental tour with his Italian piano tutor, Muzio Clementi. The pair arrived in St Petersburg in 1803, but when Clementi prepared to return to London, Field insisted on remaining in Russia. He saw the opportunity to release himself from a difficult – even abusive – master who was said to have kept his young apprentice in a state of near-starvation, paying only the most meagre stipend.[53] Field found a wealthy patron and made his formal debut at St Petersburg's new Philharmonic Hall in 1804.[54] His popularity soared, and he became a highly sought-after performer and tutor to the children of noble families, counting a young Mikhail Glinka among his pupils. In Moscow in 1808 Martha Wilmot noted that 'nothing but [his] style is tolerated', and in January 1815, having just taken up a diplomatic post at St Petersburg, Limerick-born Sir Gore Ouseley heard Field perform at a private party.[55] In Tolstoy's *War and Peace* (Book 5), the old countess, Natasha's mother, requests 'my favourite nocturne by Field'. He developed a new, tremendously popular style of piano composition known as the nocturne. This style has retained an enduring appeal for its evocative and calming, if moody, ambiance. Field married a fellow pianist, Adelaide Victoria Percheron ('Percherette'), and his son (by another partner), Leon Ivanovich Leonov, became a distinguished tenor.[56] Behind his success, however, lurked the tragedy of alcoholism. By 1835 he was on a Continental tour and in poor health when a Russian family found him in a Neapolitan hospital. They returned him to Moscow, where he died of pneumonia in January 1837. An obituary published in a Russian magazine referred to him as 'the primary harpsichord player of our age'.[57] Field performed in London in the 1820s but never returned to Ireland. Despite being recorded as British in St Petersburg's marriage register, he considered himself Irish.[58] As the childhood piano tutor of Glinka – the founder of Russian classical music – Field's influence on Russian high culture is indisputable, as is his influence on classical music more widely, as creator of the piano style perfected by Chopin. When the two met in 1832 Chopin was in awe of his idol, but Field was unimpressed by the young Polish musician, describing him as 'a sick-room talent'.[59] A year earlier Chopin told a friend that he was 'delighted' when a German composer said that he had 'Field's touch'. In a curious case of degrees of separation, Cork-born radical and novelist Ethel Lilian Boole Voynich would, in 1931, publish an edition of Chopin's letters.[60]

Irish authors and literary works inspired by Gaelic traditions were popular in Russia from the late eighteenth century. The mythical Gaelic bard Ossian came to prominence when Scottish writer James Macpherson published his controversial *Poems of Ossian* in 1762–3. They were an instant hit across Europe, even if their authenticity was questioned from the outset, and generated a new appreciation for the wild landscapes of Scotland and Ireland. The epic tales spread to Russia, with translations appearing in 1788 (A.I. Dmitriev, *Poemi drevnikh bardov* [*Poetry of the Ancient Bards*]) and 1792 (Emil Kostrov, *Ossian, syn Fingalov* [*Ossian, Son of Fingal*]).[61] In the 1770s to 1790s Irish playwrights Oliver Goldsmith and Richard Brinsley Sheridan found popularity in Russia, as did Tipperary-born writer Laurence Sterne – his *A Sentimental Journey* was available in Russian from 1779 and *The Life and Opinions of Tristram Shandy* was translated into Russian by Mikhail Kaisarov in 1804–7. In 1869 Leo Tolstoy's *War and Peace* (Book 1, Chapter 28) testified to Sterne's enduring popularity and recognizability in Russia, when Princess Mary states: 'As Sterne says: "We don't love people so much for the good they have done us, as the good we have done them."'

Introduction

Ireland's most popular literary export to Russia, however, was Thomas Moore, who achieved great popularity there in the 1820s and 1830s. Martha Wilmot was somewhat before her time when she performed one of his songs at a party in Moscow in 1805.[62] Moore's compositions were extremely fashionable across Europe, and his *Irish Melodies* (10 volumes, 1808–34) included at least two Russian-inspired poems: 'Those Evening Bells' and 'The Russian Lover'. 'Those Evening Bells' is an excellent example of how song and poetry circulated internationally at the time. The poet Ivan Kozlov made a Russian translation of the poem, which Moore claimed he had set to the tune of 'The Bells of St Petersburg', but the original song is not known.[63] Kozlov's translation, set to music by a Russian composer, remains a popular favourite in Russia, having circled back to the place of its origin. Moore's influence on Russian poetry is evident, as well-known poets like Vasily Zhukovsky, Konstantin Batyushkov, Pushkin and Lermontov produced translations or directly imitated his style.[64] In Wiltshire in January 1829 a Russian man showed Moore a translation of his *Paradise and the Peri* 'in a collection of Russian poems which he had bound together to read in travelling'. The man read it aloud for the assembly, and to Moore's ear it 'sounded very musically'.[65] In the same year the journalist and writer Petr Vyazemsky published his Russian translation of Moore's 'Whene'er I See Those Smiling Eyes' – a fitting tribute to the Irish birth of his mother, Jenny O'Reilly Vyazemskaya.[66] In 1823 Turgenev had urged Vyazemsky in relation to Moore's *Irish Melodies*, 'Get it and read it!'[67]

As folk song and dance became fashionable forms of entertainment in Europe's upper-class drawing rooms, Russian traditions made their way to Ireland. Cork sisters Martha and Katherine Wilmot made an important collection of Russian folksongs during their residence on a rural Russian estate in 1803–8. The transcriptions were only published in 1840, when Martha included four of the folksongs in her edition of her dear friend Princess Dashkova's *Memoirs*. Shortly afterwards some of the songs were published, along with extracts from the *Memoirs*, in the popular periodical *The Literary Gazette*.[68] Martha Wilmot also became the first to translate Nikolay Karamzin's celebrated poetry into English when she worked on

xxxviii

his composition, 'Dovolen ya sud'boyu / I miloyu bogat' ('Contented with my humble lot / Thy love is all my store') – unfortunately, she did not publish her translation.[69] Coincidentally, Karamzin married Jenny O'Reilly Vyazemskaya's stepdaughter.

From the 1820s Russian poetry was available in Dublin's bookshops and began to feature in the literary pages of Irish newspapers and magazines.[70] The *Freeman's Journal* – Ireland's biggest selling newspaper at the time – published a translation of the popular Russian song 'The Inexperienced Shepherdess' along with an extract from Sir John Bowring's *Specimens of the Russian Poets*. This extract was a Karamzin composition, 'The Church-Yard', which remained popular for some time.[71] Irish newspapers also advertised new products from Russia, like a 'Russian Oil' that promised the user a 'fine head of hair'.[72]

Irish interest in Russian music and dance increased in the 1820s and 1830s, with regular themed performances and variety concerts at Dublin's Theatre Royal on Abbey Street and the Grand Promenade on Suffolk Street.[73] On one occasion a 'Russian Overture' was performed immediately before Moore's 'Believe Me, If All Those Endearing Young Charms'.[74] In September 1839 Madame Rosier performed a 'Russian dance' during an evening at the Theatre Royal.[75] In November of the same year the Matweitsch family made their first Irish appearance 'to one of the most crowded houses [...] witnessed since the commencement of the season' and performed 'several of the most admired Russian marches, songs, and choruses'.[76] This continued into the early twentieth century, with the Queen's Theatre in Dublin showing *The Conscript*, a drama based in Russia, twice nightly during the summer of 1913. The marketing of Russian song and dance on the Dublin stage indicates a wider pattern of exoticizing and othering Russian culture that had mass appeal and endured throughout the eighteenth and nineteenth centuries.

Irish writers and artists were also inspired by Russian topics. Ulster 'weaver poet' and United Irishman James Orr wrote 'The Ruin of Moscow' as an allegorical response to the terrible events of 1798 with the lines: 'So Moscow fell. Now o'er her ruins weep, / Ye friends of man, with

Introduction

awe-struck anguish riv'n, / See Russia's boast a huge chaotic heap, / Her people cinders, or as outcasts driv'n!'[77] Donegal-born Frances Browne (1816–1879), the 'blind poetess of Stranorlar', was responsible for the most significant English-language artistic response to the forced removal of a million Circassians from their homelands in the 1840s. Her first published collection, *The Star of Atteghei* (1844), drew on the flurry of recent travel accounts of the Caucasus and the frequent reporting on the Circassian conflict in the British newspapers, reflecting her sympathy with nationalist movements in Ireland and Poland. Browne's response to the plight of the Circassians unmistakably situated England and Russia as oppressors, with Ireland and Circassia as nations struggling for independence.[78] Cork-born playwright Herbert Trench (1865–1923) published an English translation of Dmitry Merezhkovsky's novel *Death of the Gods* in 1901, having previously collected works of art in Russia. In 1907 the Monaghan writer and landowner Shane Leslie travelled to Russia and met Tolstoy, who he claimed was the greatest influence on his own life; the elderly Russian writer presented the nationalist landlord with a signed photographic portrait.[79] Travelling in the opposite direction, Tsar Nicholas II was a fan of Bram Stoker's *Dracula* (1897),[80] and Odesa-born writer and activist Sophie Raffalovich (1860–1960) married Irish nationalist leader William O'Brien and published a number of novels influenced by the couple's retirement in Mayo. Dublin-born writer and polyglot Liam Ó Rinn translated Turgenev's *Prose Poems* from the original Russian into Irish (*Dánta Próis*, 1933) and published a translation of Petr Kropotkin's *Fields, Factories and Workshops* for publication in serial form in the periodical *Irish Freedom* in the 1910s, corresponding with the anarchist directly on the finer points of the translation.[81]

Elizabeth Thompson Lady Butler's well-known painting *The Roll Call* (1874) remains one of the best-known artistic responses to the Crimean War. The work launched Butler's career as a painter concerned with the psychological effects of warfare and secured her reputation as the greatest 'war artist' of the age.[82] While not Irish by birth, she married an Irish Catholic who was enlisted in the British Army and moved to Wicklow with him, recording on her canvasses the global experience of imperial warfare as she saw it through his eyes. Her knowledge of Irish political and social life is reflected in her evocative Irish scenes *Listed for the Connaught Rangers* (1878) and *Evicted* (1890). Neither work shied away from the harsh realities of life in Victorian Ireland, drawing on the same compassion that defines her battlefield scenes. Later, in 1913, Dublin-born Harriet Kirkwood moved briefly to Russia with her husband, taking painting lessons from Russian neo-primitivist Ilya Mashkov in Moscow. Her work bears his influence in her bold use of colour and in the composition of her startling portraits. She returned to Dublin to study at the Metropolitan School of Art in 1919–20 and later attended London's famous Slade School of Art.[83] Around 1900, 300 Donegal women worked for three years stitching and embroidering ('sprigging') linen stair-cloths for one of the Russian imperial palaces.[84] In an enduring testimony to the cultural links between Russia and Ireland, one of twenty-six scenes painted in rural Donegal in the mid-1920s by New York artist Rockwell Kent hangs on permanent display in the Hermitage Museum, the artist having presented it to the St Petersburg gallery in 1964.[85]

This book ties together the various strands of Irish–Russian contact from around 1690 to the eve of the Irish and Russian revolutions, identifying thematic connections between apparently disparate individuals. The contrasts between Chapter 1, which focuses on male lives and careers, and Chapter 5, which focuses mostly on women's lives and careers, illuminate broader patterns in the history of Irish migration and in Irish social history. By the late nineteenth century Irish women were as likely to emigrate as Irish men, a unique pattern not repeated among any other global diaspora group. The story of Irish links with Russia offers new perspectives on the Irish abroad. It is not just a curious aside to the well-recognized and massive outflows to Britain and North America, but is part of the global Irish experience.

I

MERCENARIES AND AMBASSADORS: IRISH CAREERS IN EIGHTEENTH-CENTURY RUSSIA

The Russians may one day become what we now are, and notwithstanding our present boasted superiority, we may possibly relapse into that barbarism from which they are endeavouring to emerge.

Macartney, *An Account of Russia* (1768), p. 57

The story of Irish contact with Russia is a long one, with Irish soldiers serving there since at least 1619.[1] However, this book takes 1691 for its starting point, when the Treaty of Limerick ended the war between Jacobite and Williamite forces in Ireland, ushering in a new era of British rule and leading Jacobite soldiers to join – and even form – Irish regiments in Continental armies. Fortunately for some Irish Catholic soldiers, this coincided with the reign of Peter I ('the Great') in Russia. His ambitious modernization plan called for the recruitment of European professionals and experts in a wide range of areas, including architecture, engineering, medicine and the military and navy.[2] This section focuses on soldiering and diplomacy, reflecting eighteenth-century Russian imperial expansion and the concerns this raised for Britain – and the opportunism of Irish military families who participated in the Russian Empire's subjugation of peoples and territories. I do not detail their battlefield exploits, but instead focus on the ways in which they integrated and set down roots in Russia.

Irish-born British diplomats were part of the long history of official Anglo-Russian relations, established in the 1550s by the English merchants of the Russia Company and conducted for generations by merchants living in designated areas in the port of Arkhangelsk and in Moscow's Nemetskaya Sloboda ('foreign quarter'). Anglo-Russian relations were formalized from around 1730, when diplomats mediated the political, social and cultural worlds of Britain, Ireland and Russia. They were required to produce official reports, summarizing their experiences and observations of Russian government, laws and customs. While their task was usually to conduct tricky trade negotiations, their accounts communicated particular ideas about citizenship, statehood and the rights of the person, all coloured by their perceptions of Russia as barbaric and Oriental. As official documents, diplomatic reports were not intended for public readership but were circulated at the highest levels of the British state, informing foreign policy and embedding negative perceptions of Russia within British political circles. In this respect, these diplomats and their reports are essential to understanding how Irish images of Russia developed over the centuries. They are also part of wider eighteenth-century European currents of thought that were shaped by Classical geographies that understood national characteristics as determined by climate and therefore inalienable.

The Catholic Jacobite soldiers and the (mostly) Anglo-Irish diplomats experienced Russia in very different ways. The most successful soldiers and their families put down roots that endured in Russia until 1917, in so doing implicating themselves in Russian imperial expansion. The diplomats had largely negative experiences and saw a posting to St Petersburg as a necessary, if unpleasant, step in career advancement. There are no indications that the two groups interacted directly, but eighteenth-century diplomats were certainly aware of the disproportionate influence wielded

Mercenaries and Ambassadors: Irish Careers in Eighteenth-Century Russia

at the Russian court by the likes of Peter de Lacy in relation to the size of the Irish military diaspora there. Irish-born British diplomat George Macartney concluded his review of the reign of Empress Anna with the words: 'Munnich, Keith and Lacey [*sic*] were her generals – what an elogium!'[3] The German military engineer and Scottish and Irish generals were implicated in Empress Elizabeth's bloodless seizure of power from the infant tsar, Ivan VI, in 1741. Macartney would not allow his readers to forget the political threat formerly posed by the Scottish and Irish Jacobites both at home in Britain and Ireland and abroad.

I

EARLY CONTACTS: IRISH SOLDIERS IN RUSSIAN SERVICE

In the eighteenth century the Irish established a small but significant military presence in Russia. After the 1691 Treaty of Limerick Jacobites left Ireland to seek military commissions on the Continent, where Irish soldiers had earned a good reputation since the seventeenth century. A small number of these ventured east to the expanding Hapsburg and Russian empires due to the lack of employment in Western Europe following the Treaty of Ryswick in 1697.[1] They were also drawn to Russia by the opportunities created by modernization and territorial expansion. The number of foreign workers and residents in Russia increased dramatically from the early eighteenth century. Peter I recruited Western European architects, doctors, engineers, naval officers, soldiers, teachers and shipbuilders to implement his vision of reform and build the new capital, St Petersburg. In 1699 the tsar drafted 32,000 men into his army, creating twenty-nine regiments commanded by foreign officers.[2] In 1716 his 'military regulations' included provision for the employment of foreign soldiers and remained in force for 150 years. Irish soldiers were also drawn to Russia by the relatively favourable conditions of work, with foreign officers earning more than Russians. Limerick-born Peter de Lacy, for example, earned approximately 3600 roubles per year, whereas Russian officers received around 3120.[3] The composition of the Russian nobility was also conducive, in that many noble families were of non-Russian origin: the Yusupovs traced their origins to a Tatar prince, the Kantemirs to a Turkish pasha and the Korsakovs to a Corsican prince.[4] Alexander Pushkin's great-grandfather, Abram Petrovich Gannibal, was a Cameroonian nobleman, kidnapped and raised in the imperial household during the reign of Peter the Great, while Mikhail Lermontov claimed Scottish origins. The setting was one of opportunity for the Irish arrivistes, with noble and court society receptive to external influences.

Several Irish doctors were also attracted to work in Russia in the eighteenth and early nineteenth centuries, some with military medical experience. In 1731 Henry Smith completed his medical training in London and left for St Petersburg to take up the role of physician to the empress, having been recommended by a German professor of medicine. He remained in the position for thirty years.[5] Francis Dease took his MD at Rheims and was medic to the Russian army during the Russo-Turkish War in 1738–41.[6] Perhaps the most significant Irish doctor in Imperial Russia was James Quinlan. Educated at Louvain's Irish College, he was medic to Napoleon's Grand Army during the Russia campaign. He apparently remained in Moscow treating the wounded after the failed French invasion and went on to become surgeon-general to the tsar and chief of the Royal Hospital.[7] Lisburn-born naval surgeon James Prior (c. 1790–1869) also found himself in Russia during the Napoleonic Wars, having previously served with the Royal Navy in the Indian Ocean, South Africa and Brazil. He was part of a crew that accompanied a Russian squadron from Sheerness to Kronstadt in the summer of 1814. Uniquely among the Irish medics who found themselves in Russia, Prior published his experiences in a detailed seventy-four-page pamphlet, *A Voyage to St Petersburg in 1814* (1822). It relates how he was not only the ship's surgeon, but was also called upon to carve the huge hams served at dinner because of his presumed skill with a knife.[8]

The Irish military diaspora benefited from the influence Scottish Jacobite exiles wielded at the early eighteenth-century Russian court, as demonstrated by historians Steve Murdoch and Rebecca Wills. This is exemplified by the figure of General Patrick Gordon, remembered for effectively mentoring Peter the Great in military matters.[9] With a sizeable military diaspora in Russia – estimated to number at least 3000 soldiers in the seventeenth century, plus any accompanying family and dependants – the Scots made a number of attempts to formalize their relations with Russia.[10] Proposals ranged from a marriage between Peter I's daughter Anna and James Stuart, to an alliance between Russia and France to supply troops and aid for the Jacobite cause. In 1718 the Kildare Jacobite Charles Wogan, acting as a secret agent for James Stuart, travelled to Russia to try to negotiate a confederacy between Sweden and Russia against George I. None of these plans were realized. Finally, in 1723–4 an Irish Jacobite secret envoy named Daniel O'Brien began fresh negotiations with Peter I, but did not manage to conclude them before the tsar's death.[11] The British kept a close eye on these efforts; one letter of 1717 referred to 'several rebels at Paris who make their Court to the Czar's physician'.[12] Three years later James Butler, 2nd Duke of Ormond, found himself under surveillance during what was termed his 'secret stay in Mittau' and his negotiations with the Russian ministry in the Netherlands. The British response to a Russian report on the matter stated that 'All the world has seen the great number of rebellious subjects of His Majesty to whom the czar has given every protection and encouragement.'[13] Even if the Jacobite attempts came to nothing, the strength of the Scottish presence in Russia must have bolstered the Irish military diaspora there. Increasing religious tolerance allowed foreign Catholics to worship at a Jesuit church in Moscow, and a Jacobite club was established in Petersburg after it replaced Moscow as the Russian capital in 1713. Against this backdrop, the Irish 'wild geese' quickly gained a reputation and rose to high ranks in the Russian service.

Members of the de Lacy and O'Rourke families were particularly successful in Russia. These high-ranking soldiers and their families utilized Irish international military networks to integrate into Russian noble life. Some earned awards and promotions, noble titles and estate lands for their service, assimilating into the upper echelons of Russian society. The de Lacys and O'Rourkes retained their Russian properties and titles for generations, with their descendants remaining there until the early twentieth century.[14] Empress Anna in particular sought the support of non-Russian nobles to bolster her position in the western and Baltic borderlands of the empire, further enhancing the favourable conditions for these Irish families.[15] It can be safely assumed that they lived as Russian nobles did: counting their wealth by the number of 'souls' or serfs they possessed, generating from these people's labour the wealth required to maintain the lavish lifestyle expected in eighteenth- and nineteenth-century Russian noble circles.

Peter de Lacy (1678–1751) left Ireland for Russia via France in the late 1690s. He found success quickly and in 1725 became one of the first recipients of Russia's second-highest honour, the Order of St Alexander Nevsky.[16] Politically, he was associated with Russian military success and imperial expansion and was recognized as a representative for Jacobite exiles in Russia.[17] He famously led the Russian seizure of the Crimean fortress of Azov from Ottoman forces in 1736. De Lacy's exploits were reported in Irish newspapers, such as his orders to march on Crimea with 60,000 men and to march on Sweden with 20,000 men.[18] His retreat into Ukraine a short time after the capture of Azov, due to the loss of an estimated 28,000 Russian troops to hunger and disease, has been less well remembered. Pride in the senior command occupied by an Irishman, coupled with Islamophobia, clouded any possibility for a critical appraisal of his actions in the Irish press. De Lacy was awarded estates in Livonia valued at £10,000 for his role in the Great Northern War (1700–21), a victory that delivered territorial gains and Baltic sea-ports to Russia and greatly reduced Sweden's influence in the region. By the time of his death, de Lacy had amassed a fortune of £60,000.[19] Hoping to emulate his granduncle's success and using his family connections and influence, Maurice de Lacy left Ireland for Austria in 1756. In 1762 he joined George Browne in Russia and later became governor of Hrodna province in Belarus.[20] Maurice's nephew, Patrick O'Brien de Lacy, left Ireland in 1810 and ten years later inherited Maurice's large Russian estate, valued at £100,000.[21] Similarly, Count Joseph O'Rourke (1772–1849) distinguished himself during the Napoleonic Wars and was awarded the Order of St Alexander Nevsky; his portrait still hangs in St Petersburg's Hermitage Museum.[22] The O'Rourkes held a 20,000-acre estate populated by over 200 serfs in Hrodna, meaning they were economically well placed relative to other noble Russian families.[23]

Just like the Irish diaspora elsewhere, Irish military families in Russia made valuable connections through marriage. In Spanish Flanders, the frequency of inter-marriage within the Irish military diaspora showed how closely Irish families interacted with one another, but in France, the odds of marrying outside the Irish community increased the longer a family remained in exile.[24] Intermarriage functioned to retain estates and titles within the community and, in the Russian context, it may also have reflected a shortage of suitable Roman Catholic spouses. De Lacy women in Russia often married within the small Irish military community, such as Helen de Lacy's marriage to George Browne the younger; Annabella de Lacy's marriage to a Stuart and their daughter Martha's marriage to Cornelius O'Rourke; and Catherine de Lacy's marriage to a General Boyle.[25] Other Irish soldiers, however, married into Eastern European noble families. Peter de Lacy married a Livonian noblewoman, Martha Phillippina von Loeser, and two of his daughters married noblemen from the Baltic states.[26] Marrying into a non-Irish family could come at the cost of kinship and cultural ties, but compensation came in the shape of the material and political advantages of a legal and personal allegiance with an influential local family.

Military success was often rewarded with local government or state appointments, as well as certain privileges. As governor of Riga in 1730–51, Peter de Lacy and his family were exempt from Riga's anti-Catholic laws and were allowed to employ two priests for private worship. Peter de Lacy reached beyond local government, becoming a member of the Imperial College of War in 1723 at the invitation of Peter I.[27] His star continued in the ascendant during the reign of Catherine I: he had a place of honour at her coronation in 1725 and was always the first to sign her war college reports.[28] He retained his influence throughout the reign of Empress Elizabeth, as demonstrated in a letter from Scottish soldier General James Keith, begging de Lacy to petition the empress on his behalf for 'permission to come to Petersburg [...] that I may have the happiness to kiss H.M. hand and to

Early Contacts: Irish Soldiers in Russian Service

assure her that while I breathe I shall never forget her goodness to me, nor fail to pray for her prosperity'.[29] When the sixteen-year-old future Empress Catherine II 'the Great' married in 1745 de Lacy was her principal dancing partner at the celebratory ball in the Winter Palace; his missteps and those of the other 'people from sixty to ninety years of age' rendered the party an 'unpleasant business', in her words, that almost reduced her to tears.[30] George Browne (the younger, 1698–1792) was general-in-chief and governor-general of Livonia and Estonia in 1762–92, and corresponded directly with Catherine the Great as her direct representative in the region. Empress Anna sent an Admiral O'Brien to the West Indies to explore opportunities for Russian colonization.[31] Overall, the impact and success of the Irish in Russian service was disproportionate to their number. This was not because of any inherent talent or skill, but was more likely the result of an over-representation of Irish soldiers in Western European armies, which pushed the most ambitious towards Eastern Europe, where there was less competition.[32]

These men and their families moved in the highest circles, capitalizing financially and socially on their battlefield exploits. Frederick II 'the Great' presented John O'Rourke with a diamond-studded sword after he distinguished himself at the siege of Berlin in 1760.[33] In 1736 Emperor Charles VI presented Peter de Lacy with a jewel-framed portrait and 5000 ducats.[34] De Lacy was a fixture at the Winter Palace and was there when Elizabeth I deposed two-month-old Ivan VI from the throne in 1741.[35] His international renown was publicly invoked in a pamphlet vindicating John O'Rourke's character and military expertise (see Chapter 3), in which the latter's familial connections to de Lacy were highlighted as an indication of his good character.[36] The ease with which high-ranking Irish officers navigated Russian noble circles is clear from a few surviving testimonies. Anthony O'Hara noted that one Polish countess in St Petersburg always welcomed Irish visitors, and Princess Ekaterina Romanovna Dashkova remembered George Browne in her *Memoirs* as 'enlightened and [...] generous', having been received by him in 1782 in his capacity as governor of Riga.[37]

While they integrated and gained acceptance into the Russian upper classes, individual soldiers differentiated themselves by continuing to

Early Contacts: Irish Soldiers in Russian Service

use Irish titles and practising openly as Catholics. The de Lacys needed a special dispensation to employ Catholic priests for personal worship in Lutheran Riga, but the O'Rourkes may have found life a little easier in a more diverse region of present-day Belarus inhabited by Orthodox Russians, Jews and Catholics. After the family had been resident in the area for three centuries, Edward O'Rourke became Roman Catholic bishop of Riga in 1918 and head of the bishopric of Gdansk in 1922.

The lives of the daughters, wives and mothers who accompanied these soldiers are more difficult to piece together. As with the lives of lower-ranking soldiers and naval officers, documentary evidence offers little more than the barest of details about them. Women are completely sidelined in the family pedigrees that Irish officers obtained from Dublin's heraldic office. These documents were necessary to prove their noble descent for the purpose of gaining employment or promotion.[38] It is difficult to provide a more nuanced picture of the women associated with the Irish military migration to Russia than Jerrold Casway's depiction of a 'generally passive, or involuntary' migration shaped by 'legal and material dependencies to male kin'.[39] No surviving record has been found of the conditions under which these women travelled to Russia, whether they accompanied male family members or travelled separately, or their standard of living following the death or absence of their husbands or fathers.[40] Generally speaking, it is likely that they enjoyed a slightly better quality of life from the 1760s onwards. The early arrivals who came during the reign of Peter I experienced the effects of universal military service, meaning long periods of separation and, in the case of those in possession of land, the possible neglect of their estates. By the 1730s the administration recognized the damaging effects of lifetime universal service on the empire's vast estates, so universal service for the nobility was abolished in 1736 and officers were allowed to retire after 25 years. The 1760s saw the introduction of the first pensions for dependants of deceased veterans. Against the backdrop of the Napoleonic Wars, from 1807 the widows of those killed in battle received their husband's full salary; this was transferable to dependants in the event of the deaths of both parents.[41] These broader contexts give some indication of the gradual improvements in the standard of living and

Early Contacts: Irish Soldiers in Russian Service

financial security of the women of the Irish military diaspora in Russia throughout the eighteenth century.

It is also important to note that there was an underclass of officers of Irish birth or parentage in the Russian army and navy throughout the eighteenth century who quartered and served alongside Russians. However, records of their lives and careers are scant; we cannot know how well they integrated, or what they thought of their comrades-at-arms. We also do not know much about the relationships that the high-ranking Irish military families had with the lower-ranking soldiers, or with the serfs who worked and lived on their estates. It seems unlikely that these landowning families could have avoided contact with the serfs living on their lands, with Russian servants and tradespeople or with functionaries of the Russian state. However, the details of their relationships with and impressions of those people remain unknown.

The first generation of Irish military migrants in Russia created a group identity and community through a shared perception of their suffering as Jacobite exiles, pushed out of Ireland by British rule and anti-Catholic legislation. But by the mid-eighteenth century they had harnessed demarcations of difference honed over two generations to signify their special status as foreign nobles in Europe's armies. Elaborately decorated genealogical documents obtained from the Irish heraldic office attested to their noble backgrounds, tracing and fashioning lineages back to the ancient high kings of Ireland. Their descendants even manufactured Irish heritage or identities by seeking permission to use or retain titles such as 'Irish Count' or 'Irish Earl'; for example, Joseph O'Rourke successfully petitioned Nicholas I in 1848 for permission to retain such a title.[42] But the most striking aspect of their identities is their cosmopolitanism. They harnessed broad expressions of 'Irish' identity, from religious identity to intellectual life, forging and shaping these identities in transnational contexts and proving themselves highly mobile, strategic and adaptable.

A key element of that strategic adaptability was a willingness to assume a contrary role to the one assumed by the 'wild geese', exiled Jacobites and their descendants – put plainly, to participate and even lead in Russian campaigns of aggression and territorial expansion. In 1733 Peter de Lacy commanded the Russian forces that captured Warsaw during the War of the Polish Succession, installing Augustus III to the Polish throne, sending Stanislaus into exile in France and ultimately strengthening Russia's influence over Polish affairs. For this action, Augustus III awarded de Lacy the Order of the White Eagle of Poland. In 1772 Count Cornelius O'Rourke (1736–1800, a brother of Count John O'Rourke, discussed in Chapter 3) participated in quashing resistance to the First Partition of Poland – a move by Prussia, Russia and Austria that provoked outrage in Western Europe. He died a major-general and the Commandant of Tartu (or Dorpat, as it was known under Russian rule).[43] Count Joseph O'Rourke (1772–1849) was a captain of cavalry in the Russo-Swedish War that saw Russia claim Finland, and he commanded the cavalry corps during part of the long Russo-Turkish Wars that led to Russia's annexation of the Crimean Khanate in 1783. For his service, he was decorated with the Orders of St Anna, St George and Alexander Nevsky, rose to the rank of lieutenant general and gained 20,000 acres of Belarusian land populated by 236 serfs; by 1850 he owned 1000 serfs. O'Rourke secured for his descendants a comfortable future as landowners, generals and bishops – some of the region's most prominent figures – that endured into the early twentieth century.[44] In 1910 the centenary of the Battle of Varvarin – fought by Serbia with Russian support against the Ottoman Empire – was marked with the unveiling of a memorial to Count Joseph on the battlefield site. His grandson, 76-year-old Count Nicholas O'Rourke, travelled to Serbia from the family estate near Minsk for the event. A writer for *America* magazine described the occasion in terms of celebrating the triumph of Christianity over Islam. Count Joseph was portrayed as a defender of Christianity who, at his own expense, equipped a regiment and personally marched it south to Serbia to, in the journalist's words, 'assist the Christian races struggling for freedom'.[45] The roles played by the Irish in Russian military service must be fully acknowledged for both their impressive ability to navigate intricate social networks and structures, and for the harm their military expertise caused to the peoples whose territories were annexed through centuries of Russian expansionism.

2
ANTHONY O'HARA'S CONSTRUCTED IRISHNESS

Anthony O'Hara was born in Genoa in 1751 to an Irish father and a French mother and was brought to Russia by his parents at an early age. His life is a microcosm of the experiences of the eighteenth-century Irish military diaspora. While soldiers of Irish birth and descent were found in Russian service into the early twentieth century, Jacobitism waned internationally after the decisive Jacobite defeat at Culloden in 1745, resulting in much less contact between Irish soldiers living in Russia and those elsewhere in Europe. O'Hara found ways to maintain his 'Irish' identity, an identity that served him professionally and personally, and used what networks were available to him in the absence of the strong, transnational Jacobite network that had sustained his father's generation.

Although he had never been to Ireland, O'Hara worked to position himself as an Irishman and a foreigner in Russia. His father, Charles Hubert O'Hara, was born in Ireland but left at an early age to enter the French service. He moved to Russia in 1758, when Anthony was seven years old; Anthony himself was immediately entered into the cadets. After having served the Russian military for most of his life, he found himself

Anthony O'Hara's Constructed Irishness

in 'straitened means', as he put it.[1] He began pursuing avenues to secure a more beneficial pension from the Knights of Malta. In 1787, he had already received the Order of Vladimir, the second-highest order in Russia. The Knights of Malta, however, were drawn from Europe's oldest noble families, requiring Anthony to prove his noble ancestry. It was to this end that he contacted his cousin Charles O'Hara in Co. Sligo, writing,

> As you have been so kind as to interest yourself [...] in procuring me some information relative to my family, I hope you will still be pleased as to continue me your good offices on that head, that I might be able to enjoy the privileges granted by a law recently enacted here, to noblemen in the military service as well as for my own satisfaction.[2]

The law he refers to here is Catherine II's 1785 Charter of the Nobility, which removed the obligation of military or administrative service from the nobility and exempted them from taxation. Anthony hoped that his Irish cousin would use his political influence to obtain the Ulster Herald's seal of approval for the family pedigree, a document crucial to his future. The cousins maintained a fairly regular correspondence from 1787 until about 1796, when their communication became more sporadic. Anthony wrote his first letters to Charles in English but quickly switched to French. Born to a French mother and French-educated father, and having spent most of his life in Russia, Anthony knew that French was his stronger hand and had the added bonus of being more widely understood among his Russian superiors. His written English was not perfect, and he seems to have had only a limited knowledge of Russian, despite having lived there from an early age.[3]

Anthony's political identity was more complex than his lineage might suggest, as the son of an Irish Jacobite with experience in French and Russian service. His letters display a reactionary conservatism that may have been sincerely held, but equally may have been contrived or exaggerated to win his cousin's confidence. Charles O'Hara (1746–1822), a British-educated Whig, was returned as MP for Co. Sligo in every election between 1783 and 1822. In 1798 he led a skirmish against General Humbert's invading French force at Tubbercurry, Co. Sligo, but he was also opposed to the Act

Anthony O'Hara's Constructed Irishness

of Union and to Catholic emancipation.[4] Anthony was committed to the preservation of the old order in Europe and wrote in reference to the 1798 rebellion in Ireland:

> It grieves me sorely to see that in our own country (*notre patrie*) these same Regicides have succeeded in propagating the infernal spirit of Revolution [...] I am indeed astonished that Irish gentlemen, forgetting their Duty and their Religion, should so far dishonour their good name as to adopt the infamous doctrine of these monsters, who merit the execration of all mankind.[5]

While the majority of the archive consists of letters from Anthony to Charles, it is still possible to piece together the regularity of correspondence and measure the depth of friendship between the two men. The correspondence covers the period 1787–1810, but no communication is evident in seven of those years – whether those letters were simply lost, or military duties hampered their ability to communicate, we cannot know. Anthony initially made contact with Charles out of the need to establish his family tree, but that impetus dissolved in late 1796, when the matter was closed. From that point on the letters focused on military and diplomatic matters, and from 1799 they began to peter out. Charles's responses to Anthony became more infrequent from the early 1800s. This may be because the 1801 Act of Union would have required Charles, as an MP, to spend more time in London and away from his Irish estate at Nymphsfield, Co. Sligo. After a two-year break in communication, in 1804 Anthony somewhat pathetically begged Charles to break his silence as it was causing him 'great disquiet'.[6] In 1810 Anthony's final surviving letter listed the dates of his last three letters, all of which had gone unanswered: 14 March 1805, 17 November 1806 and 4 January 1808.[7] There is no evidence that this letter received a reply. Anthony's letters show that he greatly valued his connection with his Irish cousin. This may have arisen from his awareness of his place within the Jacobite tradition of exile, as the direct descendant of people forced to leave Ireland. He considered his father and father's peers the representatives of a religion 'for so long persecuted' and one that caused, in his words, 'their forced emigration to enter into the service of foreign powers'.[8] His own life and career embodied the Jacobite perception of their own experience of exile.

The correspondence suffered in part from Anthony's position as Russia's representative in Malta during the Napoleonic Wars. The Russian fleet was active in attempting to counter French gains in the Mediterranean islands at the time. In 1798 Russia negotiated for a Maltese garrison to be supplied by itself, Naples and Britain, but this was overruled by the Treaty of Amiens (1802), which returned the islands to the Knights of Malta, despite the objections of residents who considered the Order too weak to protect them against Napoleon.[9] After returning to Russia Anthony outlined his response to the Treaty of Amiens in a manuscript addressed to the British ambassador at St Petersburg, Lord St Helens. The opening paragraph stated: 'None of the Knights [...] will have the slightest desire to go to Malta and find himself the equal or even the inferior, according to the spirit of the Treaty [of Amiens], of a Maltese subject, who previously might have been his *valet de chambre*.'[10]

Anthony had never been to Ireland, but his letters carefully emphasized his sense of his own Irishness. He wrote to Charles, 'If fortune will be as favourable to me, to procure me the means to be able to repair to Ireland according to my constant wishes, it is certain that I will be very happy.'[11] He seems to have attempted to acquaint himself with any Irish visitor to St Petersburg. In winter 1795 he told Charles that he had hosted three Irish travellers at his home – the later MP and Clonmel native William Bagwell, William Adair and a Mr Kiely.[12] Bagwell was MP for Co. Tipperary and a privy councillor whose father went to school in London with Anthony's father; Adair was a friend of the Irish antiquary Joseph Cooper Walker. Kiely may have been Bagwell's brother-in-law. Anthony asked his cousin to send him specific books relating to Ireland, providing a list of the volumes he already owned to avoid duplication. Charles obliged by sending a few of the requested books; shortly afterwards Anthony wrote to thank him, but three years passed before he offered to reimburse his cousin's expenses via a London contact.[13]

Somehow, without much help from Charles, Anthony was able to amass a decent library of Irish titles. He reported that William Adair was particularly impressed with his library.[14] He clearly placed great value on the books and presented his copy of Sylvester O'Halloran's well-known *An Introduction to the Study of the History and Antiquities of Ireland* (1770) to Goethe in 1810; the two had become acquainted during Anthony's residence in Weimar.[15] Many of the books in his library reflect a fashionable antiquarian interest in ancient Irish history and language,[16] but others were more controversial and reveal an interest in the historical background to his father's Jacobitism. Several of the books he owned or requested were published by Catholics educated on the Continent, like the historian and Catholic priest James MacGeoghegan's pro-Jacobite three-volume *Histoire de l'Irlande* (1758–63). Books like MacGeoghegan's embody the filtering of Irish political ideas through Continental philosophy and Jacobite exile perspectives. The inclusion of some seventeenth-century works, too, shows the transmission of political and historical ideas through space and time, such as the Stuart loyalist Roderick O'Flaherty's *Ogygia, or, a Chronicled Account of Irish Events* (1685). More broadly, Anthony's reading list communicated to his cousin that he was in touch with European intellectual currents, and that even if his St Petersburg location made the acquisition of Irish-authored works difficult, he was aware of enduringly important earlier works as well as the most significant recent publications. His identity, then, was transformed from the less relevant or even passé figure of the Jacobite émigré's son, to that of a cosmopolitan reader with a fashionable interest in history.

3
JOHN O'ROURKE, INTERNATIONAL MERCENARY

John O'Rourke was born in Leitrim around 1725 and joined the British army in around 1750 but maintained that he was forced to resign after five years due to his Catholic faith.[1] He proceeded to France but claimed that French soldiers were so angered by his promotion to Captain of the Royal Scotch Regiment that he was obliged to fight four duels in the space of a few days. He resigned, informing Louis XV that it was 'a dear purchase to fight for it every day'.[2] His subsequent introduction to King Stanislaus of Poland was allegedly arranged through his close relationship with a Polish diplomat's wife but, lacking the patience to wait for the promised position to materialize, he went to Russia.[3] He resigned his Russian commission in 1764 after his success at the Siege of Berlin and, having been suitably honoured by Frederick II, returned to France. He later returned to Ireland for a short time before making his way to Russia once more. Three semi-biographical and autobiographical accounts of his life were published during his lifetime, writings that emphasize his standing as a military man and the transnational nature of his career and ambitions.

In 1782 an article entitled 'Account of the Genealogy of Count O'Rourke' appeared in *The Hibernian Magazine*. Published anonymously, it was a thinly veiled account of the glory and renown O'Rourke achieved during his long career in armies across Europe. The piece attempted to elicit sympathy from the reader and clearly demonstrated O'Rourke's enduring bitterness over his 'forced' resignation from the British Army almost thirty years previously. The reader was assured of his virtuous character and of the O'Rourke family's noble heritage and connections. This piece appears to have been mined to produce the eighteen-page pamphlet, *The Case of Count John O'Rourke*, two years later. Together, these publications emphasized his international career, his high social standing and his great achievements on the battlefields of Europe. Both publications were anonymous but may have been written by O'Rourke himself in an act of self-promotion. He had served in the armies of no fewer than four countries, even returning to one (France) for a second commission. He pursued one commission more ardently than others, however – a return to the British army.

O'Rourke has been remembered as a mercenary for his frequent changes of service, and the events of his later life add weight to this assessment.[4] He saw the outbreak of the American War of Independence as a lucrative opportunity to return to British service at the end of his career. He claimed to have approached the Prime Minister, Lord North, with an offer to raise three Irish regiments to fight against the Americans, 'declaring, now that his own country wanted his arm, he would not fight under a foreign banner', but his offer was rejected and he felt that 'in all his applications he has been treated, by the ministry, with indifference or scorn'.[5] It seems that he may have been regarded in Britain as a mercenary, mistrusted for having served too many different monarchs, and Catholic ones at that. Either way, there was a sour note to the account of events presented in *The Hibernian Magazine*.

O'Rourke published his book *A Treatise on the Art of War* only two years after he claimed to have appealed for a commission in America, and while the revolutionary war was still going strong. His preface to the volume, addressed to George III, begged:

> My profession is my delight [...] If, under the auspices of Your Majesty's countenance, and with the approbation of veteran Officers experienced in Your Majesty's service, I shall be instrumental in leading the junior Officers, and those of less experience, towards perfection in that service in which it will be their glory to excel, I shall not think my time or labor misapplied; happy in having rendered myself in any degree useful to the Military Order and Military Service of Great Britain.[6]

This offer, too, was ignored by the British authorities.

The article in *The Hibernian Magazine* publicized O'Rourke's achievements and honours, reproducing his genealogy. It emphasized that despite the humiliations he felt he had suffered, he 'still preserves all the dignity of a prince'.[7] The piece assured readers of his good character and presented evidence of the family's nobility and high connections, such as the £200 annuity he received from his friend Lord Cunningham. It emphasized his gentlemanly character as a person who 'does not game, he pays his tradesmen, and will neither lend nor borrow'. The character defence ended by stating that his youngest brother was married to the niece of Franz Moritz de Lacy, field marshal in the Imperial Service.[8] The reference to de Lacy was no accident. The family's name was well known in Ireland, throughout the Irish military diaspora and more widely; indeed, the *Belfast News Letter* printed a copy of a letter that Joseph II sent to Franz Moritz, supposedly written on the emperor's deathbed, and not long before the field marshal himself died in 1801. The emperor expressed to de Lacy his 'sense of the obligations which, on so many occasions, I owe to you. [...] Independent of my personal obligations, it is to you the whole army is indebted for its formation, its discipline, its military appearance, and the esteem in which it is held.'[9] No small praise. The appendix to O'Rourke's *Treatise on the Art of War* also emphasized his own high connections across

Europe in the military and diplomatic spheres and the esteem in which he was held during his time in Berlin.[10]

The Case of Count John O'Rourke leaned on the Jacobite narrative of exile as key to the family's experiences for generations, describing how '[his] Grand-father, finding that the tyranny intended against him was rigorous and unrelenting, quitted his native land [...] but each time his lady was ready to lie-in, he sent her for that purpose to Ireland, that her children might be born natives of the country'.[11] This anecdote was intended to enhance O'Rourke's Irish connections, clearly indicating that his father was born on Irish soil. Despite his long absence from Ireland, O'Rourke was said to have preserved 'the broad dialect, and the peculiar style of Ireland',[12] and his biography in *The Hibernian Magazine* was an undisguised attempt to re-appropriate an Irish identity after years of exile. His dream of ending his career with a glorious performance in the American War of Independence came to nothing, and he returned to Russia in 1786, where he died. His peregrine life sits curiously, like that of Anthony O'Hara, alongside a cynical reaching out to Ireland as a means of securing renown and recognition. Both of these men's migrations were opportunistic, as were their appeals to Britain and Ireland for career and financial opportunities in later life. That they looked back to Ireland when in need of assistance shows how transnational networks and flexible individual identities acted as safety valves for migrants.

4

IRISH-BORN DIPLOMATS IN EIGHTEENTH-CENTURY RUSSIA

Several Irish-born diplomats represented British interests in eighteenth-century Russia, mainly with the goal of negotiating trade agreements. Russia was Britain's most valuable trading partner in the eighteenth century: the British navy was dependent on Russian raw materials like hemp, pitch and tar, and Russia had geographical advantage in terms of Asian trade.[1] Captain James Jefferies (d. 1739) was at Peter I's court in 1718–19; George Forbes, 3rd Earl of Granard (1685–1765), was at the court of Empress Anna in 1733–4; James O'Hara, 2nd Baron Tyrawley and Baron Kilmaine (1681/2–1773), saw Russia under Empress Elizabeth in 1743–5; and George, Earl Macartney (1737–1806), was at the court of Catherine II in 1764–7. Sir Robert Gunning (1731–1816) was sent to St Petersburg in 1772 to mediate a peace treaty with the Ottoman Empire and became a favourite of Catherine the Great during his three-and-a-half years there.[2] Another, Richard Wall, was born in Nantes to Irish émigrés and from the 1720s embarked on a very successful diplomatic career that saw him represent the Spanish crown in St Petersburg (1727–8) and London (1747–54).[3]

These Irish-born British diplomats operated within a three-way process of exchange as cultural intermediaries between Britain and Russia, Britain and Ireland, and Ireland and Russia. They were importers and purveyors of ideas, artefacts and protocols. Their written accounts were relics of the process of mediation and were instrumental in shaping ideas about Russia at the highest political levels in Britain. They were required to record their impressions of Russia for presentation to the Georgian court and administration. Jefferies was diligent in sending regular updates by mail, with almost fifty letters on record in the Russian state calendars. While Forbes's is the earliest known structured account of Russia by an Irish-born writer, unfortunately, his writing remained unpublished and inaccessible to all but a small number of court officials and family members for generations. These diplomats' official accounts range from Tyrawley's 10-page manuscript to Macartney's 230-page printed volume, providing Georges I, II and III with information on Russia's climate, geography, trade, currency, natural resources, military organization and serfdom, and character portraits of the empresses and the highest-ranking nobles. Tyrawley's unpublished 'Succinct Account of Russia' delivers what it promises, providing in its ten pages a cursory overview of the extent of the empire, its climate, inland navigation, nature of government, and the highest figures at court. Forbes's 83-page account is also thin on detail and contains broadly similar types of information to Tyrawley's. In contrast, Macartney's 230-page printed *Account* is divided into 12 distinct chapters, reflecting an increasingly professional, methodological approach to diplomatic reporting. It also included as an appendix the English cleric Reverend John Glen King's authoritative account of the Russian Orthodox Church, the first of its kind in the English language.[4]

These diplomatic exchanges occurred during periods of expansion for Russia and Britain, against a backdrop of changing international relations and commercial and imperial ambitions. Anglo-Russian relations were becoming increasingly formal. The commercial interests of the mid-eighteenth-century diplomatic missions were reinforced by the inescapable influence of the merchants of the Russia Company and British Factory, with Westminster going so far as to seek Russia Company approval when choosing envoys. The British Factory at St Petersburg was represented in London by the Russia Company, who brought the Factory's interests to Parliament. The Russia Company's founding principles – dating back to 1553 – included the conduct of English foreign policy in Russia.[5]

While trade was a central pillar of Anglo-Russian relations at the time, broader geopolitics were also at play. Russia demanded more respect from Western European states following its defeat of the old regional power, Sweden, in the Great Northern War of 1700–21.[6] Concerns around Russia's increasing influence were at the heart of British insistence that George Forbes should adhere to established customs and ceremonies – orchestrated to maintain power structures – when he was presented at court, and not bow to new norms that might inadvertently elevate Russia's standing.[7] Occasionally the traditions and practices of local court and foreign embassy clashed. Forbes was instructed not to address Anna as 'empress' but instead to use the less-deferent 'tsarina'.[8] Forbes objected to the practice of kissing the Russian ruler's hand on the grounds that it was an acknowledgment of Russian superiority over Britain, but he was also keenly aware of the political importance of gestures and so waited six weeks for guidance from London on the matter.[9] This indicates that he was familiar with earlier accounts of Russia, in which merchants, envoys and observers wrangled and worried over appropriate titles and gestures to show Russia a sufficient, but not excessive, level of respect. Despite his initial stumbles, Forbes successfully negotiated Russia's first trade treaty with any European state, one that made Russia Britain's largest international trading partner. He boasted of the special treatment he received in St Petersburg, that he was lodged in one of the best houses and had been allocated more guards than any other diplomat in the city.[10]

In the eighteenth century, diplomacy underwent a revolution, laying the foundations of modern, professionalized diplomatic culture.[11] Diplomats began to communicate largely through French, those with a formal education were increasingly favoured for ambassadorial posts, and envoys began to be sent on long residential postings, in contrast to the shorter missions of the early modern period.[12] There was a growing appreciation of diplomacy as a process of intercultural contact, rather than simply a political and economic dialogue. By 1839 one writer listed the characteristics of a good diplomat: 'He must be a courtier, a linguist, a connoisseur [...] strong upon statistics, rich in reports, able to pronounce upon all, from an antique table to a treaty, from a vol au vent to a Velasque.'[13] The choice of representative also indicated the level of respect afforded to the host country. While the popular image of diplomatic life is often one of well-appointed accommodation and lavish parties, eighteenth-century envoys had little resembling a private life. Work constantly intruded, not least because there was often little demarcation between their living quarters and their reception rooms.[14]

Most of the Irish-born envoys had quite a bit of previous experience before being posted to Russia. Jefferies was envoy to Sweden in 1707–9 before being appointed British envoy to Russia in 1718. Forbes had distinguished himself as a naval officer and had previously served as governor of Minorca (1718) and the Leeward Islands (1729). Tyrawley was a field marshal in the British Army, had a seat in the Irish House of Lords and was made Baron Kilmaine in the Irish peerage in 1722. He was ambassador to Portugal in 1728–41 before being sent to St Petersburg in 1743.[15]

Still, the selection of diplomatic representatives was often informed as much by domestic political intrigue as it was by a candidate's personal merits. George Macartney, for example, was probably selected for the Russian ministry thanks to his friendship with Stephen Fox (1745–1774), son of Henry, later 1st Baron Holland. This friendship was cultivated during Macartney's tours of Europe in the early 1760s. While Macartney had no previous professional experience, he did possess desirable personal qualities. His education at Trinity College Dublin, Lincoln's Inn and the Middle Temple in London were capped with two grand tours of Europe. He was fluent in French and Italian, and his youth and energy fitted him for the social obligations increasingly demanded of diplomats.[16] A nineteenth-century biographer described Macartney as 'a graceful person, with a great suavity of manners, a conciliating disposition, and winning address.'[17]

Irish-Born Diplomats in Eighteenth-Century Russia

These characteristics and qualifications reflect the cosmopolitanism of eighteenth-century European high society and the importance of shared culture in developing and maintaining international relations.

At the time, French culture was fashionable among the Russian elite. Young Russian noblemen were sent to European universities such as the School for Diplomats in Strasbourg as part of state attempts to cultivate a Western European-style diplomatic culture.[18] Increasing numbers of Russians undertook the grand tour and attended Western European universities. All of this should have facilitated interaction between foreign ministers and their Russian hosts, especially because French was also the language of international relations. However, this 'Westernization' of Russian culture attracted much negative comment. Macartney sniped that Russians were 'conscious and jealous of the superior civilisation of foreign nations, sensible of, yet unwilling or unable to correct the errors of their own' and that they 'derive few advantages from birth or education, which claim the respect of others, or are of use to themselves.'[19] His critique of Russian high culture extended to twelve pages and is best summarized by the following passage:

> Warped by imitation of alien manners without selection, they too often appear vain, petulant, light, inconsequent, indiscreet, envious and suspicious, faithless in their engagements, traitors to one another, incapable of true friendship, and insensible to all the nobler movements of the soul: luxurious and effeminate, listless and indisposed. [...] few of them employ their leisure in polishing their minds: insensible to the charms of conversation and the refinements of literature, they loiter and sleep away life and wake but to the calls of sensuality and the grosser pleasures.[20]

His comments employed all of the stereotypes associated with Orientalism, but he also targeted Russian Francophilia, which he thought 'not only divests them of all national character, but prevents them from aspiring to the praise of all national virtue.'[21] He went further, claiming – without a hint of irony – that all progressive and civilizing influences in Russia in the previous three centuries had been the initiative of foreigners, such as the marriage of Sophia of Achaea to Ivan I, which he considered 'the deliverance of Russia [...] she invited to her court many excellent Greek officers and expert engineers'; the founding of the port of Arkhangelsk by the English; the recruitment of foreign experts and craftsmen by Ivan II; and the fact that the first great Russian poet, Kantemir, was the son of a foreigner.[22] He did not remark on the fact that the Europeanization of Russian high culture created increasingly lavish lifestyles, the demands of which were met in part through increased exploitation of the serfs – the same exploitation that was criticized by many foreign observers.[23]

Macartney's *Account* is polished and fairly comprehensive, but he did not obtain all of his information through first-hand observation. This was normal practice – many diplomats borrowed or paraphrased the observations of their predecessors, who themselves also borrowed at least some of their observations from earlier envoys and travellers. Forbes's expenditure notebooks record the purchase of one unnamed account of Russia before his departure; no Russian travelogue was found among the contents of the family library, auctioned at Sotheby's in 1993.[24] Macartney's influences are also unknown, but it is likely that he borrowed from Tyrawley's 'Succinct Account', which has a similar structure and opening remarks – so much so that Tyrawley's account has previously been wrongly attributed to Macartney.[25] Macartney also borrowed from and paraphrased parts of King's *Present State of the Church of Russia* (1761). There are remarkable concurrences between Macartney's and King's views, and the language used. Macartney nevertheless repeatedly assured his readers of the reliability and quality of his sources, employing such phrases as: 'what I observed myself, joined to very good information'; 'perusal of authentic documents, and from the information of very intelligent persons'; 'assured, from incontestible authority'; and 'having taken uncommon pains to inform myself'.[26] Despite these reassurances, his account fails to deviate in any meaningful way from previous western European diplomats' and travellers' accounts. Macartney continued the tradition of reporting a barbaric, Orientalized Russia that fit the widely held images of the country.

Their written accounts make it clear that these diplomats did not engage with Russian culture, language or traditions. Kept busy with engagements and official correspondence, they rarely left St Petersburg or Moscow. St Petersburg was home to several Anglophone clubs and a considerable British population. The English Club and the English Masonic Lodge provided St Petersburg's Anglophone expatriates and visitors with opportunities to make useful contacts, while also releasing them from the necessity of mixing with locals. This was particularly true of Macartney's time there, when the British community grew strong with the goodwill of Catherine II.[27] Operating within the rarefied world of diplomacy – in Hamish Scott's words, 'sealed off from the rest of society'[28] – these representatives were largely confined to court, and their accounts reveal little or no interest in the varieties of Russian life that existed outside that sphere. Their knowledge of and contact with non-noble Russians was superficial at best, but that did not deter them from borrowing others' observations, or making generalizations that fit with wider, mostly negative, perceptions of Russian life.

Their apparent lack of interest in Russian culture seems to have been influenced by the fact that each of them went there out of duty and in the hope of securing their future career ambitions. Macartney's letters convey an impatience to conclude the trade negotiations and return home. He took care to voice his complaints moderately, despite his clear dissatisfaction:

> [...] a seat in Parliament has long been the great object of my Ambition. I am however by no means dissatisfied at my Situation, On the contrary [...] But at this Court it is impossible to go higher [...] had I a seat in Parliament, might I not with more reason pretend to something better in the Course of Life.[29]

He was later offered an opportunity to return to Russia but excused himself due to the reluctance of his new wife, Lady Jane Stuart, and awaited something more appealing.[30] (Lady Jane was, incidentally, the granddaughter of Lady Mary Wortley Montagu, whose famous letters from Turkey were composed during her husband's period as British ambassador to the Ottoman Empire.) Regardless of Macartney's own wishes, Catherine

II's political advisor, Nikita Panin, had written to Macartney personally to say that he would not be received due to earlier indiscretions. Panin was referring to two high-profile affairs that Macartney had while in Russia, one of which resulted in one of Catherine II's ladies-in-waiting being sent home pregnant, threatened with the cloister; the other involved a cousin of Panin's.[31] The secretary to Ambassador Cathcart wrote from Moscow of how the latter woman 'has long since been this Gentleman's stumbling-block. Ever since his arrival here he visits with so little precaution, and sees her so often, that his enemies have certainly at present the fairest opportunity of laying the foundation of his ruin.'[32]

Jefferies appears to have made a little more effort to familiarize himself with Russian life and culture. At times when there was not much political news he filled his correspondence with whatever he could learn of Russian life. Within a week of his arrival in St Petersburg in January 1719 he described the scene on the Neva at the 'blessing of the waters':

> As this solemnity gives some idea of the genius of this people, I would not omit sending your lordship a short account of it: It is on the river Neva that this farce is acted; the ice is opened in a certain place on that river, where the chief ecclesiastics present themselves to bless the water. This ceremony being performed, all those amongst the people who have either a mind to wash away their sins or to be cured of some distemper, approach the sanctified place. People of distinction content themselves with washing their faces, but the common undress and plunge themselves overhead and ears with so great an assurance of relief either to soul or body, as their necessity requires, that I could not but admire both the zeal and the robust constitutions of those who, in spite of the terrible frost we have, acted in this farce. [...] This is one of the ancientest customs among the moscovites, to which His Czarish Majesty likewise submits to shew that in matters of religion he will not separate himself from one of the meanest of his people.[33]

Just two weeks later he excused the shortness of his letters, blaming the weather: 'One can hardly put one's nose out of doors without running the risk of losing it by the cold.'[34] By February he resorted to padding his

Irish-Born Diplomats in Eighteenth-Century Russia

despatches with court gossip, admitting, 'The absence of court has rendered this place so barren of news, that I have scarce anything to communicate worth your lordship's attention.'[35] He related, for example, the horrific punishments meted out to those denounced in 1718 as supporters of the exiled first wife of Peter I, Evdokia Fedorovna: the main conspirators were tortured before being broken on the wheel. His insistence on relating curious instances in his despatches only reinforced existing images of Russia as a strange and barbaric place. In the following example, Peter I himself is portrayed as behaving in an undignified manner by playing an April Fool's prank on the nobility:

> Wednesday last being the first of April His Majesty invited most of the nobility and gentry in and about this town to a comedy [...]. The time appointed being come, a great company [...] met together at the play-house, where everything seemed to be in a readiness [...]. After two hours expectation the company was not a little surprised to see a curtain drawn aside, and a machine let down on the theatre from a cloud on which was writ in capital letters, and in Russian and German characters the word 'April', the merry Andrew at the same time advancing on the stage, and with a profound reverence and an impudent face, telling the company that they were all a parcel of fools. The trick being perceived, the people began to gaze on one another, and by little and little sneaked out of the play-house.[36]

All envoys saw the Russian state as despotic and oppressive. Jefferies portrayed an ambitious but still archaic Russia; St Petersburg was a gleaming, impressive, new city, but it was filled with people who appeared to come from a past age. Forbes saw a developing and expanding Russia, whose massive extent he could not help but admire, yet he also pointed out that the 'populousness and riches of this vast dominion is not at all equal to the extent of it, which proceeds entirely from want of policy and polity in the government'. He saw the administration as haphazard and arbitrary, the government as 'confused and inconsistent'.[37] Tyrawley emphasized the despotism of the state by listing examples of individual acts of cruelty. Macartney also wrote disparagingly on the Russian government, emphasizing the need for reform and modernization and citing examples of corruption, bad governance and the despotism of previous rulers, leading him to conclude that it was to despotism that Russia owed its 'greatness and dominion'. In Macartney's view, only a change of government would allow Russia to develop its plentiful natural resources, because the 'form of government certainly is, and will always be, the principal cause of the want of virtue and genius in this country'.[38]

Serfdom was, naturally, one of the most frequently critiqued aspects of Russian life. Forbes noted that the population of Russia was between 11 and 16 million and that there were at least 11 million serfs in the country, but wrote only 3 short pages of generalizations about the character of what he called the 'commonality'. He was at least ahead of Jefferies and Tyrawley, who made no mention of them at all. The extent of Macartney's exposure to the lower classes in Russia, or his interest in them, is reflected in the proportion of space dedicated to each class in his account. Of his account's 230 pages, he devoted 4 pages each to what he termed the 'common people' and merchants; to the clergy, 1 page; and to the nobility, 12 pages. The population figures provided at the beginning of his text state that there were 500,000 nobles in the country but 12,828,200 peasants of various kinds. However, criticisms of serfdom were framed almost exclusively in economic terms, with Forbes concluding, 'This slavery of the people is one of the greatest discouragements to their industry.' He was not blind to the cruelty of the system, noting that the nobility had complete control over the lives of their serfs, to the extent that 'if they die by their hand, or by the correction which they order for them, it is not much minded'.[39] Macartney disapproved of the tributes exacted by landowners from the serfs and the brutal punishments meted out to those who would not or could not pay.[40]

While these diplomats' assessments of Russian serf life appear rather detached, both Forbes and Macartney displayed some compassion towards the Irish poor later in their careers. Forbes has been remembered as 'one of the ablest and most consistent of the reformers' in eighteenth-century Ireland and was in favour of Catholic enfranchisement.[41] Macartney was also interested in Irish welfare matters as Chief Secretary to the Lord

Lieutenant in Ireland (1769–72), questioning during a debate on the repeal of Poynings' Law: 'Shall the poor be relieved [...] Will the Irish landlord be less severe to his miserable tenant? Will the dissenter enjoy more than toleration? Will the opprest Roman Catholic be enabled to acquire fixed property or secure the little they have left?'[42] This outburst seems to represent long-held beliefs on Macartney's part, reflected in improvements he made to his estate at Lissanoure, Co. Antrim. Towards the end of his career, as governor of the Cape Colony, he discouraged the slave trade.[43]

The social, cultural and political realities of Russian life created a barrier to interactions between British representatives and their local hosts. To many Western European observers, the new north-eastern power appeared more an Oriental despotism than an Enlightenment European state, with its serfs, the deficiencies in its education system (the first Russian university was founded in Moscow in 1755) and – to Anglophone Protestant eyes – the superstition and ritual of Orthodoxy. Despite the considerable cultural gaps between these diplomats and their hosts, however, Forbes and Macartney managed to negotiate commercial treaties and to compose accounts that, in places, reveal respect for Russia. Between 1725 and 1780 the Russian population increased from 18 to 27 million, due in part to territorial gains and the improvements in nutrition and infant mortality common to other parts of Europe.[44] Within a few years of Catherine II's accession and her pronouncement, 'Russia is a European power,' Macartney admitted that the empire was 'no longer to be gazed at as a distant glimmering star, but as a great planet that has obtruded itself into our system, whose place is as yet undetermined, but whose motions must powerfully affect those of every other orb'.[45] Macartney did not doubt that Western Europe was superior to Russia in every respect and that the Russian nobility mimicked Western European norms only 'to conceal their disadvantages'.[46] However, he was not above conceding the possibility of improvement:

> [...] when we reflect on the barbarism of our own and of other countries a few centuries past, we may be induced to form more favourable conjectures of a nation who are far from being destitute of radical virtues. A docile and humane peasantry [...] may under better laws be molded

into a better people [...] The Russians may one day become what we now are, and notwithstanding our present boasted superiority, we may possibly relapse into that barbarism from which they are endeavouring to emerge.[47]

Introducing his chapter on the 'Genius and Character of the Russians', Macartney conceded that he was aware 'how little attention is paid to such general portraits' and that 'In all countries we meet with extraordinary characters, which, by their virtues or depravity, by their talents or incapacity, make exceptions to every general rule.' Unfortunately, his attempt to paint 'the shades of character which mark the different ranks of people' of Russia was, broadly speaking, unsuccessful.[48] This runs parallel to his failure to mediate his own pathway within the Russian court and high society. These failures can be attributed to over-confidence on his part as an ambitious young man and to his lack of interest in the host country. The more moderate Forbes was much more successful as an intermediary.

These envoys' difficulties in Russia may have been compounded by the question of its place in the world – whether it was Asian or European. Straddling east and west, Russia has long been considered enigmatic, more so in a period when the world was conceptualized in terms of east and west, rather than the north–south structure that emerged later.[49] Russia blurred the boundary between Asia and Europe. Forbes counted Russia amongst the 'countries of Europe', acknowledging its position as the new political and military power in Northern Europe following the Great Northern War. But thirty years later, in the aftermath of the Seven Years' War and Catherine II's coup of 1762 – the memory of Peter III's murder still fresh – Macartney raised the question of whether a rapidly changing Russia was Asian or European. He highlighted 'a strong resemblance between the Muscovites, and the Orientals'.[50] His general observations on Russian life and culture depended on a view of Asia as inferior to Europe and fed on negative stereotypes of 'Oriental' life as one of luxury, excess, cruelty and leisure.

Diplomats were among the most prolific writers on foreign countries in the eighteenth century. They shaped official British opinion on the

Irish-Born Diplomats in Eighteenth-Century Russia

emerging Eastern European power, and they knew that their observations would be read in the highest political circles. While unavailable to the reading public, their accounts had a role in the wider current of eighteenth-century British and Irish ideas relating to Russia, perpetuating lasting stereotypes of Russia at the highest levels and indicating the extent of negative Irish and British perceptions of the country. The common practice of copying or borrowing from previous accounts contributed to static images of Russia that would change little over the next century. Negative portrayals of Russia have endured with much more potency than Forbes's awe at the extent of the empire, or Macartney's concession that 'modernity' was, perhaps, just a little slower to arrive in Russia. Their observations still perform an intermediary role today; Macartney's account remains an important source for scholars of eighteenth-century Russia. A year after his death, his private secretary, John Barrow, published *Some Account of the Public Life, and a Selection from the Unpublished Writings, of the Earl of Macartney*. The work set out to provide a 'faithful sketch of the public conduct' of Macartney's various public offices, to 'afford an illustrious example for imitation'.[51] Inadvertently, perhaps, it also propagated negative views of Russia and the Russian people, by including substantial extracts from Macartney's *Account of Russia*, exposing his observations to a much wider and lasting audience.

II

To Russia with Love

This is the first of the new year and I am to spend it how distant from the place of my nativity and how far removed from Home! Yet surrounded by affection, by friendship, and kindness — my heart overflows with gratitude, and love, to the dear, the noble Princess, whose friendship is of a nature truly maternal and flattering to my heart.

Martha Wilmot, Moscow, 1 Jan. 1804

In the late eighteenth and early nineteenth centuries, while Europe was plunged into chaos by the French Revolution and the Napoleonic Wars, a number of Irish women had deeply personal experiences in Russia. These women were part of wide international networks that were forged in the mineral waters of the small mountain town of Spa. Across Europe, spa towns were important social hubs, especially for women.[1] Spa itself was very popular with British and Irish travellers, both for its proximity to Dover and for its thriving summer social scene.[2] Men and women mixed much more freely at Spa than in their normal lives, and so too did people of different classes and faiths. The Irish Protestant traveller Horatio Townsend described Spa in 1781 as 'an epitome of all the upper classes of Europe's inhabitants [...] meeting together every day in the same rooms, and on terms of apparent equality. This produced an easiness of communication and freedom of manner that banished all the insipid restraints of formality and reserve.'[3] The small but lively mountain town was 'the crossroads of Europe', with large numbers of visitors passing through it annually.

This section tells the stories of four Irish women from very different backgrounds whose links to Russia were determined by connections made at Spa in the 1770s and 1780s. Jenny O'Reilly, or Evgeniya Ivanovna Vyazemskaya, as she was later known, was launched onto Moscow's elite social scene in the 1780s after divorcing her Irish husband, shedding her old identity, migrating to Russia and embracing a new life. Twenty years later, in the middle of the Napoleonic Wars, Cork-born sisters Martha and Katherine Wilmot found themselves part of an international network of writing and travelling women that revolved around Princess Ekaterina Romanovna Dashkova (1743–1810), one of the most important women in Enlightenment Europe (Fig. 2). The diplomat George Macartney described Dashkova in 1765 as 'a woman of an uncommon strength of mind, bold beyond the most manly courage [...] and a beautiful person'.[4] Katherine's maid, Eleanor Cavanagh, accompanied her to Russia, and her impressions are recorded in her remarkable letters to family and friends in Ireland.

Shared European Enlightenment culture and the ubiquity of the French language helped middle- and upper-class women to forge international networks and lasting friendships. They identified at various times as Irish or English, but their identities and personal values rose above 'national' boundaries and were shaped by the life-changing experience of travel. The significance of travel in the lives of individual women was, of course, deeply personal and resists generalization. Some travelled out of curiosity or for education. Some of the most famous and controversial women of the age turned to travel as an antidote to dissatisfaction with everyday life. The early feminist Mary Wollstonecraft's *Letters Written in Sweden, Norway, and Denmark* (1796) publicly showcased the deep personal crisis caused by her disastrous relationship with Gilbert Imlay. Before travelling to Scandinavia at Imlay's behest, Wollstonecraft had briefly worked as tutor

To Russia with Love

to an Irish girl named Margaret King. In a strange echo of her former tutor's life, Margaret would later leave her husband, Stephen, Earl Mount Cashell, and move to Italy with her lover under the name Mrs Mason – a character from Wollstonecraft's *Original Stories*.[5] For the Wilmot sisters and Jenny O'Reilly, travel and migration offered possibilities for reimagining day-to-day life. In Russia, Martha and Katherine Wilmot were able to expand the education they had received at home from their parents. Katherine's interests came to include Russian land law and the legal status of the serfs, while Martha studied music, languages and history, drawing on Dashkova's private library and benefiting from the assistance of tutors in learning Italian, Russian and the harp. For Eleanor Cavanagh, travel opened a window into an entirely new culture and way of life. Even if she did not always approve of what she witnessed in Russia, she admitted after a month that she would 'be sorry to go back so soon as now, for to be sure this is a wonderful grand place, and I'm always very merry'.[6]

Relocation helped Martha Wilmot to recast her life on new terms. She departed for Russia a broken woman, devastated by the premature death of her younger brother a year earlier. In Russia, she developed a concern for the poor that helped her to come to terms with her loss. Living on Dashkova's rural estate, she came into close contact with serfs, who were slaves to the landowners, denied voting rights, forced to labour for free and surrender their harvests, and subject to conscription. With her characteristic empathy, Martha visited their homes and took an active interest in the so-called 'beggar's hospital' on Dashkova's estate. Following one of her first visits to the hospital, she referred to the patients as 'my young family (as the princess calls them!)'.[7] Martha made four sketches of Russian people – two of women in elaborate traditional dress and two of bearded, shivering beggars (Fig. 3). That she concentrated such attention on those pitiful figures shows how large they loomed in her visual impressions of Russia.

Her understanding of the condition of the serfs was cast in a transnational mould. She already knew these people, in a sense, because she had met them before in Ireland – the Irish poor were widely acknowledged

To Russia with Love

as among the worst off in Europe.[8] She often compared what she saw in Russian noble homes with circumstances in Ireland, writing after one dinner party, 'The profusion is beyond any thing I ever saw – many a time I wished, the wasted food of their fatiguing feasts, transported to little Erin; which too often wants, what is here despised.'[9] In Martha's lifetime, Ireland suffered frequent national and regional shortages of corn and potato, the staple foods of the poor. Scarcity was recorded in seven of the years between 1778 and 1801; this is not to mention the widespread distress caused by conflict in 1798.[10] Martha's interactions with Russian serfs placed the condition of the Irish poor in sharp relief and prompted her to reflect on her own position: 'The equality and comforts attending middle life are inestimable, when attended by a sufficiency, to avoid debts, and share the little over plus with those less fortunate.'[11]

The realization of her relative privilege helped Martha to overcome her crippling grief, and after two years she declared herself 'happier now than I have ever been'.[12] This transformation took place within the limits of 'traditional' women's work of caring for the poor and the sick, but her reaction to poverty transcended national boundaries and reflected an international, comparative perspective that was enriched by the depth of the personal relationships she forged in Russia.

5

THE MYSTERIOUS IDENTITIES OF JENNY O'REILLY OR EVGENIYA IVANOVNA VYAZEMSKAYA

In 1782–3 Prince Andrey Ivanovich Vyazemsky (1754–1807) made a tour of Western Europe, visiting Scotland, England, Portugal, Spain, Italy and the mineral waters at Spa. He was from one of Russia's most prominent noble families. Details are scant, but it seems that during this tour he met an Irish woman named Jenny Quin or O'Reilly (d. 1802), starting a relationship that would launch her into Moscow's elite social scene and that would be immortalized in their passionate private correspondence. Her story is a fascinating example of the shedding of an old identity and assumption of a new one and represents a rarely studied element of the Irish diaspora: the middle-ranking woman embedded in eighteenth-century Continental cultural life. She represents a largely hidden group of eighteenth-century Irish women who saw travel and migration as an opportunity for personal reinvention.

Very little is known of Jenny's life prior to meeting Andrey, and much uncertainty has surrounded the details of the couple's introduction.[1]

My research has uncovered evidence that points to the small mountain town of Spa, in present-day Belgium. Spa was a meeting place for the fashionable from all over Europe, and the Irish were well represented among the town's seasonal residents. It was a likely destination for both an Irish woman of middling rank and a Russian nobleman.

The people of Spa were so proud of the calibre of visitors their town attracted that every year between 1750 and 1798, a local publisher produced *Listes des Seigneurs et Dames Venus aux Eaux Minérales de Spa* (*Lists of Lords and Ladies come to the Mineral Waters of Spa*). The volumes were simply lists of foreign visitors, along with the name of their hotel and the date of their registration (which was close to, but not precisely, their date of arrival), accompanied by advertisements for local businesses.[2] The *Lists* are an extremely valuable source for recreating and understanding the social circles that were formed and maintained at the little mountain town and provide vital clues in piecing together the early relationship between Jenny and Andrey.

Tradition holds that Jenny had divorced a Mr Quin to marry Andrey, and in some of the pair's early correspondence, Andrey refers to her as 'Madame Quine'.[3] The *Lists* record a 'Mr le Baron de Quin' lodging in Spa's *l'Hotel de Russie* in August 1783.[4] Vyazemsky is also recorded at Spa between 8 and 10 August 1783.[5] It is therefore possible that Jenny and her husband were at Spa that summer, and that it was there that she and Andrey were introduced. A contemporary noted that Andrey had 'womanising tendencies',[6] and the prince's letters make obscure references to a young woman he met in Spa. His friend went walking with her husband so that Andrey could be alone with her, and she treated him 'coldly' afterwards. They barely spoke the following day but did agree to meet again in Brussels, where she ordinarily lived.[7] Could this have been Jenny? Where more appropriate than Spa for the pair to meet, as a renowned meeting place for Europe's most fashionable nobles and the aspirational middle class?

Jenny herself has proven an elusive figure, and her family background is cloaked in confusion and uncertainty. Her portrait depicts a dark, curly-haired woman with an expressive face and the delicate features that were

The Mysterious Identities of Jenny O'Reilly or Evgeniya Ivanovna Vyazemskaya

admired at the time.[8] At the end of one frustrating day's research, I even found myself wondering whether her story was the figment of her son's creative imagination – Petr Andreyevich was a very significant figure in the nineteenth-century Russian literary world.

Nothing is known of Jenny's early life. A Russian source gives her date of birth as 1762, but it has not been possible to verify this due to the absence of birth or baptismal records.[9] Vyazemsky family tradition holds that her birth name was O'Reilly and that she divorced an Irishman named Quin before marrying Andrey. Russian historians have generally accepted that she was the daughter of a linen draper and the granddaughter of a Jacobite in Spanish service, Alexander O'Reilly (1725–1794), ultimately linking her to the great O'Reilly clan of Breifne.[10] The O'Reilly family's official genealogy, however, fails to mention her at all.[11] The omission of wives and daughters from the genealogical records of Irish military families was not unusual. In the absence of any other evidence, I have had to take at face value Jenny's family background as asserted by Vyazemsky family tradition.

In the mid-1780s Jenny followed her heart to Russia, married Andrey and made Moscow her home, defining herself for the rest of her life through her husband and his pursuits. She travelled back to the Continent at least once, visiting Italy in 1786.[12] It is unlikely that she had any formal education, but she knew English and French. Bilingualism was not uncommon among the Irish military diaspora in France, so this may further hint at her family background. Andrey, for all his dissoluteness, recognized the value of appearing as an educated man. The couple's estate at Ostafyevo, near Moscow, became a centre of literary sociability, and Jenny found herself immersed in Russia's most influential cultural circles. The colonnaded palace was a statement of wealth and cultural capital. Designed inside and out to impress, its library contained an estimated 5000 volumes – the couple's grandson would later augment the collection to 22,000[13] – a mineralogical collection and a collection of Italian art. (The library was removed from the palace in 1929 and is now housed in the Russian State Library, Moscow; the palace was used for a variety of purposes during the Soviet period, and in 1994 it opened to the public as a museum.) Andrey

The Mysterious Identities of Jenny O'Reilly or Evgeniya Ivanovna Vyazemskaya

was a friend and patron of the celebrated writer and historian Nikolay Karamzin, who in 1804 married Andrey's daughter Catherine (Jenny's stepdaughter). Jenny and Andrey's son, Petr Andreyevich (1792–1878), was evidently influenced by a childhood spent in such company and went on to become a Romantic poet, a friend of Russian literary greats including Turgenev and Pushkin, and a noted journalist. Later, Pushkin dubbed Ostafyevo the 'Russian parnassus' for the succession of literary visitors who passed through its doors.

Like the Irish soldiers discussed in Section 1, language was one of the means by which Jenny fashioned a Russian identity. She and Andrey corresponded in (imperfect) French, she addressed letters to him in Russian and she utilized her small but ever-growing Russian vocabulary in the letters.[14] This was more than just a tool used for external appearances or to fit in – it was a vital component of her project to create a new persona. To marry Andrey, she had to convert to Russian Orthodoxy. As part of the same process, she had to adopt a Russian name, becoming Evgeniya Ivanovna. This included taking her husband's patronymic (Ivanovna = 'daughter of Ivan') and completed the process of her dissociation from her family and her assimilation into Russian life. From the moment of her arrival in Moscow, it seems she made little or no attempt to maintain contact with her family. Her correspondence with Andrey makes it clear that she had given herself over completely to him. In one letter, she confessed that a letter from her father had left her feeling 'indifferent', that she had no desire to have anything further to do with Ireland or her family and that she would prefer to devote all of her energies to her husband.[15] Her letters constantly assured Andrey that he was the most important thing in her life, and she consistently referred to him as '*mon meilleur ami*'. Indeed, the correspondence is so dominated by their personal relationship that little space remains for other topics, save some Moscow society gossip and a little information about the health and wellbeing of the children.

Her son, Petr Andreyevich, rarely discussed his Irish blood and had only the slightest awareness of his mother's background.[16] He was ten years old when she died, and at the age of thirty-six he was still trying to piece

The Mysterious Identities of Jenny O'Reilly or Evgeniya Ivanovna Vyazemskaya

together her background. He wrote to his friend Ivan Turgenev, who was then travelling in Western Europe:

> Do me a favour, find me my relatives in Ireland: my mother was of the surname O'Reilly. She had previously been married to a Frenchman and divorced him in order to marry my father, who was then travelling. They got together, it seems, in France, possibly in Bordeaux. [...] Perhaps I shall have to seek civil hospitality in Ireland. It would be even better if there was a rich uncle or rich aunt for my children. Here is a glorious romantic adventure! Be the Walter Scott of our romance. [...] For the love of God, take me to Ireland![17]

These comments were made at a time when Petr was thinking about leaving Russia. As a liberal journalist and writer, he had been deeply affected by the recent death of Maria Feodorovna; as empress consort and dowager empress, she fostered foreign links and oversaw charitable institutions and public architectural projects with flair. He reflected sorrowfully: 'She was our best administrator, and the places under her jurisdiction would be ruined without her. She was also the last link with the past.' He was already under state surveillance for his literary objections to serfdom and Russian oppression in Poland; he was also personally close to members of the revolutionary Decembrist movement. His interest in his Irish background must be understood in terms of his desire for an alternative to the stifling of speech and press freedoms in Russia. He spent long periods abroad in the 1830s but does not seem to have visited Ireland or established contact with his mother's family. He revised his liberalism after the revolutions of 1848.[18]

Jenny's marriage to Andrey granted her access to the highest echelons of Moscow society, but she felt lonely and isolated during her husband's long absences.[19] Her daring act of divorcing her first husband only resulted in her attaching herself to an absent partner, raising the children and mourning her loneliness. She appears to have had only a limited number of acquaintances among Moscow's expatriate community. This may have been by choice, but her circle was further circumscribed by the fact that most of Russia's Irish and British residents were based in St Petersburg. One O'Hara mentioned several times in her letters is very likely Anthony O'Hara, an officer in

Russian service (see Chapter 2).[20] With his dual Franco-Irish parentage and Jacobite upbringing, O'Hara's friendship may have given Jenny contact with the Francophone culture that she was evidently comfortable with. It is worth bearing in mind that O'Hara's career ambitions may have motivated him to befriend Jenny; Andrey was very well-connected politically.

Despite the family's wealth and social standing, being a Vyazemsky was not always an asset. Princess Ekaterina Romanovna Dashkova may have known Jenny, but it is not likely that they were friends. Andrey's father, Ivan, was a first cousin of Aleksandr Alekseyevich Vyazemsky (1727–1793), one of the most senior Russian administrators of the age.[21] He was Minister for Justice and Chancellor of the Exchequer and had responsibility for establishing territorial boundaries within Russia. He and Dashkova had a less than cordial relationship, and she remembered him as 'ignorant and vindictive'. According to her memoir, it was Aleksandr Alekseyevich who, as Minister for Justice, requested that Dashkova be sworn in in the same manner as any other state employee when she took up the directorship of the Russian Academy in 1783. This caused her a great deal of offence, as one of Russia's most celebrated noblewomen and a close personal friend of Catherine the Great. Furthermore, as Chancellor of the Exchequer, it was he who held the purse strings to the state fund to which the Russian Academy was in arrears at the time of Dashkova's commencement as director. She decided to reduce the price of Academy publications by 30 per cent, which increased sales and thereby paid off the institution's debts – but also caused Aleksandr Alekseyevich to 'create difficulties' for her in her role as Director of the Academy. Further, her memoir recounts how he ignored her recommendations for the promotion of subordinates and neglected to supply her with information about provincial boundaries, of which she wished the Academy to publish up-to-date maps. The relationship became unworkable and resulted in Dashkova tendering her resignation to Catherine II. The empress mediated a resolution, rejecting Dashkova's resignation and requesting that Aleksandr Alekseyevich apologize.[22]

It may be most appropriate to refer to Jenny not as an Irishwoman, or as an Irishwoman living in Russia, but as a transnational woman. Histories

The Mysterious Identities of Jenny O'Reilly or Evgeniya Ivanovna Vyazemskaya

of eighteenth-century Russia commonly emphasize the importance of French and English fashion and mores in upper-class culture. Yet there is little evidence that O'Reilly was particularly celebrated for her foreignness, or that she sought to cultivate prominence on that basis. Rather, she embraced Russian life through her flexible identity as a woman whose personal experiences of travel and personal drama appear as a prelude to the sensational marital breakdown and elopement of Margaret King, Lady Mount Cashell, (a close friend of Katherine Wilmot; see chapter 6) twenty years later. But Jenny was not only defined by her private relationships. Rather, she exerted agency through her decisive rebirth as Evgeniya and her intentional estrangement from her family. Her life was transnational, in keeping with the European Jacobite circles that her kin-group – the O'Reillys of the Irish military diaspora – moved in and depended upon. Local and international networks were crucial to the success and enduring power of the Irish military diaspora. As part of that diaspora, she was raised to speak both English and French and to conceive of her cultural heritage and of the political world in terms that transcended national borders.

6

THE WILMOT SISTERS AND PRINCESS DASHKOVA: FRIENDSHIP ACROSS GENERATIONS

While Jenny O'Reilly/Evgeniya Ivanovna Vyazemskaya was negotiating her admission to the highest ranks of Russian society, other Irish women forged international friendships through connections made while travelling. As a result, one of these women, Martha Wilmot, would later be thrust into the international spotlight as editor and translator of one of the most important women's memoirs of the Russian pre-revolutionary period. This network was the Wilmot–Dashkova circle, whose signature production was the collective enterprise of composing, translating and editing Princess Dashkova's famous *Memoirs*, first published in two volumes in 1840. This ranged from the initial impetus for the project – with which Dashkova credited Martha Wilmot – through Dashkova's painstaking and often pain*ful* work of recollection and composition; Martha and Katherine's roles as translators; Katherine's safe conveyance of copies of the politically sensitive manuscript from Russia to Ireland in 1807; Martha's task of translating, editing and selecting supplementary material;

and finally, in 1840, the publication of Martha's annotated translation. Martha's role as editor of the published volume made her name known in international literary circles and ensured her and Katherine's enduring legacies as Dashkova's closest companions in her later years. Even if they remained mostly unpublished until the early twentieth century, Martha and Katherine Wilmot's observations – along with their translation and edition of Dashkova's *Memoirs* – are now recognized as one of the most important English-language sources for early nineteenth-century Russian life. How the sisters came to be acquainted with Dashkova and to be counted among her closest confidantes in her later years was the result of an encounter at Spa in 1770.

It was at Spa that Dashkova first became acquainted with one of her dearest friends, Irishwoman Catherine Hamilton (*née* Ryder, d. 1805). The pair formed a devoted bond and would meet on several occasions in Ireland, England, on the Continent and in Russia. Little is known of Hamilton aside from her relationship with Dashkova, but she was key to the establishment of the Wilmot–Dashkova coterie in the first instance. She introduced Dashkova to her cousin, Captain Edward Wilmot, during the Russian princess's residence in Scotland and England in the 1770s. During a spell in Dublin in 1779–80 Dashkova became more closely acquainted with the Wilmot family and with the Irish philanthropist Lady Arabella Denny (1707–1792), with whom she maintained a warm friendship until Denny's death.[1] She made a splash in Dublin society, with the renowned artist Francis Wheatley depicting her leaning from a window of a house on College Green, watching a parade by the Dublin Volunteers. Hamilton visited Dashkova's Troitskoe estate in 1784–5, and Martha and Katherine Wilmot followed in 1803–8. Martha Wilmot later recalled that she went to Russia because she had always wanted to travel and had wished to meet Dashkova, having heard so much about her from Catherine Hamilton – she was a young child when Dashkova was in Ireland.[2] (Indeed, Dashkova's name was well known in Ireland; in Moscow in 1807 the young Irish gentlemen Arthur Pollock, John Ladeveze Adlercron and Welbore Ellis Agar, Viscount Somerton, met the Wilmots, but were disappointed not to meet 'the famous Old Princess Dashkoff'.[3]) For her part, Dashkova later recalled, 'I was very well placed in England and Ireland with the Wilmot family, and their parents, all the very best of people, the best friend that I ever had [Catherine Hamilton] persuaded her young cousin M[artha] W[ilmot] to come and share my solitude.'[4] Learned and accomplished women of Eastern and Western Europe reached out to one another through this international chain of friendship. Their connections were formed and maintained on the strength of a shared literary culture within the tradition of the 'republic of letters', of which Dashkova was a respected citizen.

The printed lists of visitors to Spa that yield such valuable clues relating to the lives of Jenny O'Reilly and Andrey Ivanovich Vyazemsky also record the formation of the first connections in the Wilmot–Dashkova coterie. Dashkova is found in the *Lists* in July 1770, under a pseudonym. 'Mme de Michalkaw' was her homage to her dearly beloved late husband, Mikhail Ivanovich Dashkov (1736–1764), and while they are not mentioned in the *Lists*, her two children did accompany her.[5] The party also included a nanny, Mlle Kamensky, and a relation, Mr 'de Worontzow'.[6] It was not unusual for high-profile travellers to go by a pseudonym, and it was part of the princess's assumption of a simultaneously modest and celebrity persona. But eccentricity, rather than modesty, was the impression Dashkova made on the famous English diarist and courtier Mary Hamilton (1756–1816) when they met in Spa in 1776. She noted that Dashkova's 'usual morning dress' was formed of men's clothing and that the princess was unable to sing or play music in public because of illness and nerves.[7]

For her part, Dashkova later described Spa as 'a place of most delightful recollections' and as the foundation site of some of her most deeply valued friendships – those with Catherine Hamilton and Elizabeth Morgan, which, in Dashkova's words, 'stood the test of time and absence, and all human casualties, for five and thirty years'.[8] Dashkova named one of her villages 'Gamiltonovka' in honour of her lasting friendship with Hamilton.[9] She delighted in recollecting the progress she made in the English language with the assistance of Hamilton and Morgan, and the trips she made in winter 1770 to France and Switzerland with Hamilton and to England with Morgan.[10] Hamilton and Dashkova would meet again at Spa in 1775 or 1776, honouring an engagement made in 1770–1.[11] By contrast, Dashkova's visit to Paris in winter 1771–2 was spent in relative isolation, except for making the acquaintance of the philosopher Denis Diderot and indulging in the city's arts and architecture.[12] Dashkova's portrait of Spa as a meeting-place corresponds with the experiences of Irish women travellers and with the historical reputation of the town as the 'crossroads of Europe'.[13]

Most importantly, the Irish connections Dashkova made in Spa laid the foundations of the most important personal relationship of her later life – her friendship with Martha Wilmot. Historian Elizabeth Eger has shown how bluestocking friendships were the culmination of early feminist thought that emphasized the cultivation of personal independence through correspondence, and whose attachments found expression in objects and gifts – this certainly describes Martha Wilmot and Dashkova's relationship.[14] Spanning generations, with a thirty-year age gap, Martha Wilmot and Dashkova's friendship was partly modelled on what Amanda Herbert describes as the 'idealized, classically inspired friendships' that were familiar to Enlightenment readers through the fashionable circulation of the classical texts of Plato, Aristotle and Cicero.[15] Yet there was also a familial element to the relationship, with Dashkova adopting a maternal role. She referred to Martha by the diminutive 'Matouchka' and wrote of her as 'mon enfant cheris, mon ange, mon tout'.[16] She also wrote to Empress Dowager Maria Feodorovna in July 1806 with a request that in the event of her death, Martha Wilmot would be placed under the Empress Dowager's patronage and to ensure the donation of £5000 to the foundling hospital in Moscow in Martha's name.[17] The strength of Dashkova's attachment to Martha led to conflict with her daughter Anastasiya, culminating in a public scene at Dashkova's son Pavel's funeral in 1807, during which Anastasiya verbally attacked Martha and Katherine.[18] Dashkova thereafter cut Anastasiya from her will.[19]

Martha, for her part, felt a mixture of filial obligation and intellectual admiration for the older woman who had accomplished so much and had shown her so much kindness. The question of Martha's return to Ireland

The Wilmot Sisters and Princess Dashkova: Friendship across Generations

became pressing in 1807, when Britain and Russia were no longer allies and her elder sister Katherine had already departed, leaving Martha in defiance of her parents' wishes that she also return home. Tortured by indecision and feelings of guilt in relation to her 'Russian mother' as well as her own parents, Martha considered herself 'a prisoner in the true sense of the word, tho' the prisoner of friendship' and prayed for 'a speedy peace'.[20] She had declined an opportunity to sail to England in late 1807, stubbornly and loyally refusing to leave the ageing and ailing Dashkova until she became an object of Russian government suspicion and came to fear for her own safety due to (not entirely reliable) reports of the war. The decision to remain overshadowed her final year in Russia. Reflecting on events a year later, she cursed herself

> for suffering the single sentiment of gratitude, to master my reason, and all the affections which bind me to my native land for blinding me to the very peculiar circumstances which entangle me here, and were I to lose any of my family or near friends before I see them, a thousand self reproaches would aggravate the loss, and embitter my existence.[21]

Responding to others' admiration for the devotion that tied her to Russia, Martha wrote bitterly, 'Dearly as I love her [Dashkova] I cannot accept as praise, what I look upon as madness.'[22] The continuing war exacerbated an already difficult situation, torn as she was between the family she had not seen for five years and an ageing friend to whom she had grown much attached over the same period, a friend passing her final years virtually in exile after an illustrious and active youth. An opportunity to return to Ireland came in late September 1808. Martha, in no little distress and convinced that she would miss her last opportunity of passage to London, left her 'Russian mother' and the palace that had been her home for five years. Friends and acquaintances reported Dashkova's continuing and unabated distress at Martha's departure; the older woman was, at the time, also grieving the death of her son.[23] Martha vowed to return to Russia after spending an appropriate amount of time with her family, but did not manage to do so before Dashkova's death in 1810.

The Wilmot Sisters and Princess Dashkova: Friendship across Generations

While new freedoms were opened to the sisters during their travels, Martha re-burdened herself by assuming filial responsibilities towards Dashkova. She may have established such deep, meaningful personal relationships to create a homely or safe place in a time of war. As she left Russia with a heavy heart, Martha took consolation in the company of her little 'Russian dog', Krasota ('Beauty'). She had received the puppy – which she described as an 'atom of a Dog' – two months earlier and had looked forward to 'teaching it to know nothing but Russ, and having a living memorial of a Country where so many years of my life have been spent, and in it a memorial of one of Princess D's great passions'.[24] The King Charles spaniel represented the possibility of having a constant reminder of Russia and of her 'Russian mother', who particularly favoured that breed of dog. A few days before Martha's departure, however, Krasota, 'who was growing so Comical, so playful, and who began to know me, and to amuse me excessively' was found to be 'paraletic by inheritance'. Krasota began to recover, but Martha was devastated to find that during the journey to St Petersburg the animal had been 'smothered with bed clothes in the Calash during the Night'. She and her travelling companions buried the dog under a birch tree. The grief she recorded in her diary at the death of the 'dear little creature' makes for striking reading.[25]

Dashkova showered both Martha and Katherine with gifts, which Martha and her daughter Catherine catalogued in a 'green book' in 1859.[26] There were gifts of money; diamonds and jewellery; shawls and sables; books, watercolours and prints; miniatures representing Russian and other European royals; a fan and a pink snuffbox that once belonged to Catherine II; an opium pipe, schnapps cup and watch formerly owned by Peter I; an opal once belonging to Christina of Sweden; and portraits of both sisters made by a Russian artist, in which Katherine was depicted cloaked in furs. Martha described her feelings on being presented with Catherine II's fan 'as one of the most valuable memorandums of friendship which I possess'.[27] The monetary value of the objects was incidental. Katherine concluded: 'Tis all a chance when [Martha] gets really valuable things, for whether it is a diamond or a flower I think the princess seems to know no difference,

The Wilmot Sisters and Princess Dashkova: Friendship across Generations

and would not give it, if she thought there was any other value attached, than what her affection ensures.'[28] The symbolic power of gift-giving was even clearer in the things that Dashkova treasured, for what can be given to a woman who has no material needs? Dashkova famously wore to threads a dress that had previously belonged to her old friend Catherine Hamilton and kept a pair of Martha's gloves to remember her by.[29] Their value was as material symbols of strong relationships that were maintained largely through correspondence, with only intermittent – if intense – periods together. Before Martha's departure, Russian acquaintances asked her for locks of her hair. Tellingly, she refused one noblewoman she did not know very well because, as 'being part of myself', she would only give her hair 'as the highest compliment to those who loved me and *who made it valuable or not by their affection for me*'.[30]

From Martha's point of view, the greatest gift she received from Dashkova was the editorial rights to the princess's memoirs. In 1935 H. Montgomery Hyde, historian and biographer of Dashkova, Catherine II and the Wilmots, stated that Dashkova's *Memoirs* had been 'long out of print and forgotten',[31] but at the time of their publication in 1840 they created something of a sensation. The book had been much anticipated and, as the historian Simon Dixon notes, was 'doubtless made the more enticing by Bantysh-Kamenskii's declaration, in his 1836 *Dictionary of Famous People* that they were "unpublishable in our time"'.[32] Martha Wilmot's friends and acquaintances, particularly those who had also known the princess, pressured her to publish the manuscript from the time of Dashkova's death in 1810. The potential for controversy in the memoir was such that three years after Dashkova's death her brother, Count Simon Vorontsov, entered into a rather hostile correspondence with Martha, demanding that she wait another thirty years to publish the book.[33] He died in 1832, but Wilmot respected his wishes, referring in her editorial introduction to a 'near relative' of the princess who had 'feelings unfavourable' towards the publication, despite Dashkova's elder brother, Count Aleksandr, having already given approval for the first volume.[34] The considerable delay between composition and publication did not go unremarked upon, with one review opening with the lines: 'Much of the interest belonging to these *Memoirs* has been superseded by Time. If they had been published thirty or forty years ago, the recollections of the profligate Catherine would have appealed to a generation which knew something of her and her period; but these have passed away.'[35] There were, though, positive responses too. One reviewer considered the volumes 'well worthy of perusal both for their personal and national sketches' and particularly commended Katherine Wilmot's 'admirable letters [which] form parts of the illustrations which enrich the Memoirs. We know not if we read anything more delicate, terse, and vividly descriptive.' Indeed, the same reviewer valued the book for its collaborative nature, 'on account of the glimpses which the notes and illustrations collected from various quarters afford of their several writers.'[36] The Irish novelist Maria Edgeworth was moved to congratulate Wilmot personally:

> Her [Dashkova's] character alone would have been sufficient to make
> the book very interesting [...] such indisputable evidence and bearing
> eternally and naturally the stamp of truth make the work of historic value
> and besides its popularity must ensure its lasting as a notice *pour l'histoire*.
> We are very glad that justice has at last been done to that noble Princess
> Daschkaw's memory – she has been sadly misunderstood.[37]

Despite Edgeworth's praise for Martha Wilmot's editorial work, she disapproved of some of the content, especially Dashkova's continued contact with the soldier and statesman Count Alexei Grigoryevich Orlov (1737–1808), given his role in the death of Peter III as one of the key conspirators in Catherine II's plot against her husband. She wrote to Wilmot: 'The only point I dislike is the Princess's ordering or accepting a ball from that Orloff the actual murderer – tho so many years had elapsed not 40 or 50 or any number of years can wear out the stain of blood – I wonder that she could bear to see him.'[38] Edgeworth was, however, more forthright in a letter to another friend:

> After reading the book I wrote to Mrs Wilmot, and after homage due
> to her talents and her truth, I ventured to express, what I am sure you
> will feel if you read the volume, some horror, towards the close, at the

The Wilmot Sisters and Princess Dashkova: Friendship across Generations

> Princess Dashkoff's accepting for herself or her sister, or for whoever it
> was, a ball from Orloff the murderer – that Orloff who with his own hand
> strangled his emperor. Mrs Wilmot made me but a lame apology for her
> dear princess, I think, and an odd answer for herself. In the first place,
> she said, It was so long ago. As if such a murder could be a by-gone tale!
> or as if thirty or forty or any number of years could purify or cleanse a
> murderer in the eyes and sense of Humanity or Justice![39]

Edgeworth seems to refer to a passage from Katherine's letter to her
sister Alicia of 18 February 1806, reproduced in the *Memoirs*, in which she
describes the 'Moscow ghosts', the 'grandees [...] of another world', with
whom she became acquainted in Moscow. Orlov, with his 'hand which
strangled Peter the Third [...] covered with its recompence of brilliants',
was among their number.[40]

But Martha's role was more than that of editor and translator – it was
thanks to her that Dashkova ever embarked on the project. On 10 February
1804 Martha recorded in her diary: 'The Princess has begun to write her
life. Her motive for so doing is friendship to me, as she says she will give
me the manuscript and liberty to publish it.'[41] Indeed, Wilmot's influence
over the project was such that the extent to which Dashkova tailored the
text to 'suit the manners and morals of her immediate reader [Martha
Wilmot]' has been questioned.[42] Later, in her editor's introduction to the
work, Wilmot publicly reinforced her role in encouraging Dashkova to pen
the manuscript, writing that the older woman 'appeared to me a being of so
superior an order, that I listened earnestly to every word she uttered which
threw any light on her early life, and longed to hear more of it in detail.
I thought also she owed it to herself, and to those who loved her, to let her
character be known.'[43] The text was intended not only as a record, but a
vindication – obvious to readers at the time, as indicated by Edgeworth's
comments above. Indeed, Dashkova claimed that she had never wished to
record her life story until she met 'my young friend for whose sake I have
overcome my repugnance at the idea of writing these memoirs.'[44] Dashkova
had come to consider Wilmot as a daughter, so dedicating the *Memoirs* to
her and crediting her with their creation can be considered an expression

of the eighteenth-century Russian norm of composing a memoir for private circulation within the family.[45] Giving Wilmot the rights to the manuscript was also a gift – a path into public literary life. Martha then chose to honour her late sister Katherine alongside her 'Russian mother' by publishing her witty and incisive letters as an appendix to her edition of the *Memoirs*, a decision that reflected her characteristic sensitivity to the importance of family and friendship.

The Wilmot–Dashkova circle coalesced around shared activities and intellectual interests, and intense personal relationships. For this circle of friends, correspondence was a way of sharing ideas and holding the group together. They were so accustomed to interacting with each other on paper that while Martha Wilmot lived with Dashkova on her rural estate, the pair habitually communicated by short notes carried around the palace by servants. One of these simple notes touched Martha so deeply that she planned to keep it 'as a memorandum of the inestimable affection which I am happy enough to possess.'[46] These women's lives were defined by mobility and travel and were characterized by the constant exchange and circulation of ideas, writings and gifts.

Martha Wilmot's long relationship with Russia found a later echo through her son. In July 1812 Martha married Reverend William Bradford, who had recently returned from service as a British Army chaplain in the Peninsular War. They had a long and happy marriage, enjoying shared interests in history and travel. Making their home at William's parish of Storrington in Sussex, they had three children: Catherine Dashkov (1813–1882), Blanche Elizabeth (b. 1814) and Wilmot Henry (1815–1914). In 1819–29 the family lived in Vienna, where William was chaplain to the British Embassy and Martha devoted herself to her children's education. Their son, Wilmot, later became a senior officer in the British Army, commanding a battalion of the Rifle Brigade and the Royal Canadian Rifle Regiment in the Crimean War, including at the siege of Sebastopol.

7

A VIEW FROM DOWNSTAIRS: ELEANOR CAVANAGH, A LADY'S MAID IN RUSSIA

In 1813 *The Universal Magazine* published two letters from Russia that the editor considered valuable because they 'expressed the native unsophisticated feelings of an uneducated Irish girl [...] and present an amusing instance of the impression produced by novelty upon such a mind'. The correspondent, identified only as 'M.S.', stated that the letters displayed 'that shrewd simplicity which marks the Irish character'. These letters were by Eleanor Cavanagh, lady's maid to Katherine Wilmot, and *The Universal Magazine* published her letters long before the Wilmot sisters' own observations ever became publicly available. It is unlikely that Eleanor's permission was sought or given for the publication. The purpose of publicizing the letters was not to enhance British knowledge of Russia, but to poke fun at a lower-class Irish woman.

The author of this cruelty seems to have been Lady Maria Josepha Stanley, who may have been given a copy of Eleanor's letters by Sarah 'Serena' Holroyd. In 1812 Holroyd told Stanley that Martha Wilmot had let her read some Russian letters after meeting her in Bath, but only 'on condition of keeping the secret', which she evidently did not.[1] Private correspondence suggests a widespread mean-spirited interest in Cavanagh's Russian letters. In 1810 Princess Dashkova's old Dublin friend, Mrs Morgan, requested that Martha Wilmot not omit Cavanagh's Russian letters from her edition of Dashkova's memoirs, 'over which bit of perfection [...] I read and laughed, over and over, till tears rolled from [my] eyes'.[2] In the end Martha did include one of Cavanagh's letters in the appendices to the *Memoirs*. Remarkably, the lady's maid's letters were published alongside correspondence between Dashkova and Enlightenment public figures.[3] Today, the letters can be appreciated for the unusual perspective they provide from 'below stairs' and for Eleanor's unselfconscious wonder at her new experiences in Russia – but at the time, they formed part of the caricaturing of the Irish as foolish, naïve and uncouth.

Almost nothing is known of Eleanor's early life. She appears to have been born and raised in Cork, possibly in Glanmire, and had four brothers. In summer 1805 she travelled to Russia as Katherine Wilmot's maid, remaining there with her until they returned to Ireland together in July 1807. Her original letters – one to her father and one to Henrietta Chetwood, a neighbour of the Wilmots – have not been located, but two manuscript copies made by Martha Wilmot and her sister Alicia survive in the Royal Irish Academy.[4] The letters record Eleanor's understanding of Russian life and culture, but just as importantly, they show the friendship that existed between a maid and Henrietta Chetwood, daughter of a better-off, middling-sort family, one of the younger of the nine children of the local Church of Ireland rector. Eleanor signed off her letter to Henrietta with the touching words, 'I like to think of you very much, Miss Henrietta, and would be glad you wouldn't forget me, no more than I'd forget yourself.'

Eleanor's first letter was written within a few weeks of her arrival in Russia and tells us that Henrietta Chetwood had asked her to 'send my love to you, all the way from Russia [...] to tell you, how I liked Russia'. She relates her impressions in a conversational manner, using memorable turns of phrase, beginning her account by emphasizing the strangeness of

A View from Downstairs: Eleanor Cavanagh, a Lady's Maid in Russia

the things she had seen in London and in St Petersburg: 'If I know no more than a Fool, how to make it out! But tis quair things I have been seeing!' The passage through the Baltic was smoother than crossing the Irish Sea; hens aboard ship provided fresh eggs during the voyage, and there was a good-natured manservant on board who she said 'did everything like the father of a family'. Arriving in Kronstadt, near St Petersburg, she was delighted to find English maids in the house of Mr Brooker, the English agent, but she was unimpressed by local fashion: 'Why wouldn't they content themselves to dress like Christians? Miss Henrietta, twou'd sour one, to look at the craitures, with their blue, and yellow, and green cloth Petticoats, bound with gold, and bouncing bobs or air-rings in their airs, and shift sleeves, like Men's shirt sleeves! 'twould make one ashamed to think how they'd ape the quality!' She was astonished at the scale of the palaces of St Petersburg but did not enjoy the hot Russian summer, joking that 'the Sun here, I believe, is a bigger one and more Scalding one than in Ireland!' Walking about the city with the servants of the palace in which she and Katherine Wilmot were staying, she was startled by the lifelike quality of the famous equestrian statue of Peter the Great, whom she referred to as 'some old Snake of a man, that they call Peter! or Peter the Great, or something like that'.

Eleanor's second letter was addressed to her father and, like the one she wrote to Henrietta Chetwood, she was aware that it would be passed around family, friends and neighbours. Her greeting conveyed fondness and excitement – 'Tis best my dear Father, to begin by mentioning that I'm in Russia!' – and the following lines reassured him that she was comfortable during the long overland journey from St Petersburg to Dashkova's Moscow residence. On Eleanor's arrival, Martha Wilmot presented her with a silk cloak lined with fur and fabric to make a new gown. Martha's Russian maid, Sophia, welcomed Eleanor to the palace with a warmth that must have helped her feel at home in her new, grand surroundings.

Eleanor forthrightly admitted the difficulty she had in engaging with the Russian servants, struggling to accept that the maids wore jewellery – she thought it was above their station – and finding the men's beards and ponytails frightening. She did not know how to relate to the African servant, or his Russian words for everyday things like bread, telling Henrietta Chetwood that it would 'turn one's heart into a curd, fairly, to hear them say DA instead of YES, and NIET instead of NO'. Lacking her mistress's Enlightened anti-slavery perspective, Eleanor was short on sympathy for Russian serfs, telling Henrietta, 'They call them slaves tho, but never the bit of a chain do I see hanging about them any way.' It is possible that she did not fully understand their legal position, as she naïvely described to her father the population of Dashkova's estate: 'There is 16 Villages, all belonging to the Princess, here, and them that lives in them, comes to the number of 3000 men and women, all her subjects, and loving her as if she was their Mother. There is 200 servants that lives in and out of the House.' This vision of Dashkova as a mother to her serfs mirrored Catherine II's self-image as a 'little mother' (*Matushka*) to her subjects. While Dashkova endeavoured to portray herself as a benevolent mistress, she undoubtedly viewed the serfs as her property.[5] Eleanor's perspective may have been coloured by her excitement at meeting Dashkova, whom she had 'heard talk of so much in Ireland, and all through Russia'. She was not disappointed as the princess introduced herself with a kiss, 'smiling and looking as good natured as a child'. Dashkova treated the Irish maid kindly, giving her gifts of money, silks and a shawl. When Dashkova's household relocated from rural Troitskoe to Moscow for the 1805–6 winter season, the princess ensured that Eleanor was able to fully enjoy the sights and sounds of the assembly by guiding her to a 'maid's gallery', from where she had a good view of the glittering noble crowd.[6] The Wilmots also involved Cavanagh in their activities, bringing her to see a traditional wedding ceremony, for example.[7]

Life at Troitskoe was very different to life in the Wilmot family home in Cork. There were 200 servants employed in the palace to wait on just four women: Dashkova, her niece Anna Petrovna, Martha Wilmot and Katherine Wilmot; another 2500–3000 serfs were indentured on the estate. In her classic study of Russian estate life, Priscilla Roosevelt notes that because these households had such huge numbers of servants, they were allocated extremely specific responsibilities; in Dashkova's Moscow palace, one man's sole purpose was to walk from room to room, perfuming the air with a censer.[8] Eleanor thought that she and the Russian housemaids lived 'like queens'.[9] The palace was vast; Martha Wilmot had four rooms at her disposal, one in which her maid Sophia slept, and one for her wardrobe.[10] The palace library contained, in Katherine Wilmot's words, 'I know not how many thousand Volumes in half a dozen Languages.' Dinner on an average day at Troitskoe went as follows:

> You must first eat Egg pattys with your Soup and then drink Hydromel to wash them down or else Quass. With your roasted meat you must eat Salt Cucumbers, and then Caviare made of the roe of Sturgeon. Young Pig and Curdled Cream is at Your service next, and lachat which is the general name for all grain baked with Cream. Fish soup do you chuse? Fowls? Game? Vegetables? or Apple bread? or raw Apples from the Crimea? or the Siberian Apples? or the transparent Apples? or the Kieff sweetmeat? or Honey comb? or preserved rose leaves, or pickled plums? In the name of goodness eat no more, for in six or seven hours you will have to sit down to just such another dinner under the name of Supper.[11]

Such luxury and plenty depended on an economic system founded on the servitude of the vast majority of Russians. Injustice on this scale did not go unchallenged – the Pugachev peasant revolt of 1773 remained fresh in the minds of the Russian nobility, who feared that the peasants armed against Napoleon would turn those same arms against their masters once more. Indeed, Troitskoe palace was burnt to the ground during the Napoleonic invasion of 1812 by 'enraged or needy peasants'; Dashkova did not live to witness this.[12] Today, little remains of her rural retreat, save the listing and crumbling front gates.

Eleanor's correspondence portrays a woman who was keenly aware of the interest her letters would generate in the small community of Glanmire. She would have known to expect them to be read and shared widely, and that they would form a lively subject of conversation among family, friends and neighbours. Her letters relate anecdotes that show her rising to the moral challenges presented by overseas travel and access to a

A View from Downstairs: Eleanor Cavanagh, a Lady's Maid in Russia

higher standard of living, and her resistance to any perceived corrupting influences. She made certain to relate her continued dedication to Catholic religious observances, her careful maintenance of distance between herself and 'her betters', and her rejection of male attention. She asked Henrietta Chetwood to 'tell my Father and Mother, that I often thinks of their advice, and follows it', and to tell 'my people below in the village' that Martha Wilmot had found a Catholic priest to hear Eleanor's confession. Her pride in her work was obvious, particularly when she told Henrietta that she had been asked to make a gown for Countess Osterman to wear to the imperial court, modelled on a gown of Katherine Wilmot's. Alongside the excitement of her new experiences, she missed her family and told Henrietta Chetwood that she was 'often thinking of everybody in Ireland'. She worried about their wellbeing while she was so far away and asked her father whether any of her four brothers were ill, as she had been having recurring dreams about them. Nothing is known of Eleanor's life after her return from Russia, but I like to think of her regaling her family and friends in Cork with tales of the glamour, feasts and unusual experiences she had over those two years. She wrote, 'Russia! and good luck to you, you are a comical place! and you'll give me something to talk of, many a long day!'

III
Jaunts to Inter-War Russia

Some travellers will see in Russia a paternal and mild government; strict, but just laws; brilliant and polished society; benevolent and charitable institutions: while others (and among them the generality of modern authors) will see in Russia a vast charnel-house, a terrible prison, where confiscation, the knout, and Siberia, are for ever in constant view, and whose hideous forms present themselves to the stranger at every moment; where laws are but licenses for oppression; society but a smooth and dark surface, that hides the horrors that lurk beneath; and the educational establishments of the country but vast manèges for the breaking-in of youthful slaves. My intention is not to enter deeply on these subjects, but merely to relate, for the amusement of the reader, a few incidents of travel, leaving him to form his own opinions as to the truth or falsehood of his former impressions. A galloping and steaming tour of eleven weeks, cannot contain much real information; but I fain would hope that its results may afford something that may help to while away an idle hour.

Richard Southwell Bourke, *St Petersburg and Moscow* (1846), pp. 12–13

If you were wealthy and in search of adventure in the 1830s or 1840s, your eye might have travelled eastward across the pages of your atlas. Early Victorian interest in Russia and Central Asia was shaped by Britain's growing concern with the integrity of India's borders. The Russian Empire – occupying much of the space between Western Europe and the jewel in Victoria's crown – emerged reborn from the conflagration of the Napoleonic Wars, the first 'world war'. For a time between 1815 and 1855 Russia and Britain managed a peace of sorts, each empire cultivating its own expansion until their borders crept to within an uncomfortable touching distance in Central Asia. Irish perceptions of Russia in this period were coloured by growing excitement about the possibilities offered by the East, even if these primarily existed in the Western European imagination. Russia was considered part of this imagined Orient, with visitors seeking evidence of barbarism and autocracy. Those who travelled through Russia en route to the Middle East, Central Asia or India used it not only as a land-bridge, but as a cultural stepping-stone to the Orient of their imagination. The rapid expansion of European colonialism, trade and exploration from the 1760s created a vast body of information relating to every continent. Asia's importance for British global trade and India's symbolic importance in the British Empire gave the region prominence, so that by the 1850s, when a European spoke of anything as being 'Oriental', they were automatically understood as placing Europe in the dominant position. Russia was absorbed into this power structure.

Young Irish gentlemen like Arthur Pollock and John Ladeveze Adlercron, both from Co. Meath, and Welbore Ellis Agar, Viscount Somerton, all visited Russia in 1806–7 (Fig. 4).[1] In 1845 Corry Connellan – a barrister who would in 1846 become private secretary to the Lord Lieutenant of Ireland – travelled from St Petersburg to Krakow via Warsaw, possibly as part of a bigger tour to the ancient city of Palmyra via Constantinople and onwards to Egypt.[2] Irish-born John Ross Browne travelled from the US to St Petersburg to make a tour 'along the borders of the Arctic Circle' encompassing Finland, Norway, the Faro Islands and Iceland.[3]

This section focuses on four very different Irish experiences of Russia in the period between the end of the Napoleonic Wars and the outbreak of the Crimean War. The perspectives and experiences of John Bloomfield, William Hartigan Barrington, Arthur MacMurrough Kavanagh and Richard Southwell Bourke converge and diverge in interesting ways. All were from landed and titled families with considerable interests in Ireland. Barrington (aged twenty-two), MacMurrough Kavanagh (aged eighteen) and Bourke (aged twenty-three) were all unmarried young gentlemen; all were dependent on parental financial support; all were of wealthy, Irish landowning families; and all had been well educated. Career diplomat John Bloomfield was attached to the British Embassy in St Petersburg in the 1820s and in 1839–51, witnessing a devastating cholera outbreak in Russia while hearing about the Great Famine ravaging Ireland at the same time. William Hartigan Barrington was the son of a self-made landowner whose business acumen and legal prowess helped him to re-instate the family noble title, which had long been extinct. He traversed social boundaries to investigate poor relief and social conditions in Russia in 1837, in light of his father's philanthropic activities in Ireland. Arthur MacMurrough Kavanagh, unimpeded by being born without limbs, travelled through Russia as part of a wider tour covering Scandinavia, Central Asia and India in 1849–51 with his brother Thomas and Reverend David Wood in a journey that contains all the elements of a classic adventure story. His position as a person with a disability meant that he could neglect no gentlemanly rites of passage – he had to prove himself. Finally, Richard Southwell Bourke's journey fulfilled the function that the grand tour had in the eighteenth century, putting the final touches on an exclusive education but with the added spice of a destination considered more morally challenging.

Together, these journeys to Russia are important records of how Victorian masculinity was constructed in destinations that were specifically chosen for the geographical and cultural difficulties they were thought to present. All of these young gentlemen used travel as a means of securing their social positions, their journeys indicating the significance of outdoor pursuits, physical endurance and social skills in the formation of the Victorian landed gentleman – all elements that could be honed during a difficult and costly journey through Russia. These challenges were in evidence when Meath native John Ladeveze Adlercron and his Irish companions (a Major O'Shea and a Thomas White) were robbed three times while travelling from Vienna to Moscow via Krakow and Minsk in 1806.[4] But it was also important that Russia was considered Oriental, and therefore a completely different cultural experience – an image that was enhanced by the Great Exhibition of 1851. Reports of this large-scale public event, with 14,000 exhibitors crowded into London's Crystal Palace, emphasized Russian luxury goods and riches over its technological or military power to confirm popular preconceptions about the vast empire.[5]

When the great powers came together to reshape Europe at the 1815 Congress of Vienna, Russia re-established itself as one of the most important European powers, gaining new political respect. Change came both in terms of external perceptions of Russia and in the Russian state's cultivation of its own image. However, this international political transformation was not accompanied by internal reforms. The continuation of serfdom epitomized this failure. On the one hand, Alexander I appeared to have a reforming agenda, allowing missionaries from various religious groups to enter the country for charitable work – including a small group of Irish Quakers who visited prisons, schools and hospitals, and, shortly afterwards, Waterford-born Reverend Robert Walsh of the Christian Bible Society, who published an account of the annual blessing of the Neva and other Orthodox practices.[6] Despite the tsar's aspirations of introducing a free press, a parliament and the reorganization of Russia as a federation, the combination of Russia's annexation of central Poland, the endurance of serfdom and ongoing restrictions on everyday freedoms diverted international attention from his reform programme which, in the event, was not realized by the time of his death in 1825. Thereafter, Nicholas I's reactionary and oppressive rule – characterized by censorship, restrictions on societies and regulations aimed at stifling opposition – left Russia without a friend in Europe by 1850.[7]

8

AN IRISH GENTLEMAN EXPERIENCES RUSSIAN POVERTY

In 1833–7 Sir Matthew Barrington funded his son William's travels around Western and Central Europe, Scandinavia, Russia, Spain and North Africa. Sir Matthew had not been born into the peerage but earned his title in 1831, with the revival of a baronetage that had been dormant for two centuries in recognition of his philanthropic work. Allowing his son to spend so much time away from the family's new estate – and to spend so much money – indicates the social and cultural importance of travel for well-to-do families of the period. William was expected to learn languages and familiarize himself with European history and high culture. As the son of a progressive, newly titled landowner, he was also expected to acquaint himself with social problems and philanthropic provisions in the countries he visited. He recorded his experiences in diaries that have never been published but are part of the National Library of Ireland's collections today.

Limerick-born William Hartigan Barrington (1815–1872) visited Russia and Scandinavia in 1837, at the age of twenty-two. This itinerary was not uncommon at the time, an alternative to the centuries-old formula of the grand tour of France and Italy. Travellers to Northern and Eastern

Europe retained elements of the traditional grand tour – visiting sites of architectural importance, museums, antiquities and theatres, and forming suitable connections and networks – and applied them to destinations that were seen as carrying less cultural heft. This gave rise to a slight shift in focus, giving travellers like Barrington the opportunity to explore social themes in his diaries. His father may even have actively encouraged him to gather information on poverty, supports for the destitute and the poor laws in the countries through which he travelled. The Anglican Matthew Barrington was widely known and celebrated for his charitable work, particularly for founding Barrington's Hospital in Limerick, an important resource for the poor of the district prior to the establishment of the Poor Law in 1838.[1] Sir Matthew's endeavours were informed by international models – the charitable pawnbroker's he founded in Limerick in the 1830s, the *mont de piété*, was based on a Napoleonic institution. It is likely that he wished his son to collect information and ideas from Scandinavia and Russia, too.

Overseas travel played an important social and cultural role for eighteenth- and nineteenth-century genteel and landowning families.[2] Many of them visited Western Europe on a regular, even annual, basis. Cities like Paris and Rome naturally attracted large numbers of well-to-do Irish, but smaller towns like Spa in Belgium were lively in the summer months, as shown in Chapter 6. The ability to travel for pleasure or curiosity demonstrated wealth and a cosmopolitan outlook. Matthew Barrington intentionally secured a noble title for himself and his heir, ensured that his sons received the best possible education, built a rural mansion (Glenstal Castle) and shared his wealth and good fortune in ways befitting a gentleman of his standing.[3] He also permitted his heir, William, to travel extensively in the name of polishing his exclusive education in languages, history, politics and the classics. For its educational value and the social capital it engendered, travel was an essential rite of passage for the Victorian gentleman.[4] Maria Edgeworth's father, Richard Lovell Edgeworth, wrote in 1809 that travel would afford the country gentleman 'a large stock of agreeable and useful ideas, which may serve for future employment and amusement in the many leisure hours he will pass in retirement' and that the productive manner in which he had spent his time abroad should be evident in his manners and conversation.[5] William seems to have been well aware of these expectations, because he searched the bookshops of Hamburg for a history of Denmark, wished to improve his German by extending his stay in Dresden and (by his own account) took care to appear well-informed when making new acquaintances during his journey.[6]

Gentlemanly travel had another characteristic that was less frankly discussed but was certainly taken for granted – sexual freedom. At liberty to associate with whomever he chose, Barrington met with several young women during his tour, as his diary records. In Hamburg, one young woman presented him with a ring made by her father, a carver of coquilla nuts. In contempt for her father's lowly occupation – and, possibly, her forwardness – he dubbed her 'Miss Coquilio', never recording her real name. In Sweden, he was given a lock of hair by a young woman named Tilda and learned the language from some local girls who he thought took 'great pleasure' in teaching him.[7]

William did not wish to be seen merely collecting the same stories or experiences as others. He complained after one St Petersburg dinner party that 'nothing Russian' was served and claimed that 'people always fancy the English wish to live when abroad as much as possible in the style of an English farmer or John Bull. With me I know it is quite the contrary. I should wish as much as possible to avoid our English customs.' He wrote that he was determined to 'try everything', but in the end, he only attended a few Russian Orthodox church services and visited a *banya* (sauna).[8]

His desire for experiences outside of the norm (as he perceived them) led him to explore itineraries that brought him to the edges of Europe and to the fringes of society. His Russian itinerary was far from original, taking in only the cities of St Petersburg and Moscow, but his interest in Russian efforts to deal with widespread poverty makes his diaries stand out from other Irish accounts of the country in the period. (That said, English churchman and travel writer William Coxe published an account of Russia in 1778 that included detailed descriptions of Russian prisons and hospitals.) While it may be unthinkable today, in the eighteenth and nineteenth centuries personal travel diaries were often shared with family and friends. William's father may have intended to read his journals after his return home, and William may well have focused on information that he knew would be of interest to his father.

William approvingly recorded the extent and success of private philanthropy in Russia, noting that Moscow had more charitable institutions and 'schools for all classes and all at very moderate expense, some for nothing' than any other city he had visited. He visited the famous foundling hospital founded by Catherine II in 1763, for example, noting that they had 'even more funds than they want' and that private donations were supplemented by a charitable pawn shop comparable to his father's *mont de piété* in Limerick.[9] He made detailed notes on the foundling hospital, the rules by which the children lived and how they were employed. It was just one part of a complex of institutions, including a maternity hospital, a children's cholera hospital and a home for widows. William also visited one of Moscow's two military hospitals, finding it clean and efficiently run and noting how well the soldiers tended to the well-fed patients.[10] What William failed to note, however, was the fact that private benevolence was in fact the source of most welfare provision in Russia, to compensate for state failures.[11]

The positive impression generated by such generous private philanthropy was eroded by the realities of Russian life. Like so many other nineteenth-century visitors, William noted the 'melancholy sight' of shackled prisoners taking leave of their pastor to begin the long march to Siberia (Fig. 5). Nor could he ignore the crowds of beggars outside every church, or the poverty so visible even in the smaller towns on the road between St Petersburg and Moscow. He noted that 'beggars seem to increase in number as we advance into the country' and that crowds of them surrounded every church. This was due to a lack of private philanthropy outside of the major cities and neglect by landowners.[12]

While he spent most of his time in St Petersburg and Moscow, William did manage to learn a little about the dire conditions of everyday life for

An Irish Gentleman Experiences Russian Poverty

the majority of the rural Russian population. In a letter to a friend, he emphasized the gross inequalities maintained by feudalism:

> The grand scale of the houses and the number of equipages tend to give one an idea of wealth and opulence, numerous splendid government institutions for the poor and sick and for the education of the poor classes of nobility and military – but in the country I am told, and from what I have seen, I believe it to be very different. The unfortunate boor or slave who is obliged to work once or twice a week on his master's land for nothing has sometimes to walk 20 or 30 versts to the work while his own piece of ground wants his labour and can become good for nothing. These fellows sleep during a cold damp night in their sheep skins at the doors of the inns with a stone for a pillow and all huddled together to keep themselves warm, and their chief food is bad black bread and water. Scarcely one of them can read or write. [...] The people have not the same gay merry faces that you see in all other countries. They appear timid and cowed, and if you strike them they make no resistance. Every slave is obliged to give his master a certain sum yearly out of his wages for permission to earn his bread, and the demand is in the power of the master who, if he is poor, exacts all he can from his slave until he is left scarcely enough to buy himself black bread.[13]

William's disgust at the conditions under which these oppressed millions lived is clear. Irish landowners' positions on the abolition of slavery were mixed, but Barrington's response to Russian feudalism has a visceral quality. His views may have been influenced by his father, a liberal and a benevolent landlord. William was clear in his disapproval of Russian feudalism, but his diary does not contain any criticisms of Swedish or Danish feudalism and colonialism. Later in life he established a girls' school in rural Tipperary, indicating that he inherited at least something of his father's philanthropy and liberal outlook.[14]

It is also possible that William's views were informed by his father's friend, Daniel O'Connell.[15] An advocate for freedom from subjugation for all peoples worldwide, O'Connell was a vociferous critic of Russia, particularly in relation to the partition of Poland. He is said to have refused on principle to give an autograph requested by Tsar Nicholas.[16]

As demonstrated in Róisín Healy's book *Poland in the Irish Nationalist Imagination* (2017), the plight of Poland was understood by nineteenth-century Irish nationalists as analogous to the cause of Ireland – arguably, most Irish people knew of Russia as Poland's oppressor and little else. Whether or not William was influenced by O'Connell's internationalism, the parallels between Russian serfdom and transatlantic slavery were not lost on him, and he compared the legal position of the Russian serfs to hereditary slavery in America and the Caribbean.[17] But two more threads indicate possible O'Connellite influences on William: he sympathized with the Norwegian poor and, like O'Connell, drew comparisons between them and the Irish. With a predominantly rural economy dependent on farming, forestry and fishing, and subject to a more powerful neighbour, William observed that the poorest Norwegians 'live much as in Ireland, [they] travel from farm to farm and beg a subsistence'.[18] Like many other Protestant observers, however, William also acknowledged the role of the Orthodox Church in failing to ameliorate the plight of the Russian people, observing at Moscow's fourteenth-century Simonov Monastery that the erection of 'an immense octagon tower' was a 'disgusting' waste of money that might be better spent on poor relief.[19]

William's experiences in Russia can be understood as part of a long tradition whereby comparisons were sought out between the Irish poor and their Russian counterparts. Without the benefit of statistical evidence, his impression was that the Irish were materially no worse off and that they carried themselves with more pride than the enslaved Russians.[20] His conclusion may be surprising, given the prevailing image of Ireland presented by nineteenth-century travellers of damp, dark, crowded hovels inhabited by livestock and clutches of filthy, malnourished children.[21] William's focus on poor relief in Russia may have been motivated by concerns for the needy, influenced by his father's philanthropy and his association with Daniel O'Connell. But it must also be understood as an important part of his identity as a gentleman in the making, a future barrister and benevolent landlord cast in the same mould as his father.

9
Arthur and Thomas MacMurrough Kavanagh's Eastern Expedition

Arthur MacMurrough Kavanagh was born without arms or legs into an aristocratic, landed Anglican family in 1831, and raised in the family's vast eighteenth-century Tudor Revival country house in Co. Carlow. Lady Harriet Kavanagh spared no expense on her son's education and medical care, and the family physician demonstrated particular dedication in helping the boy to live an active life, designing a special saddle that enabled him to ride a pony around the lush estate from the age of two. Arthur learned to write by holding a pen in his mouth and excelled in his studies at a private academy in Celbridge, Co. Kildare. His mother was a keen traveller, Egyptologist, antiquary and accomplished artist whose progressive views influenced the way she chose to raise her youngest son, who absorbed her curiosity, love of travel and adventure, and Orientalism. For the sake of their education, she brought Arthur and his older brother Thomas to France and Italy and included them on a long expedition to Egypt, Syria, Jordan, Israel and Palestine in October 1846–April 1848. This experience of travelling through deserts by horse and camel must have served Arthur and Thomas well during the journeys they undertook later. So too must have the example of their fearless, pioneering mother, who was one of only a small number of Western European women to have travelled in the Middle East at this time.

Shortly after returning to Ireland from Egypt and the Middle East in 1848, Arthur had an affair with Frances Irvine, the daughter of a local landowner. Appalled, and acting on the advice of family friend Reverend David Wood, his mother sent him into exile in June 1849 while the scandal blew over. He was to make a long journey through Russia, Central Asia and India in the company of his brother Thomas (Tom) and Reverend Wood.[1] These circumstances are glossed over in the otherwise detailed biography published by Arthur's cousin Sarah Steele in 1891, but a letter from Reverend Wood to Lady Kavanagh in April 1849 is unequivocal about the affair's potential to harm the family: 'Any suggestions that Arthur is pursuing undesirable friendships with unsuitable females cannot fail to make both him and the family look ridiculous. It remains to be seen whether a lecture or a prolonged period of travel overseas may do the maximum required to restore a sense of proportion.'[2] Wood's comments must be understood as falling within the norms of the age, but at the heart of the scandal was not the fact that a young gentleman had an affair – something that would have had much greater consequences for the woman in question – but rather the fact that a person with a disability was a sexual being. The scandal set the tone for the tour, and Orientalism's emphasis on sexuality and sensuality made the choice of destination apt. Janet M. Hartley has demonstrated how the Volga acted as a dividing line between Western (Christian) Russia and the Islamic East.[3] At Nizhny Novgorod, Arthur wrote a highly charged letter to the wife of the family banker, seething with anticipation of the Orient and its imagined treasures. His request that the married woman trace his route on a map with her finger appears intentionally suggestive:

> I shall try to give you an insight into our future plans. There are two courses open to us [...] so if you will be kind enough to spend a few

> minutes in looking at the map of Russia and lay your finger on Nijny Novgorod fair where I am at present visiting then follow my directions with your finger in your mind I think you will be able to understand me.[4]

The Kavanagh brothers' three-year excursion contains all the elements of a *Boys' Own* adventure – indeed, the series was first published in 1828, shortly before Arthur's birth, so it is possible that he and Tom encountered the books in early life. Travelling south on the Volga from Moscow to the Caspian Sea and on to Persia, Arthur lived in a *harim* at Mosul for a time before continuing through Kurdistan and through the Persian Gulf to Bengal, where he hunted tigers from an elephant's back and worked as a despatch messenger for the East India Company. It would be easy to read his travels as the fulfilment of Victorian colonial fantasy, were it not for the liberty that the journey offered a man who at times required the assistance of others. During his time in India Arthur had the opportunity to support himself by working for the East India Company; he returned to Ireland only on the news of the death of his brother, who had been running the family estate. The trio's visit to Kurdistan was certainly outside the norm for travellers of Irish origin, but more importantly, as a person with a disability participating fully in the norms of Victorian, male, titled life, Arthur's experiences bear testimony to the cultural importance and symbolic power of rites of passage like travel, sexual liberation abroad and the hunting of exotic animals.

Indeed, Arthur lived his entire life on those terms. He played an important role in Irish public life as an MP and as a benevolent landlord to his Carlow tenants. Known as an able horseman and yachtsman, he made three voyages to Norway in the 1860s with Henry Gore-Booth (see Chapter 15). He published an account of a shooting cruise along the Albanian coast in 1865, illustrated with colour tints made from photographs he took himself and providing 'new, or very nearly new ground [...] for, although many have visited the same places [...] they have kept their adventures to themselves, leaving that coast an unknown region to all'.[5] In other words, he did not define his contribution to travel writing or his own status as a traveller as that of a person with a disability; rather, he considered his book original for its detailing of the little-known hunting grounds on the Albanian coast.

It is revealing that another Irish gentleman traveller had a similar itinerary to Arthur's, and similar experiences, too. The politician and horse-trainer George Henry Moore (1810–1870) spent the years 1834–7 travelling with his friend Charles Kirwan of Dargan Park, Co. Mayo, in Russia, the Caucasus, Persia, Syria (where his route diverged from Arthur's), Egypt and Greece. His biographer and descendant, Maurice Moore, suggested that George burned many of his diaries because 'it appears from other evidence that, like St Kevin, he did not escape from the woman, the love of his youth'. He, like Arthur, travelled in search of freedom and adventure – becoming one of the first Western Europeans to visit the Dead Sea – and following a love affair that met with the disapproval of his parents.[6] A remark from his surviving observations in the Caucasus highlights the sexual liberation he sought in travel and the racialized sexual hierarchies at play when Western European men travelled eastward:

> We walked by the river-side and saw some women treading mortar, holding their petticoats at an unconscionable height, and disclosing a foot, ankle, calf, and knee, *plus ultra* [...]. I went home and made a sketch of the scene I had just witnessed, and got quite in love with my own ladies' legs but could not, however, like Pygmalion, warm them into life.[7]

Arthur corresponded with his mother for the duration of his Russian, Central Asian and Indian tour, not only to maintain the mother–son relationship (which was close, if strained) but to attempt to regain her favour. Furthermore, he was financially dependent on Lady Kavanagh. His surviving letters are copies made by Lady Kavanagh herself; private correspondence was commonly copied for sharing with family and friends. As if to emphasize Arthur's chastisement and exile, Reverend Wood communicated separately with Lady Kavanagh to assure her of her wayward youngest son's wellbeing, religious observances and good behaviour, and the value he was deriving from the tour. Wood shared with Lady Kavanagh his understanding of the tour as part of 'the same great work (although in a narrower sphere and on a smaller field) of winning souls to Christ' and that he would 'always endeavour to lead my young friends and by all possible Sabbath observances profitable reading and improving conversation I will do my part towards building them up in one most Holy Faith'.[8] Arthur's letters, intended at least in part to mollify and reassure his outraged mother, are sometimes rather stilted and formulaic. Occasionally Tom or Arthur attempted to entertain her with anecdotes, including one account of Wood falling for an Italian governess during the Baltic crossing and Tom having to 'pull him by the coat-tails' from a supper at her residence on their last night in St Petersburg.[9] The letters are an important record of a region infrequently visited by Irish travellers in the period, but are most valuable for the insights they provide into the ways in which Arthur's tour shaped him as a 'gentleman' and influenced the interest in outdoor pursuits and adventuring that characterized the rest of his life.

Just how much Arthur and Tom learned about Russian history and culture is questionable. Their capacity for cultural engagement was checked by their river voyaging – with limited capacity for landings en route – and Arthur's focus on hunting. Early in the tour he wrote, 'Tom and I both find it very stupid being sick of pallaces [sic] and churches which Wood revels in from morning till night.'[10] His devotion to hunting partly arose from the difficulties he experienced with accessibility in urban settings. Arthur very clearly sought adventure, and while he had developed ways of managing his independence from a very early age, at times he remained frustratingly dependent on others. He admitted to his sister that he was unwilling to remain more than ten further days in St Petersburg, as he had been left alone indoors all day, every day, while Tom and Wood went sightseeing. Similarly, in Moscow, he rather poignantly reported that he was 'as usual a solitary bird, Wood and Tom being out sight seeing. This sort of life nearly kills me.'[11]

While the tour was conceived as a form of exile, a punishment for Arthur's transgression, its function as a gentlemanly exercise is revealed in Arthur's inventory of the luggage they carried on the steamer from Moscow to Astrakhan:

> [...] six portmanteaux, two cases of sherry, one of brandy, one of tea, four gun-cases, three bundles of beds and cloaks, two carpet-bags, two hat-boxes, two leather bags of shot, and innumerable small parcels. The voyage down the Volga, it was supposed, would make at least one case of sherry look foolish, so, that excepted, the above list was our outfit for Persia. [...] Gun-cases and shot, if we had been gifted with prophetic vision, would certainly have been left behind. But, allured by vivid expectations of every kind of sport, we would as soon have left the guns as Wood his collection of *Murray's Handbooks* [...] Three pocket-knives and forks constituted our canteen outfit, and of everything else we had to take a chance.[12]

The excessive – even ridiculous – gentility of the cases of sherry and tea is counterbalanced by the trek through Persia, which emerged as no gentleman's sporting adventure but instead was a test of physical endurance. Arthur's journal demonstrates the shift in the party's mood, declining from anticipation to desperation as they progressed southward. The Volga, for centuries a key trade route, was marketed by the Russian state as a destination for scenic tourism from the late 1830s, emphasizing its majesty and scale.[13] In 1836 one 'Rayford Ramble' – clearly a pseudonym – published his account of a journey made in 1819 along the Volga from Nizhny Novgorod to Yaroslavl and Moscow. While nothing more is known of the author, he refers to himself as 'an Irishman' in the text and published his book in Dublin.[14] But Arthur was deflated by missing opportunities for hunting on the Volga riverbank – 'as the steamer would not stop for us, we had to forego the pleasures of the chase' – and on the approach to Baku Arthur sardonically remarked that a report of yellow fever raging at the city served 'to brighten our present gloomy prospects' of the journey.[15] From Tarki on the Caspian shore, the expedition descended into chaos, with stormy weather, bad food ('cabbage boiled in oil for soup') and the boatmen suffering such ill-effects from a night spent enjoying Arthur's brandy that they were unable to chart their course to Baku.[16] Shortly afterwards, at Astrabad, the party was rather bizarrely held responsible for a stray dog killing a chicken. Kavanagh painted the incident in intemperate language:

> The inhabitants, a bigoted tribe, received us most inhospitably. On entering the gate, one of the dogs which had followed us from the factory, being nearly as hungry as ourselves, killed a chicken, which occasioned not a little stir, and led to our being caged up for the best part of the day in the middle of the only square, and pelted diligently by the inhabitants with rotten eggs and bad oranges [...] We were put up for the night in the cock-loft of the worst caravanserai (it not being allowed for Christians to enter the better ones), and there got a sort of breakfast which we sadly wanted.[17]

The following day the party embarked on an eleven-day ride. Arthur records their poorly provisioned group eating little save sheep's head porridge (or soup), sleeping in the open under heavy rain and being swarmed by clouds of mosquitoes. The awfulness of the journey lies in contrast to the clear pleasure Arthur derived from challenges such as negotiating a dangerous mountain pass: 'The scenery was beautiful, but the road villainous [...] a precipice of five or six hundred feet [...] Twice my horse slipped one of his hind feet over the side, and only that he recovered himself in a miraculous manner, he and I were dashed into a thousand pieces.'[18] Having survived the trek to Tehran, the whole party almost immediately fell ill with fever and was forced to remain there for two weeks before proceeding through snow to Soltanieh in present-day Iran. En route, their companion William 'threatened to die' if they did not stop and almost lost two toes to frostbite. For his part, Arthur succumbed to such a severe attack of diarrhoea that he was unable to accompany Thomas and Wood to Tbilisi, instead spending 'the most miserable of Christmas Days' in Soltanieh, suffering from dysentery and an unspecified liver complaint.

It has been speculated that at this point Arthur spent at least a fortnight in a *harim*. His diary only states that on 2 January 1850 he was 'moved to Malichus Mirza's [Malik Qasim Mirza] house for a change of

Arthur and Thomas MacMurrough Kavanagh's Eastern Expedition

air' and remained there until 15 January. In a biography of 1891 that includes extended extracts from his journal, his cousin interpolated:

> His life under the Prince's roof he long afterwards described [...] He was semi-conscious when the move took place, and, on coming to, he found himself lodged in the harem, where he was nursed by an old black slave who became devoted to him, insomuch that when to a certain degree convalescent she would convey him for recreation into the ladies' apartments. There he met with every kindness, and was entertained by the stories of the former lives of the inmates, many of them most touching in their descriptions of how they were carried off from their homes. One of them – a beautiful fair-haired Armenian – awoke his deepest compassion by her pathetic longing for her own relatives and home.[19]

The suggestion seems to be that Arthur replicated his previous pattern of illicit sexual behaviour. Arthur's own narrative skips over this period, but Wood was less circumspect in his account of the missing fortnight:

> The women in the harem are horribly confined in a state of abject imprisonment. I understand they are far from beautiful and that the harem itself is a little better than a claustrophobic jail. They have only a small and dirty courtyard in which to exercise and I hear disturbing accounts of a mysterious room which is always kept locked. I intend to raise the matter with the Minister so that no future Christian visitor may fall into such a trap. Unhappily, Arthur Kavanagh is not forthcoming in his accounts of what transpired there and is inclined to treat the whole affair with levity and even, I regret to say, some amusement and to show an uncalled for affection for the inmates. [...] By oriental standards the Prince may be a man of enlightenment; superficially he is civilised and well mannered. But I fear he used his influence in a corrupting fashion and gave Arthur instructions in matters of which he would best have been left in ignorance. [...] The prince made a most strange remark to me. He said that Arthur would go out into the world much better equipped to understand the ladies and that his education had been completed by instruction in the arts of the *kama*. I find that *kama* means 'pleasure' and that there is a most unchaste oriental tract called *Kama Sutra*, which

the Prince, again joking in the worst taste, says might have been written specially for an innocent Englishman.[20]

Wood's account scrapes the gloss from the Western fantasy of the *harim*, emphasizing a lack of physical and moral hygiene while retaining the essential element of mystery through the image of the locked door. Arthur's unwillingness to share his experiences at the *harim* render him complicit not only in the suffering of the female inmates, but also in the entrapment of any unwitting 'future Christian visitor'. At the time, 'harem' was understood to mean brothel, and the dominant image of *harim* life was 'that of a lascivious world where women waited idly, lying around on sofas, smoking pipes, eating sweets, waiting for the master to come and choose one of them'.[21] Arthur's stay at the *harim* only served to reinforce Western male fantasy, the obscure references to locked rooms and mysterious sexual techniques forming a tantalizing canvas, blank for the reader's projections. As a person with a disability, Arthur's sexuality was doubly taboo, unspeakable and unimaginable. He uses silence and circumspection to great effect, amplifying the possibilities of the *harim* and using it to unequivocally declare himself a sexual being. However, through the lens of Orientalism, he is debased and corrupted by his experiences, and Wood may have been left uncertain whether the 'innocent Englishman' that the prince referred to was Arthur, or himself.

Arthur's narrative diversion from the events at the *harim* transports the reader to the crossing of Lake Urmia, which he describes as 'the most disagreeable voyage we ever made [...] humanly speaking – *we owed our lives to our Russian fur cloaks* and four bottles of the Prince's best arrack'.[22] Russia was part of Arthur's Oriental fantasy. Roughing it in Russia served as preparation for the expedition into Persia and onwards to Central Asia and India. Writing from St Petersburg, near the beginning of the journey, Arthur confessed to his mother that they had already found the tour 'much more tedious expensive and dangerous than we thought before we left Ireland'.[23] To Arthur, Tom and Wood, Russia was the Orient, and this is demonstrated in moments of disappointment during the journey. Arthur was dissatisfied with the sight of shackled prisoners leaving Moscow for the long march to Siberia because they did not appear sufficiently distressed by their fate. He had wanted to witness the authoritarianism associated with the Orient at its worst:

> [...] certainly I never saw any thing less worth seeing in my life. About 12 fellows and the same number of women were started with a quantity of soldiers. None seemed unhappy or sorry to go. They walk the whole way a journey of about 5 Months and a half.[24]

Similarly, the great annual fair at Nizhny Novgorod disappointed Tom because the assembled traders did not fulfil the exotic, Oriental vision of his imagination:

> We were told that we should see Indians Arabs and Chinese. I have only seen one Turk and a few Jews from Bokhara [...] and no Chinese as they are not allowed to cross the frontier of their own country.[25]

Russia acted as a land-bridge between Continental Europe and Asia but, more importantly, it functioned as an opportunity for the traveller to culturally acclimatize, honing their resilience to the increasing absence of familiar foods, languages, clothing and habits. The Russian furs that the travellers wore while crossing Lake Urmia acted as a marker of the trials already endured, their incongruity on a ride through the Middle Eastern desert enhancing the strangeness, novelty and danger of the experience.

Arthur did not overstate the physical danger in which they found themselves at points in the journey – the expedition proved fatal to both Thomas Kavanagh and Reverend David Wood. Tom had originally planned to leave Wood and Arthur at Nizhny Novgorod and return to Ireland, but he lost a wager over a game of billiards and so had to accompany them to Mumbai, where he developed a chest complaint. It was decided that removal to a less humid climate would improve his condition, so he and Wood departed for Australia, but Tom died en route in Batavia in January 1852. Wood decided to continue on to Australia but was killed in an accident shortly after arriving there. Arthur was the only one of the three to survive their long journey. Left in India with few resources, he took a paid position with the Survey Department of the Pune District under the East India Company. He remained in this post for about a year before returning to Ireland.[26]

To focus solely on Arthur's physical characteristics – as his biographers have done – is, I feel, to do him an injustice. He never allowed himself to be treated differently to others, nor did he define himself by his physical ability. His letters, and those of his brother Tom and Reverend Wood, are an important record of a fairly unusual itinerary for the period, and demonstrate the ways in which people with disabilities were limited by the expectations and qualms of others. Arthur consistently defied those expectations by embracing new experiences and one of the most challenging itineraries possible.

10

BLIGHT AND CHOLERA IN TIPPERARY AND ST PETERSBURG

In 1845 a microscopic spore made its way to Ireland. *Phytophthora infestans*, potato blight, caused 2 million people to flee Ireland and a million more to die when the potato crop that they depended on rotted in the ground over several successive summers. Meanwhile, in 1847 the bacteria *vibrio cholerae* swept through the Russian population, killing a million people over the next three years through dehydration and kidney failure. If 1847 became 'Black 47' in Ireland, 1848 was the most fatal year for Russia's cholera victims, with over 1.7 million cases and 690,150 deaths in a population weakened by famine.[1] Pathogens have powerful, even catastrophic, impacts on human life. Cholera and the potato blight contributed to the decisions and movements of one diplomatic family in Russia, the Bloomfields of Tipperary, and shaped their legacy.

In 1839 Tipperary-born Anglican John Arthur Douglas Bloomfield (1802–1879) was made secretary to the British Embassy in St Petersburg. He was a career diplomat for life, beginning at just sixteen years of age, when he was assigned to Vienna as attaché to the British Embassy. He clearly had the right personality for diplomatic life. Shortly after his move

Blight and Cholera in Tipperary and St Petersburg

to Vienna, Cork-born traveller and diarist Martha Wilmot (see Chapter 6) followed as wife of the new chaplain to the embassy, Reverend William Bradford. Previously acquainted with John and his parents, she and her husband grew close to the young attaché, judging him 'a very fine sweet young man, handsome and much admired. William is very fond of him and feels towards him as if he were his own son.'[2] Martha wrote to her sister Alicia in May 1821 with news of John's upcoming visit to England and describing him as having a 'handsome, artless, sweet, unassuming exterior.'[3] The Bradfords thought so highly of Bloomfield that William sketched his portrait and was the only person to visit the young man when he was contagious with scarlet fever in spring 1823 – all other friends had abandoned him for fear of contracting the dangerous disease.[4] Life at the embassy in Vienna prepared John well for his five decades as a diplomat. The city was the epicentre of European politics and offered a glittering social calendar. He was first appointed to St Petersburg in 1823 as private secretary to the ambassador. Doubtless, Martha Wilmot would have been a useful informant who would have supplied him with reliable information about Russian social and cultural life before his departure.

John Bloomfield was just one of a number of Irish-born diplomats at St Petersburg's British Embassy in the nineteenth century. In July 1814 Limerick-born Sir Gore Ouseley (1770–1844) completed his term as British Ambassador to Persia and travelled from Tbilisi to St Petersburg with a 200-strong escort of Cossack guards, his wife, two children and household staff through the treacherous mountains and lush valleys of the Caucasus, which he noted had 'always been famous' for 'the most shocking cases of rapine and murder'. He thought the north Caucasus the finest country he ever saw but remarked that it was 'a complete desert in the hands of the Russians, and nobody can settle in it from the fear of the constant incursions of the Circassians'. On entering the ruined city of Moscow, still in ashes after the French invasion two years previously, he felt 'greatly affected [...] to see such horrid proofs of French atrocity'.[5] Corkman and later MP John Brabazon Ponsonby (c. 1770–1855) was attaché to the British Embassy in St Petersburg in 1832; he may have been responsible for

84

the display of a pair of large Irish gold torcs at the All Russia Industrial and Art Exhibitions in 1829–33.[6] In 1834 Dublin-born Charles Vane, 3rd Marquess of Londonderry, was appointed British ambassador to Russia, but opposition from the House of Commons was such that he was forced to turn down the position. He travelled to Russia in a private capacity with his wife, Frances (who had family connections to Co. Antrim), and son in 1836–7, publishing his experiences in *Recollections of a Tour in the North of Europe* (two volumes, 1838). Dublin-born Sir John Fiennes Twisleton Crampton (1805–1886) was British attaché at St Petersburg in 1828–34 and returned as ambassador in 1858–60 (Fig. 6). Robert Ffrench of Monivea, Co. Galway, was secretary to the British Embassy in St Petersburg in 1863, during which time he met and married Sofia Alexandrovna Kindyakova, whose family owned extensive properties in Simbirsk (now Ulyanovsk), St Petersburg and Moscow. The pair had a turbulent relationship; their daughter, Kathleen Ffrench, born in Brussels in the following year, was raised on her grandparents' Simbirsk estate.[7] Meath native and lifelong career diplomat Francis Richard Plunkett (1835–1907) was attaché to the embassy at St Petersburg in 1859–63, returning in 1877–81 in the higher office of secretary before representing Britain in Constantinople, Tokyo, Stockholm, Brussels and Vienna. Towards the close of the century, Roscommon-born Sir Nicholas Roderick O'Conor (1843–1908) was ambassador to Russia in 1895–8, where he clashed with the Foreign Minister, Count Muravyev, and allowed his direct personal manner to get in the way of improving relations.[8]

While young John Bloomfield was earning his diplomatic stripes in Vienna, his father, Benjamin (1768–1846), found his status and political influence greatly reduced when a murky conspiracy at the British court saw him lose his position as private secretary to the Prince Regent in 1822. Shortly afterwards he was despatched to Stockholm as minister plenipotentiary, where he remained until 1833. Father and son met in St Petersburg in summer 1825, when Benjamin went to Russia on a two-month tour. John's wife, Georgiana (1822–1905), later published Benjamin's diary from this time.

Blight and Cholera in Tipperary and St Petersburg

The family had a complicated relationship with Ireland, like many of the landed and titled nobility of the nineteenth century. Benjamin was born in Co. Tipperary but was whisked off to England at an early age to be educated. He entered the British Army and fought against the United Irishmen at Vinegar Hill in 1798, one of the bloodiest chapters in Irish history. After three years as MP for Plymouth he was knighted and served for five years as private secretary to the Prince Regent, before falling from favour and being reassigned to the diplomatic corps. After ten years in Stockholm he returned to Britain, where he commanded the Woolwich Garrison until retiring in Ireland. He was buried in the family mausoleum at Borrisnafarney, Co. Offaly.[9]

Benjamin Bloomfield was a deeply religious man whose convictions were born during his exile in Sweden. In St Petersburg in July 1825 he described attending an Anglican service for the first time in two years: 'I heard an excellent sermon, and had the comfort of receiving the sacrament of the Lord's Supper [...] I cannot describe my feelings.'[10] It may seem strange that St Petersburg offered the opportunity to reacquaint himself with his faith, but by the 1790s there were 20,000 Protestants in the city, and they were largely permitted to worship freely.[11] During his time in Stockholm, Benjamin became acquainted with a Wesleyan Methodist preacher and attended his services, held in a makeshift church. He became devoted to his faith and maintained his new habit of regular prayer on return to London, where acquaintances noted a sign frequently hanging on his front door: 'At prayer.'[12]

During their two months together in Russia, father and son spent a month in St Petersburg and the rest of the time visiting Moscow and Nizhny Novgorod. Sitting at the confluence of the Volga and Oka rivers, Nizhny was easily – if not always pleasantly – reached from Moscow by boat, and started to feature more often in visitors' itineraries as a fairly accessible, exotic city where the visitor could see people from many different cultures assembled together for the annual great fair. The fair was the largest in the Russian Empire, drawing traders from Western Europe, the Far East, Persia, and the Far North. Benjamin Bloomfield clearly enjoyed seeing the merchants from Bokhara, Persia and Armenia – in his words, 'people so strange to Europeans'. He especially enjoyed the horse fair, where Kirgiz and Kalmuc people were camped, all looking 'perfectly Oriental'. He dined with 'the Chief of the Boukhars', enjoying an 'excellent' traditional meal of rice and mutton, noting that he was provided with cutlery, while the Bukhars ate with their fingers in the traditional way. Nizhny's emergence as an important centre of manufacturing in the nineteenth century is foreshadowed in Benjamin's account. He bought a vast amount of soap from one manufacturer and remarked, 'Russia ought to be a clean country if judged by the quantity of soap I saw.'[13]

As career diplomats whose lives were dedicated to public service on the international stage, John and Benjamin Bloomfield were obliged to spend their time in appropriate company and polite pursuits. Their attendance was expected at public and private events, and their calendars were too full to permit much independent exploration of Russian life. However, Georgiana Bloomfield's memoir contains some personal insights. She married John in 1845 during his posting to Russia; he briefly returned to London for the wedding. Her first impressions of Russia were not good. With John in a hurry to resume his diplomatic work, the couple had to travel from Lübeck to St Petersburg in a second-class cabin, much to the distress of the former maid-of-honour to Queen Victoria. On arriving at the River Neva, Georgiana was struck with the city's wintry appearance – it was October and the first snow had fallen – and with what she called the 'savage' appearance of the Russian boatmen, 'all dressed in their sheepskins, fur caps, and enormous tan fingerless gloves'. She quickly learned about serfdom and the state of the poor from other English residents in the city, recording what she learned in her diary and noting incidents of hunger and famine. In Moscow, she saw prisoners in chains embarking on their long march to Siberia and was deeply affected by the sight of 'so many fellow creatures doomed, in consequence of fearful crimes, to spend the rest of their days in hardship and suffering'. It is not known whether her husband shared her pity.

In summer 1847 reports of the Irish Famine started to reach the couple. Before the full horrors of the calamity unfolded, Georgiana's concern was largely for her landed friends and relations. English-born, she was now the wife of an Irish landlord. She wrote, 'Our last accounts from Ireland were a little less hopeless than they have been, and we trust the worst of the famine is nearly over […] for our resources are well-nigh exhausted, and I cannot think what those landed proprietors who have nothing to depend upon but their rent will do.' She unfeelingly viewed the Famine as an opportunity for mass conversion from Catholicism to Protestantism, that 'our poor fellow countrymen [may be] raised from the abyss of moral and physical degradation and misery in which they have been so long'. There was violence in Tipperary during the famine, with evictions, food riots, and attacks on landlords, agents and bailiffs, while landlord responses varied; some lowered their rents and set up soup kitchens, while others evicted the impoverished.[14]

In 1847 and 1848 Russia was visited by its own horror, with cholera outbreaks resulting in a reported 1100 deaths per day. In summer 1848 Georgiana followed medical advice to leave St Petersburg and boarded a ship bound for England within two days. It is likely that she wished not only to avoid infection, but also the riots that flared up in response to quarantine measures. John's letters during their separation described the terrible scenes of suffering, the endless processions of coffins and people in mourning. In 1850 the couple were advised that John was to be posted to a location 'less trying to [Georgiana's] health', and relocated to Berlin in May 1851.

In the preface to her memoir Georgiana stated, 'Just as every pawn is necessary in a game of chess, so the humblest individual fills a part on the great stage of life which no other person, however superior in talent and capacity, could fill.' It is debatable whether this holds true for her and John's time in the British Embassy in St Petersburg, but this landed Irish family's experiences in Russia over the course of almost four decades provide interesting glimpses into court intrigue, the function of diplomacy as exile and how news of the catastrophic famine in Ireland was understood by those who were far from home.[15]

11

IMPERIAL PRISON SYSTEMS AND THE MURDER OF LORD MAYO

On the evening of 8 February 1872 Lord Mayo was standing on the shore at Port Blair on Great Andaman, about to board the ship where his wife Blanche was waiting. Night had shrouded the island's palm trees and low-lying wooden buildings. The Viceroy of India had spent the day inspecting what would become the British Empire's largest penal colony, receiving a total of 83,000 Indian and Burmese convicts in the period 1858–1939.[1] Established after the 1857 Indian Mutiny, the island prison was infamous for its treatment of both political prisoners and criminal convicts. As Mayo prepared to depart, he was fatally stabbed by one of the convicts, Sher Ali Afridi. This was the first assassination of a sitting viceroy, but the incident was downplayed by an imperial administration fearful of amplifying Indian nationalism and anti-colonialism, or of generating any perception of weakness of the British grip on the subcontinent. Sher Ali was hanged a month later.

Almost thirty years earlier Mayo – then known as Richard Southwell Bourke – had travelled to Russia as a young graduate. One of the most striking moments in his account of the journey occurs during a visit to the

Imperial Prison Systems and the Murder of Lord Mayo

infamous Shlisselburg fortress, about twenty miles west of St Petersburg. Having visited St Petersburg's other main attractions, Bourke sailed down the Neva on a day trip to the island. The fortress had been a frontier defence for the western reaches of the empire since the medieval period, and the first line of defence for the eighteenth-century city of St Petersburg. But the imposing structure had a second purpose – as a political prison. The fortress symbolized the differences, as Bourke and other Western Europeans saw them, between Russia and the rest of Europe: an unfree press, autocracy, feudalism, Siberia. Suddenly, he paused his walk around the walls to consider the fates of the political prisoners held inside, their miseries pricking his conscience. We cannot know whether he recalled this memory on that February day, three decades later in the Bay of Bengal, but the injustices of Russian absolutism and British imperialism became entangled in the moment that Sher Ali's knife entered the earl's back.

Published by Henry Colburn of London, arguably the Victorian era's most important publisher of travel accounts, Bourke's two-volume account of his visit to Russia stretched across 750 pages and sold well. Lengthy extracts appeared in *The University Magazine*, whose reviewer appraised the book as 'pleasing and unpretending' and its author as possessed of 'powers both of observation and of judgment, which only require to be matured and exercised'.[2] The modern reader might not be inclined to heap such praise on the book, but the journey described in its pages was just the opening chapter in a life and career shaped – and ended – by the major international political events and the imperial and trading rivalries of the age often referred to as the 'Great Game' between Russia and Britain. Similarly, his brother Lieutenant-General John Jocelyn's career in the British military included action in two of the most sensational conflicts of the mid-Victorian period: the Crimean War and the Indian Mutiny of 1857 that resulted in the establishment of the penal colony on Great Andaman. Russia loomed large throughout Bourke's life, from his first tentative step towards independence as a travelling graduate to becoming the British Empire's most senior servant, Viceroy of India, at a time when Britain and Russia competed for primacy in Central Asia.

Imperial Prison Systems and the Murder of Lord Mayo

Bourke was born in 1822, the son of an MP and landowner. He and his seven siblings had a fairly typical genteel country childhood at Hayes, Co. Meath, their private tuition supplemented by suitable outdoor pursuits. Their education was enriched when the family moved to the Continent for a period in the late 1830s, their mother anxious that the children's Irish country upbringing might not be sufficient preparation for life in more cosmopolitan settings. They spent long periods in Paris and Florence, where the boys had a strict daily routine of language lessons, followed by a period in Switzerland, where they enjoyed the emerging sport of mountain climbing. Bourke returned to London in 1840, aged nineteen, and entered Trinity College Dublin the following year. As a student, he lived at his uncle's grand seat at Palmerstown as the childless 4th Earl's heir, spent several months each year in London and moved in politically conservative circles in Dublin.

On finishing his degree Bourke made a short visit to Russia. His biographer, W.W. Hunter, speculated that he made the journey because his great-aunt had died and he was therefore unable to go out in society with any propriety. Bourke himself denied being either 'in love nor in debt' – the two most common reasons, to his mind, that young men travelled – simply stating that he was 'obliged to leave for a time [London's] giddy whirl'.[3] He returned to Ireland ready to step into the role of a major landowner and peer as the tragedy of the Great Famine unfolded. Running the family estate on behalf of his father and great-uncle, he provided assistance and relief in the locality and promoted a cottage industry in knitting, selling the products in London. He also arranged charitable performances to raise money for the relief effort.[4] In 1847 – the worst year of the Famine – he was elected to parliament, retaining his seat until 1868 while also acting as Chief Secretary for Ireland in 1852, 1858 and 1866. In parliament, he spoke mostly on Irish questions at a time when these were of a difficult nature, particularly against the backdrop of the Famine and the Fenian campaign of the 1860s. Meanwhile, his personal life developed along the expected trajectory for a man of his means and class, with his marriage to Blanche Julia Wyndham, a former lady to Victoria's bedchamber; they had four

Imperial Prison Systems and the Murder of Lord Mayo

sons and three daughters. The success of his political career was confirmed in 1869, when he was appointed Viceroy of India.[5]

Bourke's account of Russia set out to explore whether the negative images of the country were founded in fact – in his own words, 'whether the country was a pleasant land or a hideous tomb'. He referenced the dominant negative images of Russia, such as the French travel writer Marquis de Custine's popular 1839 account of millions living in terror of the knout and Siberia, a book critical enough to be banned in Russia. Indeed, after just a short time in St Petersburg, Bourke felt that he had already learned enough to judge de Custine's book as one suffering from 'egotism, vanity, superficialness, and disregard of truth'. However, by his own admission, his visit was a 'galloping and steaming tour of eleven weeks' that may not have provided sufficient opportunity for gathering and verifying information on the world's largest empire.

Overall, the book is light in tone, pitched in the author's words at 'idlers, gapers, and little thinkers, like myself'. He appealed to a broad readership by tapping into the age-old stereotypes that he claimed to have rejected. For example, he described Orthodox religious practices as 'antics that are daily practiced in the streets, under the name of prayer'. His encounters with the Russian language betrayed the superior attitude so common among European travellers of the period. Dazed by introductions to new acquaintances at a ball, he exclaimed:

> [...] their names are the devil! In ten minutes I was fairly bewildered [...]
> as fast as a sound somewhat resembling a Russian surname trembled on
> my tongue, another totally unpronounceable one startled my frightened
> ear [...] For the first week I was in Russia, I never dared to call any of my
> new friends by their names, and used to describe them as tall, or short,
> dark or fair.

A tongue-in-cheek footnote notified the reader that Bourke would 'not be answerable for the proper orthography of any Russian name'. Despite – or perhaps due to – his lack of knowledge and understanding of the language, Bourke felt confident in his assessment of the country's arts as 'quite imaginary'. He was clearly not acquainted with the poetry of

Imperial Prison Systems and the Murder of Lord Mayo

Vasily Zhukovsky or Ukrainian-born Nikolay Gogol's ground-breaking experimental prose.

While his aim was to challenge the dominant negative image of Russia in the English-speaking world, Bourke did not shy from using some well-established or, by then, outworn images of Russia. The preface to the book stated that he wished to tell readers 'of a new country, and a new people, governed on old principles – principles that have long since been discarded and condemned by most of the enlightened nations of the world'. Whether or not his readers accepted his classification of Russia as a 'new country', given its foundations in the ancient state of Kyivan Rus', the majority would certainly have agreed with his assessment of its system of government. Indeed, he claimed that before his departure, some friends hinted darkly at the threat of Siberia, secret police and spies. Lacking the maturity and insight to comprehend the conditions of daily life under autocratic rule, the young gentleman found these intimations exciting. The thrill returned when, aboard the steamer from Lubeck to Kronstadt, he heard Russian spoken for the first time and felt 'as if we had already touched the confines of another world' – a world that conservative Bourke was ready to embrace. Other travellers to Russia complained of having to provide the authorities with details of their internal travel plans, but he acquiesced to the state's concerns and considered 'persons who complain of such trifles [...] hard up for grievances'. The young gentleman was bowled over on meeting Nicholas I at a royal concert, gushing: 'Never in any rank of life, have I seen a man so admirably fitted for the position in which he is placed; and when we consider what that position is – the absolute monarch, the wielder of the destinies of a seventh part of the habitable globe [...] Truly Nicholas is the first gentleman of the age.'

Bourke's light-touch approach and his naïve readiness to accept the grim realities of life under absolutism crippled his stated aim of challenging negative stereotypes of Russian life and government. He only registered these realities when he was confronted with the sight of prisoners departing Moscow for the long, often fatal, march to Siberia and the misery of their accompanying wives. However, in a bizarre defence of Russian absolutism,

Imperial Prison Systems and the Murder of Lord Mayo

he claimed: 'Notwithstanding the terrible feeling the name of Siberia bears to the mind of every one in Europe, the convicts are not subjected to such severe labour as those in our Australian colonies [...] the horrors of Siberia, and the frequency of unjust exile, is greatly overrated.' There is a poetic irony in his observation, as similar injustices meted out by the British imperial penal system later cost him his life.

The book's most memorable moment takes place when a shocked Bourke comes face to face with the absolutist state and its unmoving justice system during a visit to the notorious political prison at Shlisselburg fortress, lying low on the shore of Lake Ladoga near St Petersburg. Conditions were so bad there that in 1887 convicted St Petersburg revolutionary Mikhail Grachevsky self-immolated in protest. Former Russian naval officer Ivan Youvatshev, convicted in 1883 of suspected dissident activity, published details of the harsh regimen in his prison memoir, *The Russian Bastille or the Schluesselburg Fortress* (1909). The book describes the terror struck in the prisoner's heart on discovering that he was bound for Shlisselburg and the physical and emotional toll of his long solitary confinement. Bourke acknowledged that the prisoners' 'treatment is a mystery – their existence unknown – their fate uncared for; and they linger out their days, in a captivity as dismal as it is hopeless'. But one inmate invoked his pity more than any other: Ivan VI, the infant tsar deposed during the coup that placed Empress Elizabeth on the throne and who died a prisoner in Shlisselburg at the age of twenty-three, and whom Bourke romantically compared to the Man in the Iron Mask. While insisting that all inmates were guilty of serious offences like treason and therefore deserving of severe punishment, Bourke experienced a moment of enlightenment while standing on the parapet. He suddenly became aware of the contrast between his happy, laughing party enjoying the sun and open air and the doomed inmates on the other side of the wall. Realizing that 'our merry voices even might fall heavy on the doomed one's ear', he vowed to never again visit the 'dark, mysterious' place. Could the memory of that day have crossed Mayo's mind as he performed the last professional duty of his life, inspecting the Andaman Islands penal colony?

Bourke closed his book with the following wish:

> I only hope that what I have said may not be judged by works lately published on and against Russia. I know that few of their statements will be corroborated in these pages, but this I little heed. I went not to Russia for the purpose of discovering the best manner of abusing or praising her people, government, institutions and laws, or with the design of writing. I went for the sake of amusement, and instruction, and if I have succeeded in making any one, who has thus far accompanied me, a sharer in the smallest part of the pleasure of my short tour, my whole end is gained. A book on Russia, written in a dispassionate manner, is at least a novelty, as few have attempted the subject lately who have not given utterance to the deepest flattery, or to the most unmeasured abuse. Mine has, I hope, done neither.

He did not succeed in his ambition to produce a novel account of Russia or to challenge negative stereotypes. For either to have been possible, he would have had to embark on a much more daring itinerary, rather than confining himself to the easily accessible western part of the empire. He would have had to readjust his entire worldview as a conservative imperialist and monarchist and set aside the tendency to understand peoples and cultures in a fixed, biologically predetermined hierarchy. Within that worldview, to be Russian was to be Asian and, therefore, lesser. The same reasoning was applied to indigenous people worldwide who came under colonial rule – the colonial rule that he later embodied as Viceroy of India.

Lord Mayo was appointed Viceroy of India more than twenty years after his visit to Russia. Anglo-Russian relations had become increasingly strained as British Russophobia focused on the threat Russian imperial ambitions in Central Asia posed to India, the so-called 'jewel in the crown' of the British Empire. In the decades between Mayo's graduate jaunt to Moscow and his arrival in India as Viceroy, Russia had extended its grip on Central Asian territories, establishing military settlements and extending telegraph communications as far as Issyk Kul Lake on the Chinese border.[6] Russian expansion into Tajikistan meant that by the 1860s, the two empires shared a narrow, mountain-walled border, present-day Afghanistan's

Wakhan Corridor. It was believed at the highest levels in the British administration that Russia intended to invade India to gain access to warm-water ports along the crucial Indian Ocean trade route. As a British official, Mayo was bound to oppose Russian expansion in Central Asia, and he did this by working to improve Indian relations with Afghanistan. In the year after Mayo's death, Britain and Russia reached an agreement defining the extent of Afghan territory and each power's sphere of influence in Central Asia – an agreement that lasted only five years, when the Second Anglo-Afghan War was triggered by British and Russian jostling for position at the court of Sher Ali Khan.

Bourke's life as a public figure was bookended by two strangely interconnected events. In Shlisselburg Prison in 1845 the conservative, pro-imperialist graduate was confronted by the devastating realities of life under absolutism, its inequalities and injustices mirroring those inflicted globally by British colonialism. The brutality of tsarist summary imprisonment and exile was replicated at the British penal colony on Great Andaman, of which Mayo was ultimate overseer three decades later. His killer, Sher Ali, voiced the anger of oppressed millions globally and their shared suffering under the yokes of imperialism and autocracy.

VI

ADVENTURERS AND INNOVATORS
AFTER CRIMEA

Peace! the most blessed sound that angel voices ever uttered over a strife-tossed world – peace was proclaimed. We left you, my friends, some rejoicing, some sorrowing: the one looking forward in the gladness of hope to happy meetings with heroes of the Crimea; the other shrinking with redoubled pain from the sights and sounds of triumph and joy, thinking only of the earth-mounds that ridged the Crimean soil where lay the cross-marked graves of Christian soldiers who fought and died with and for the unbeliever. Peace was proclaimed; but as we moved slowly up the clear rushing Neva, we could not forget that the war had only just ceased its horrid din, for, independently of all other causes for recollection, there were with us a band of Russian prisoners whom we were escorting home to St Petersburg.

Selina Bunbury, *Russia After the War* (1857), pp. 1–2

On 22 October 1856 one of Dublin's largest buildings was transformed for a special event. The massive cast-iron columns of a tobacco warehouse on the north bank of the River Liffey were painted red, white and blue and festooned with banners and ribbons. Over 3000 Crimean War veterans

Adventurers and Innovators after Crimea

trooped into the venue to be feted as heroes, together with a thousand invited guests and paying spectators. The diners consumed 3 tons of potatoes, 200 turkeys, 200 geese, 250 joints of beef, 250 hams, 230 legs of mutton, 500 meat pies, 100 rice puddings, 260 plum puddings and 2000 loaves of bread. The celebration shows the importance of the Crimean War in Ireland, not only as a much-needed source of employment in the aftermath of the Great Famine, but also as one of the most significant international events of the nineteenth century and one in which the Irish played no small role.[1]

After the half-century of peace that followed the Napoleonic Wars, Crimea unleashed a barely dormant Russophobia. Western European observers returned to the fear and mistrust of the expansionist Catherinian era. The sizeable gains Russia had made in Poland–Lithuania through the Congress of Vienna symbolized the threat posed to all small nations by their larger neighbours. On the eve of the Napoleonic Wars Walpole had referred to Catherine II as 'the imperial vulture of Russia', and these fears surrounding Russian territorial ambitions were hardly forgotten by later generations.[2] The Russo-Circassian wars, a series of battles between the expanding empire and the Caucasian ethnic group that had been ongoing since the 1760s, became a focal point for critics. The *Irish Examiner* editorialized in 1844 that British foreign policy in respect of Circassia was no more than 'truckling to the despot', adding, 'We are determined and decided enemies to the merciless tyrant who inflicts the punishment of the knout, who tramples upon Poland, who depopulated Lithuania, and who annually sends thousands of miserable exiles to perish amidst the eternal snows of Siberia.'[3]

However, the Crimean War brought an unprecedented volume of information about Russia to Anglophone readers, including the groundbreaking work of Irish journalists William Howard Russell and Edwin Godkin. The war brought the Crimea and the southern portions of the Russian Empire to the attention of curious Irish and British travellers. Dark tourists visited the peninsula's battlefields and mass graves. James Creagh had served as a captain in the war and returned to the region en route

Adventurers and Innovators after Crimea

to Jerusalem in 1867, and an unknown Irish woman travelled overland – partly by pony treks of up to sixteen hours per day – across Europe to St Petersburg, Moscow and Nizhny Novgorod before continuing south through Crimea, Turkey and Asia Minor. Her anonymously published *Sketches of Travel in Russia, Turkey, Greece, &c, &c, in 1869* (1870) includes a visit to the English graveyard at Scutari, the resting place of many of those killed in the war.[4] Journalist Selina Bunbury, travelling in Russia in the immediate aftermath of the war, published a brutally honest account that laid side-by-side the Muscovy of her imagination and the modern, centralized state embodied by the eighteenth-century city of St Petersburg.

Irish travel to the Russian Empire took on a more adventurous edge in the final decades of the nineteenth century. As mountaineering took off as an elite sport, climbers like Belfast-born James Bryce – who was still climbing in his seventies – made ascents of Caucasian peaks. Irish journalist Edmond O'Donovan travelled through Georgia and Azerbaijan in 1879–81 as part of a wider itinerary taking in the Middle East, Turkey and Persia. In 1895–6 Tipperary native Sir Michael Francis O'Dwyer took an eighteen-month career break from the British Civil Service to learn Russian and travel around Russia and Central Asia. The celebrated horse trainer Corkman Captain Matthew Horace Hayes made four visits to Russia in 1897–8 at the invitation of the Imperial Horse Guards, publishing *Among Horses in Russia* in 1900. In 1909 Dublin publisher Joseph Maunsell Hone and mountaineer Page Lawrence Dickinson visited Persia and returned to Ireland via Georgia. Their published account emphasized the 'violent and [...] unscrupulous' hand of the Russian Empire in the Caucasus.[5] In 1905–13 Offaly-born soldier and explorer Charles Howard-Bury travelled from Western Russia to Tibet through what is now Tajikistan, Uzbekistan and Kyrgyzstan, collecting plants along the way. In 1912 he travelled the breadth of the Russian Empire by rail, from Warsaw to Omsk and onwards by boat to Semipalatinsk and the border with China, photographing Kazakh and Kirghiz nomads and making a pet of a bear cub named Agu that he took back to Ireland via the Caucasus and Turkey; he was later part of the first British expedition to Everest in 1921.[6] Alongside these more adventurous itineraries, the classic St Petersburg–Moscow jaunt that was established in the early nineteenth century remained an option for those seeking something more accessible, like Irish-born and American-resident banker and oil magnate Samuel Gamble Bayne, who visited St Petersburg and Moscow in 1907.[7]

The Victorian age was one of exciting innovations in transport, communications and industry. From the 1850s onwards Russia embraced what Simon Sebag Montefiore calls 'breakneck industrialization'.[8] From medics like Roscommon-born doctor Sir David Barry, who investigated a cholera outbreak in St Petersburg in 1831, to engineers associated with Crimean War infrastructure, a small but notable group of Irish scientists and industrialists found their way to Russia. Towards the end of the period the eastern reaches of the Russian Empire began to open up with the laying of the Trans-Siberian Railway. Begun in 1891, by the time of its completion in 1916 it was the longest railway in the world, stretching over 6000 miles from St Petersburg to Vladivostok. Irish journalist George Lynch travelled eastward by rail to Port Arthur (Lüshun Port) and back to Moscow in 1902, publishing his observations in *The Path of Empire* (1903), a title that leaves no doubt as to his views on the significance of the line. Developments in transport and communications went hand-in-hand with imperial domination but proved useful to Far Eastern travellers, too. George Lynch hurried from Moscow to Beijing to report on the Boxer Rebellion of 1900 and Lizzie le Blond, one of the most prominent female mountaineers of the age, travelled partly by the almost-completed line from Korea to St Petersburg in 1913. Some of these Irish travellers, visitors and professionals are implicated in nineteenth-century Russian economic opportunism, territorial expansion and imperialism.

12

A 'CHILLING EFFECT': SELINA BUNBURY REPORTS ON RUSSIA AFTER CRIMEA

At the age of nine, the daughter of a rural Irish pastor read a description of St Petersburg that stayed with her for life. Selina Bunbury's parents had allowed her 'an unrestricted course of private reading, and an unfettered exercise of the right of private judgment.'[1] The freedom and range afforded to the child's imagination gave birth to a prolific writer and dedicated traveller whose account of Russia interrogated the myths and realities of life in the empire.

Born in Kilsaran, Co. Louth, in 1802, Bunbury was one of the fifteen children of Reverend Henry Bunbury, a Church of Ireland clergyman. Her father went bankrupt in 1819, forcing her to seek employment as a teacher. Simultaneously, she wrote in secret, concealing this fact and her additional income from her disapproving mother. Eventually, she would support herself, her sister and her nephew with her earnings as a writer. Her first book, *A Visit to My Birth Place* (1821), was hugely successful and went into twelve editions in her lifetime. Like so many Irish at the time, the family moved to Liverpool in around 1830, and from 1845 Bunbury began to travel. She visited almost every country in Europe, gathering inspiration and material for her many publications. She selected her destinations with an eye to what would be of interest to her readers. She published around a hundred books, pamphlets, and articles, including no fewer than fifty articles in the high-circulation Tory favourite *Fraser's Magazine* in the years 1836–50.[2]

Bunbury departed for Russia in July 1856, four months after the end of the Crimean War, and when the country was still reeling from its after-effects. Luckily, her visit also coincided with the coronation of Alexander II. She was aware of the lively British interest in Russia in the immediate aftermath of the war, writing in the opening scene of her account, 'There are few countries on which British imagination has been more freely wasted, especially in late times, than Russia.'[3] She understood that a book titled *Russia After the War* had commercial potential in this context and wasted no time in writing up and publishing her experiences and observations. Her book was released at a time when more information than ever was available about Russia in the English language. Over fifty English-language books relating to the country were published in the years 1854–9 alone.[4]

In 1850 Bunbury published *Anecdotes of Peter the Great*, a didactic work intended 'to exhibit [...] the results of laborious exertion in overcoming difficulties, and thus to stimulate young persons to energy and perseverance in the acquirement of knowledge.'[5] The images of Russia conjured in her young mind by the course of childhood reading referred to at the opening of this chapter had clearly stayed with her into adulthood – *Anecdotes*, intended for young readers, is full of positive lessons drawn from the tsar's determination to modernize his country and his ascendancy to the imperial throne at the tender age of ten. But she found on visiting Russia six years later that her early 'imaginations of the world and its wonders' were to be 'disappointed by the realities of what they depicted'. Her childish imagination had latched onto the Summer and Winter Palaces as 'icy palaces and gardens, and Babylonian palaces, and Babylonian gardens'. Even with the passage of four decades, a tinge of those impressions remained until 'The actual St Petersburg was to obliterate that trace.' She was disappointed to find that the new city 'banishes the old idea of Muscovy completely from the mind' and that 'most things natively Russian' were 'out of repute' there. Like almost every foreign visitor to Russia in the eighteenth and nineteenth centuries, she noted that the nobility was more interested in French culture and Western European fashions, and that the Russia of her imagination was to be found among the lower classes: 'The upper branches of the social tree are more exquisitely exotic, more completely foreignized, than the great Reformer of Russia could ever have dreamt of seeing them; the lower and the lowest remain pretty much what they were before the light of Peter I dawned on barbaric Muscovy.' The city's mix of nationalities and ethnicities, Bunbury felt, diluted its Russianness further: 'This is not a national city; its population, composed of all nations, is moreover constantly changing.' Surely diversity was to be expected in the capital of an extensive empire, but it may not have sat comfortably with Western Europeans' prior expectations.[6]

Bunbury was recommended to search for her idea of Russia and reprieve from St Petersburg's 'terrible ennui [...] of white houses and stately monotony' in the small towns of the interior, but she did find some of what she was searching for in the capital's markets. There, she wrote, 'you plunge back into an epoch that existed long before Peter [the Great]' and find yourself 'in old Muscovy, in a crowd of old Muscovites; in Russia.'[7] She revelled in Moscow from the moment she arrived and was in raptures with her first sight of the Kremlin under a crimson sunset:

> Wonderful – beautiful scene! One Russian gem at last for my mental kaleidoscope, to which so many lands have contributed a particle! [...] it was so sweet to stand there and see for oneself what one had partly fancied, partly been told of [...] It is an old and oft-repeated saying, that Moscow is the heart of Russia, and the Kremlin is the heart of Moscow – a heart within a heart.[8]

She dismissed any comparison with other European cities, finding that 'Moscow is only like itself, and quite unlike anything else I have seen in Europe.' At the core of her pleasure on visiting the Kremlin was the pulse of history beating through its walls, where 'Strange memories of the past, of Muscovites, Mongols, Poles, who ruled therein, rise up.' Delving further, Bunbury found the Kremlin a 'mausoleum of the buried past, to the real Muscovite' – that of the pre-Petrine era – but the red colour of its walls was a reminder that 'the earth has been drenched in blood'. This echoes her observation that the foundations of the slave-built city of St Petersburg 'may be said to have been laid in human blood'.[9]

One aspect of Russian life was universally decried by foreign observers – serfdom. Bunbury sympathetically observed, 'Their step may be free, their look easy and cheerful enough [...] but the chain is around them [...] an order from the proprietor recalls them to their former drudgery.' She visited Russia in 1861, five years before the abolition of serfdom, and her book clearly advocates not only for abolition, but also for universal education. She was surprised to find the rural peasantry 'quickly intelligent' and wondered 'what [they] might be made of by cultivation'.[10] While her book indicates that she spoke a little Russian, the extent to which she was able to converse with ordinary Russians is questionable. She found evidence of the brutalizing effects of serfdom in the villages outside Moscow, where

> the few [people] we saw, whether men or women, had not at all the same ferocious and vicious appearance that abject poverty among us, with its usual concomitants vice and crime, so generally exhibits. [...] Here the people were not quite so ragged nor so black as such beings among ourselves; but their faces were paler, and had an almost indescribable expression [...] It was the expression of a class more than that of an individual; a cast of countenance that was hereditary, rather than derived from passing circumstances of harshness or distress; a perfect resignation to an inexorable and inevitable destiny might be its characteristic, and this mingled with a quiet subjugation of manner, a complete acquiescence in the allotment to them of a fate so cruel.[11]

However, her short time among the rural peasantry only served to complicate rather than confirm her existing opposition to serfdom. She compared Russian serfdom and American slavery, attempting to untangle the moral and psychological results of each:

[...] serfdom [...] does not even in its darkest present us with the full horrors of negro slavery. It does not wear in Russia, despotic Russia, the cruel, revolting character of slavery in that 'home of liberty', as an American writer, who decries despotism in his travels in that country, calls America. But the despotism of democracy is of all others the worst. Still, though not so bad as slavery, though as an institution it guarantees the poor from sinking into that frightful abyss of poverty and vice, which is, alas! to be seen in free, rich, happy England – still, when its darker features came into view, we forget the brighter; we groan in our very hearts [...] When we see a man, a strong man, dressed grandly it may be in his lord's livery, turn white, white as death – and that strange look of fear which ever seems lurking beneath the sunniest gleam of a Russian eye [...] his terror caused by an offence for which an English servant would scarcely submit to the merest reproof – then we see a glimpse that places the servitude of freedom and of serfdom in clear opposition.[12]

But the effects of the war were the main focus of Bunbury's book. Her deeply held pacifism informed her response to a country reeling from the after-effects of recent war. On a short trip to Finland's Sveaborg Fortress, occupied by Russia since 1808, Bunbury reflected: 'Prince of Peace, when shall Thy kingdom come, and Thy will be done on earth as it is in heaven? Then only shall men learn war no more.' As an experienced traveller and writer, Bunbury had a keen eye, and she challenged from the outset popular British and Irish images of Russian soldiers to elicit sympathy and empathy from the reader. She emphasized that the 'terrible looking specimens of Russian humanity' – surly guards accompanying the port's revenue officers – strongly resembled the 'type of what was presented to most English imaginations during the recent war as the Russian soldier or the Russian peasant', but in reality they were probably galley slaves. She acknowledged her own prejudices, noting, 'It is astonishing what a change the peace has wrought in many of our imaginations' and reminding the reader, 'We also were invaders; and though Sebastopol and Sveaborg were not on the holy soil of Russia the Great.' Her crusade to humanize a recent enemy stretched from the lowliest serf to the very apex of power. Shortly after arriving in St Petersburg she attended the festival of the patron saint of the guards at Tsarskoe Selo. There, her eyes dramatically locked with the tsar's piercing blues, finding that the 'miserable war' had 'mark[ed] his brow with care, and his countenance with dissatisfaction.'[13]

For all Bunbury's sympathy for the Russian people and her attempts to humanize the erstwhile enemy for an Anglophone readership, her book is not free of the negative stereotypes that feature in so many travel accounts. Her descriptions of Moscow's architecture, Orthodox religious practices and traditional dress are steeped in an Orientalist perspective. She described a 'wild-looking priest with his un-European air' officiating at a military ceremony; she thought Moscow's Boyar women looked like 'the descendants of an eastern race'; and she referred to the pilgrimage site of Troitse monastery as 'a half Asiatic land' with 'a quite un-European air'.[14]

The modern, centralized Russian state is embodied by the eighteenth-century city of St Petersburg – a city of 'stately uniformity' and a 'somewhat chilling grandeur' – and emerges from her book as all-encompassing and controlling. The immaculate walks around Tsarskoe Selo, 'kept without speck or spot, being cleaned, brushed, it might be said dusted, from morning to night', symbolized this order and discipline. The Summer Palace's outdoor statues were a metaphor for the unbending power of the state: 'All the Grecian and Roman figures, so abundant around St Petersburg, appear to want a much warmer climate. The snow and ice of Russia are by no means suitable to these naked divinities [...] Yet even they must learn to submit to over-ruling power.' Among the people, she found, exaggerating for effect, the lack of liberty and free speech meant that 'laughter is seldom long or loud'. Even the nobility was not free, for 'all their privileges are reversionary at the will of the Tzar, on which they are even more dependent than the inferior class'.[15]

What can *Russia After the War* tell us about Bunbury herself, in the absence of any unpublished personal writing or correspondence, as an independent woman who never married and supported herself through writing? While she certainly did travel a lot, she did not go to Russia alone, but was accompanied by two male relatives and a Russian maid named Violette. She must have been aware of her position as one of the few Irish women of the age to make a living from writing, portraying herself in *Russia After the War* as strong-willed and taking opportunities to comment on the status of women. Passing under the Moscow Kremlin's sacred Spasskaya Vorota ('Saviour Tower'), she noted that despite the snow falling from the arch above, men must go bareheaded, but that it was 'one of the few places in this world where the privileges of womankind are to be felt. Bonnets are not to be taken off. Alas! it may be that some lingering trace of eastern theology teaches that women have not souls.' She offered some similar thoughts on the status of women in Russia, emphasizing that 'a female Russian peasant is not "a soul" [...] The males only are rated, and they are called by the term "souls". In all respects women hold that subordinate place which law, if not sentiment, everywhere assigns them.' During a short excursion to Finland she expressed her exasperation at being denied entry to Sveaborg Fortress: 'And that refusal if it did not excite our national combativeness, sorely irritated our feminine self-will [...] We held ourselves accountable to the women of England; and just because the permission was not granted became doubly resolved to get in.' Later the same day Bunbury refused to acquiesce to local norms that dictated that women should not go into society unaccompanied, and convinced a young Finnish female acquaintance to come with her to a party. The following day, she and her companion tried again to access Sveaborg Fortress, where her companion, a Miss Malvina, demonstrated that she was 'the only one of our party who possessed the prerogative of her sex – the use of the tongue – the only weapon universally conceded by the so-called stronger sex to the weaker'.[16]

Bunbury's sharp sense of humour pervades her travel writing. She thought that a soldier she was standing close to at a parade might have been 'one of the many fragmentary parts that willingly or unwillingly compose the mighty empire of all the Russias', but it turned out to be the tsar himself. On witnessing a funeral for three Lutheran children, she distastefully joked that a piece of paper was placed in each coffin, 'commonly called the passport, giving the stranger the rather droll idea that even the dead cannot leave the Russian dominions without this all-important document'.[17] Her Irish roots emerged when she related the following anecdote:

> A writer, celebrated for her records of Irish wit, in speaking of one of those vehicles that are so much in esteem with the natives, relates how a driver informed her of the means by which he knew a married couple from a pair that were only coortin'; 'When they are married', he said, 'they sit one on each side to balance the car; but when they are only coortin they sit together and let me balance it myself.'[18]

Indeed, Bunbury drew many comparisons between the Russian and Irish people, and the two countries. These not only communicated her enduring affinity to her home, but also reflected the Victorian British reading public's appetite for descriptions that cast Ireland in a particular light. She found similarities between the Russian *droshky* and the Irish jaunting-car, particularly at ports and other locations where the drivers competed for business:

> [...] like the descent of a flock of crows, an innumerable crowd of droschkies swooped around us. As if by magic the whole silent, deserted street was crowded with a mass of these wild-looking little equipages and their wilder drivers [...] In short, it was completely an Irish scene; and had all the droschkies been changed into those equally droll vehicles called 'jaunting cars', we might have thought we had landed at Kingstown in mistake. The long skirted coat, the long shaggy hair, the old hat, and sundry other personal appearances, recalled the recollection of the Irish car driver; but it was the look of good-humoured roguery, the boisterous yet humoured contention for our possession, and their sly, laughing, cajoling manner, that made the resemblance complete.[19]

She joked that the drivers' cries of 'Pady! pady! which, Irish-sounding as it is, signifies only – clear the way', and found that 'poor Paddy' and the Russian poor favoured wearing their coats in a similar manner, tied around the waist with cord. On a more serious note, she compared the Polish revolution of 1831 with the Irish rebellion of 1798, for the brutality of the state responses to both events, the bloodiness of the violence and the use of agricultural implements as weapons by the rising peasantry. She also criticized the landlord absenteeism that blighted both countries as 'the bane of true civilization' and the cause of 'so large a part of the miseries of Irish tenants, and the ruin of Irish landlords.'[20]

Bunbury's aim was to produce a balanced account of Britain's recent foe for a wide readership. While she was keenly aware of the dominant stereotypes about Russia, she did indulge in some of the more facile tropes, such as relationships with alcohol. For example, on seeing an almost-drowned sailor revived with cognac, she remarked, 'Life must perhaps be extinct when a Russian soldier can no longer swallow spirits.'[21] While she was disappointed by aspects of her experiences in Russia, she was conscious of the role her own expectations – forged in childhood – played. Perhaps her greatest disappointment was the approach to St Petersburg on the Neva, a first impression of the city lauded by other travellers:

> We have arrived at St Petersburg and written from St Petersburg without even attending to that which is the common and usually the first theme of most of our travellers and summer tourists, the approach by water to this far-famed capital. Which of them has not told of golden domes, flashing like balls of fire in the sunlight; of spires of gold trembling and glittering in mid air; of palaces and towers, and all that is magnificent and magical, which rise to the stranger's view as he passes up the Neva to St Petersburg? It looks as if one must have been sulky, disagreeable, or sea-sick, not to have seen all this in the same way; nevertheless I have gone from and returned to St Petersburg many times, and the impressions on my eyes and mind have always been the same, namely, that the glittering spires and golden domes were very beautiful and curious in effect; but that if they were taken out of the picture, it would remain a very uninteresting, cold, and dreary one. [...] Flat, swampy, and barren shores appear as low as the waters they bound: these have a chilling effect on the expectations of the visitor, too much excited perhaps by the reports of those who have gone before him.[22]

The 'chilling effect' on Bunbury's impressions was not St Petersburg's location, but rather the weight of history, both distant and recent. Bunbury's alertness to the bloodshed and loss of life on the hillsides of Crimea and in the foundations of St Petersburg's palaces disposed her to a

A 'Chilling Effect': Selina Bunbury Reports on Russia after Crimea

gloomy outlook on a vast empire bound by absolutism. Self-aware as ever, though, she suddenly reflected: 'Hush! my pen is stopped. We did not come to Russia to complain of past or discover present despotism. There are always lights amid shadows [...] Perhaps we may do greater good than by railing against the darkness, or bringing forward the shadows in the hope of dispelling them.' As an experienced writer and traveller, Bunbury sought to provide her readers with some new insights. She challenged popular images of Russia in the post-Crimean context, pointing out that economic progress and industrialization were underway in the country in the same way as elsewhere, and questioned assumptions that 'the spirit of progress' in Russia was a function of 'aggression' or 'the icy chains of despotism'. She emphasized the change in regime since the passing of Nicholas I, whose long reign (1825–55) was marked by absolutism and repression, noting that 'Thousands, millions, rejoice at the change in the iron rule that was latterly so heavily felt.' Her attempts at optimism were, however, tempered by the soberingly prescient observation that 'The horrors that may attend an outbreak of the Russian peasants is a fearful matter of thought.'[23]

13
JAMES BRYCE, THE MOUNTAINEERING VISCOUNT

Until the 1700s Europe's highest mountain peaks were considered the preserve of deities, their crags and caves the hiding places of demons and spirits. Even miners and shepherds who worked in the mountains for generations dared not climb to the summits. The Alps had long been conflated with sorcery and mystery, partly because some traditional beliefs linked glaciers to occult powers; for example, a seventeenth-century bishop exorcised demonic glaciers to stop them creeping over the town of Chamonix. Accordingly, the rise of the sport of mountaineering required a fundamental shift in thinking. People had to want to reach a peak, and to think of such a feat as a real possibility.[1]

By the 1820s the formerly unapproachable Alps were fully measured and mapped, represented in guidebooks and board games. The eighteenth-century sublime – the exultation of solitude and challenging landscapes – was sinking under the weight of consumerism and nationalism as new rail lines made formerly remote locations much more accessible. By the mid-nineteenth century tourists buzzed around Europe's mountains, attracted by climbing clubs, commercialism and spectacle. An

James Bryce, the Mountaineering Viscount

'age of conquest' took place as mountaineering increased in popularity among the upper and middle classes. Lines of people trudged up and down Mont Blanc's (sometimes) dangerous paths, rewarded afterwards with a certificate confirming that they had reached the summit. The more adventurous sought out new challenges, looking east to chains like the Caucasus and eventually turning to the Himalayas' offer of space, distance and overwhelming greatness of scale.

The Irish were active in nineteenth-century international mountaineering circles. The Dublin-born politician and naturalist John Ball was the first president of the Alpine Club (1857) and author of the bestselling *Alpine Guide*. Carlow scientist John Tyndall visited the Alps regularly and was part of one of the first teams to reach the peak of the Matterhorn in 1868. Louth aristocrat Frederica Plunket pioneered women's mountaineering, publishing her experiences in *Here and There Among the Alps* in 1875. In the 1880s Youghal native William Spotswood Green famously made and attempted ascents in New Zealand and Canada, with Mount Green in Canada named in his honour. Wicklow-born Lizzie le Blond, too, made pioneering ascents and innovations in snow photography (see Chapter 15).

Victorian mountaineering mania set James, 1st Viscount Bryce (1838–1922), on the path to a life of adventure. The politician, historian, jurist, chief secretary for Ireland and mountaineer was born into a Belfast Presbyterian family that moved to Glasgow when he was eight, so that his father could take up a new teaching post. Encouraged by his parents, he developed an early love of hillwalking, mountaineering, botany, swimming and fishing. He maintained these interests throughout his university education at Glasgow, Oxford and Heidelberg, and after becoming an Oxford law professor and being called to the bar. Finding that work too often interrupted his writing and travelling, he gave up his legal practice to scale peaks all over the world. He campaigned for public walking rights in the Scottish mountains and was a member of the Alpine Club, serving as its president in 1899–1901. He made ascents in Ireland, Scotland, the Alps, the Dolomites, Iceland, the Pyrenees, the Rockies and Hawaii; of Mount Etna, the Tatras in Carpathia and finally – at the age of seventy-five – Mount Myogi-San, Japan. In 1898 English mountaineer J. Norman Collie named Mount Bryce in the Canadian Rockies after him. Bryce made tours of America in 1870, 1881 and 1883, publishing his observations about what he saw as an exciting new society in *The American Commonwealth* (1888); he also published *Impressions of South Africa* in 1897, after travelling there in 1895–6. By the time of his death he had visited every continent except Antarctica.

Throughout these adventures, his mind was also occupied with legal and political matters, particularly liberal causes. He opposed racial prejudice, supported women's advancement in education (but not suffrage) and denounced the 1876 Turkish massacres of Bulgarians, arguing that Britain had a duty to protect Christians living in the Ottoman Empire. During his twenty years as an MP (1885–1906) he supported Irish Home Rule, protested the Armenian genocides of 1896 and 1915 and criticized the severity of British tactics during the Boer War. His final book, *Modern Democracies* (1921), remained popular into the 1950s.[2] His views on the Caucasus – informed by his knowledge of international politics and his extensive travels – were influential, and his hefty, 526-page illustrated book *Transcaucasia and Ararat* (1877) was quoted at length in an account of Armenia by Irish military captain and travel writer James Creagh. Creagh returned to Sevastopol en route to Jerusalem in 1867, having previously captained a British Army regiment during the Crimean War. Creagh also spent almost a year living in Armenia and published a two-volume work titled *Armenians, Koords, and Turks* in 1880, a work that was really about 'Russian intrigues' in the Caucasus, as he termed them.

Transcaucasia and Ararat sold well. It documented Bryce's journey from Nizhny Novgorod down the Volga to Kazan, Saratov and Rostov-on-Don, from there to the spa town of Pyatigorsk, and on to Vladikavkaz in the northern foothills of the Caucasus.[3] He then made his way from Tbilisi to Yerevan and Ararat before returning to Tbilisi, then turning westward to the Black Sea coast and on to Constantinople. He set out on his Transcaucasian journey in the summer of 1876, on the eve of the 1877 war between Russia and Turkey; when his book went to print, the war was still ongoing.

James Bryce, the Mountaineering Viscount

During his tour Bryce made the first recorded Irish ascent of Ararat. However, contrary to claims made elsewhere, he was not the first European to scale the iconic peak but was in fact the sixth. In *Transcaucasia and Ararat*, he acknowledged that the title had belonged to German-Russian scientist Friedrich Parrot since 1828. By the 1870s Ararat had slipped down the list of the world's highest peaks, as the staggering scale of the Himalayas was revealed by surveys made in the 1850s. Today, it does not even feature on the list of the 100 highest peaks.

Bryce's ascent of Ararat was inspired by his boyhood reading of Bible tales and a conviction of the region's historic importance. He wrote: 'From the beginning of history the Caucasus is to the civilised nations, both Greek and Oriental, the boundary of geographical knowledge – indeed, the boundary of the world itself.' His journey explored his own prejudices as well as the rich history of the meeting-point of the Russian, Ottoman and Persian empires. He understood the mountain's shared veneration by both Christians and Muslims as evidence of the general level of religious tolerance he found in the region, which he contrasted with Irish sectarianism:

> No Irish Protestant venerates the sacred island in Lough Derg; but here the fanatical Tatars respect, and the Persian rulers formerly honoured and protected, Etchmiadzin and many another Christian shrine; while Christians not unfrequently, both in the Caucasus and farther south through the eastern regions of Turkey, practice pagan or Mohammedan rites which they have learnt from their neighbours, and even betray their awe for the sacred places of Islam.[4]

To promote his journey as something novel, he opened his account with the unlikely claim that north-western Russia – including Moscow and St Petersburg – was still 'very little visited by travellers' and that the south was 'hardly visited at all [...] all the way to Tiflis or Constantinople, one does not see a single stranger travelling for pleasure, and discovers from the attentions which the western visitor receives, how rare such a visitor is.' However, he found that the famous fair at Nizhny Novgorod was no longer a spectacle worth travelling for because the pervasiveness of Western fashions had diluted the characteristic, traditional dress of the different peoples of the Russian Empire. Globalization had made the merchandise mundane, no different, he claimed, to what was available in shops in St Petersburg or even on London's Regent Street. But he was hopeful for the potential of the remainder of the journey to fulfil his fantasies. For Bryce, Nizhny was the gateway to the eastern part of the Russian Empire. Leaving the city by steamer, he and his companion 'felt as if entering a new world, borne along by the strong majestic stream [the Volga] to the mysterious East'. On leaving Tbilisi for Yerevan, he finally felt that 'we were going far afield into a really curious and seldom visited country'.[5] The 'east', for Bryce, was both an imaginary land conjured up by Victorian Orientalism and a shorthand for non-Christian countries.

The bulk of Bryce's long book was dedicated to the Greater and Lesser Caucasus chains and the nations living in the countries now known as Georgia and Armenia. Georgia and eastern Armenia had both been part of the Russian Empire since the early nineteenth century. Bryce acknowledged the role of the Crimean War in bringing the wider region to the attention of Western Europeans, but noted that the small increase in Anglophone visitors to Transcaucasia did not equate to improved knowledge or familiarity:

> In the days of the Crimean War, when the Caucasus first drew the attention of the Western world, Englishmen mostly thought of it as a chain of snowy mountains [...] inhabited by a race of patriotic heroes and beautiful women [...] Since then travellers have begun to penetrate it, and some of our own countrymen have even scaled its loftiest summits. But our conceptions are still so vague.[6]

Bryce had travelled around America five years previously and felt that both it and Russia were 'new' countries simmering with potential, where 'things are still pretty much in the rough, have what we should call a colonial air about them [...] there is a mixture of magnificent designs with imperfect accomplishment. [...] Both are countries whose interest lies in the future rather than in the past.' In Transcaucasia, he felt the intersection of 'many cross-currents, so many diverse associations of the past and possibilities for the future', with the echoes of an ancient past reverberating still. However, while American settlers had a claim to the English past – one that was venerated by Victorians – he thought that 'Russian history lies in a dim twilight [...] in the main it is an uncertain as well as dreary record of family quarrels between savage princes and incessant border warfare with the Tatar hordes.' Indeed, much of his account was set on demonstrating that Russia was still awaiting civilization and that an imaginary Scythian spirit lived on in the steppes. Bryce was enchanted with the simple lifestyle of the Kurds he encountered in the plains at the foot of Ararat and thought the mountains were 'much in the same state as they were in the time of Herodotus and Strabo.'

Bryce speculated that while the Russian Empire was rich in natural resources and tracts of fertile land, for it to 'become a tremendous power in the world' it would have to become 'a nation one in sentiment and faith, swayed by a single will'. His comments are reminiscent of author Selina Bunbury's, when she noted Moscow's multiculturalism (see Chapter 12). It seemed to him that the peoples of the Caucasus had a 'complex and almost unexplored past' and that, situated at the meeting-point of three empires, the region had 'a considerable part to play in history'. However, these factors gave him no hint of Transcaucasia's destiny – whether it would form part of the Russian Empire, or its peoples would be 'melted down into one nation'. Despite his awareness of resistance to Russian oppression among the nations of the Caucasus, he never considered the question of their living as independent nations, reflecting the fact that even as a liberal politician, Bryce only came to support Home Rule for Ireland from 1882.[7]

He made his initial ascent of Ararat in the company of six Cossack guards, a group of Kurdish porters and his travelling companion, the Scottish lawyer Aeneas Mackay. The party was equipped with a compass, snow glasses, gloves and umbrellas (for sunshades); the Cossacks were fully armed, while Bryce and Mackay carried pistols and were prepared to use their ice-picks in self-defence should the need arise. As he began the ascent, Bryce recalled the busier paths he had climbed within the previous five years – the Schreckhorn in the Bernese Alps and the Maladeta in the

Pyrenees – thinking 'how unlike this cavalcade of ours was to the parties of loud-voiced Englishmen and stalwart guides that issue from an Alpine inn before daylight to "do" some stimulating peak or pass'.[8] While he was keen to portray his climb as an unusual one, far removed from Alpine tourism, Bryce's ascent was rushed and not without incident. The party began its ascent in the middle of the night, intending to reach the summit with enough daylight to spare for the return to base camp. From the outset, Bryce had some difficulties with the Cossack guards, as it was feared that the Kurdish guides might, if left unsupervised, take the opportunity to rob or murder the climbers, but the Cossacks kept stopping to rest when Bryce wanted to press onwards. Bryce grew tired of waiting for them and took off by himself at eight o'clock in the morning for the summit; two Cossacks and a Kurd followed, out of curiosity, pity or amusement. At 13,000 feet, Bryce found a piece of timber that he thought looked hand-hewn, so he took a piece of it away on the absurd basis that it may have been a fragment of the biblical ark. Shortly afterwards the Kurd and the two Cossacks – poorly equipped and unfamiliar with the mountain – gave up on the climb, and Bryce proceeded alone, claiming to have reached the summit after almost six and a half hours. He reached basecamp by nightfall, and the entire party descended the mountain in the dark. At the summit, he wrote, 'There was a sense of expanse, solitude, vastness, which I never before experienced on any other mountain summit.'[9]

Bryce's unwitnessed solo ascent is unverified and unverifiable, recorded only in his own book and a paper he read to the Royal Geographical Society, but his observations and experiences are nonetheless of interest as a rare nineteenth-century Irish view of the Caucasus. In his concluding chapter, he admitted that he 'went with a mind which, so far as it was prejudiced, was prejudiced against Russia, which I had learnt from childhood to look upon as the enemy of freedom, the power which oppressed Poland, and had enabled Austria to crush Hungary'. He closed by arguing that 'the power and the ambition of Russia have been greatly exaggerated', that its imperial ambitions were no different to those of other European countries, and that Russia's interference in Turkish affairs was the result of Western European

James Bryce, the Mountaineering Viscount

indifference to the situation of Christians in the Ottoman Empire. Indeed – and surprisingly for such a strong defender of democracy – sections of his book read as an apology for Russian imperialism, suggesting that Russia's power had been greatly overstated because of a mistaken assumption that geographical extent correlated to political potential. As he saw it, Russia had 'undoubtedly the elements of one day becoming a very powerful monarchy. But for modern warfare, which is, above all things, a matter of money and science, she is probably less strong than the weakest of the three other great military states of the Continent.'[10]

The liberal Bryce's encounter with the long-troubled southern fringes of the Russian Empire prompted him to reflect on the British Empire. His positive impressions of the Caucasus led him to the improbable conclusion that the Russians tended to get on better with conquered nations than the British, Dutch or Spanish did. He did not find among Georgians or Armenians 'so much bitterness of feeling among the subjects as there is towards ourselves, among certain sections of the better-educated class in India, or to the French in Algeria now' and wondered whether this was 'partly because the Russians leave their subjects more to themselves, while we try to improve them'. This was not a signal of benign intent, but rather evidence of the Oriental barbarity of the Russian state, as Bryce saw it – uncivilized itself, it was unable to civilize. However, within twenty years, Bryce had to update the fourth edition of his book with an appendix detailing the rise of national feeling among Georgians. His idealized vision of Transcaucasia as an earthly haven of multi-ethnic harmony skewed his viewpoint to the extent that he claimed that the persecution endured by religious minorities in the Russian Empire was 'trifling compared to those [hardships] which we were recently inflicting on Roman Catholics in Ireland' – an astonishing suggestion in the context of the widely acknowledged anti-Semitism of the imperial Russian state, its treatment of indigenous Arctic peoples, and the oppression of politically dissenting and reformist voices.[11]

14
SCIENTISTS AND INNOVATORS

Irish scientists were active on the world stage in the nineteenth century, making discoveries of lasting importance and embedding themselves in international and imperial scientific networks. These global networks secured invitations to visit, work and share knowledge and expertise in other countries. For example, Sligo-born chemist and physician Bryan Higgins (*c.* 1737–*c.* 1818) opened a medical practice and a school of chemistry in London after studying medicine at Leyden. His public lectures and chemistry demonstrations were hugely popular, and he became a celebrated figure. London was as important for Higgins as it was for countless others of the Irish diaspora. Living in Soho, he found himself at the heart of the city's scientific community, counting among his neighbours Sir Joseph Banks, president of the Royal Society. His reputation soared internationally; in 1796–1801 he visited Jamaica at the invitation of the House of Assembly to advise on the sugar and rum industries. Unconfirmed reports assert that he visited Russia in the 1780s and was received by Catherine the Great – perhaps not so far-fetched, given her interest in modernization and Higgins' international reputation?[1]

Scientists and Innovators

The earliest Irish scientific professionals in Russia were medics. A number of doctors – mostly military – were recruited to work there from the eighteenth century on, as noted in Chapter 1. This tradition continued throughout the nineteenth century, when Roscommon-born doctor Sir David Barry (1780–1835) spent four months in St Petersburg investigating a cholera outbreak, and when Irish nurses and doctors tended to the sick and injured on the Crimean frontline. In 1831 the British government sent Barry to Russia with his colleague William Russell to investigate a worrying cholera outbreak. Barry had previously worked as a British military surgeon in Portugal and in private practice in Paris. Cholera was a deadly constant in Russian life from 1823 to 1926; over 236,000 died in the first outbreak, which lasted until 1834, and other European countries monitored the situation closely.[2] Barry and Russell compiled a 151-page report, focusing on clusters of infection at military barracks, factories and residential institutions. Their investigation involved an effort to establish whether the St Petersburg outbreak was linked to an existing cholera strain found in India in 1817 and whether, like previous outbreaks that had taken place periodically since the mid-fourteenth century, it had made its way to St Petersburg via the Volga trade route.[3] International and imperial networks were crucial to the investigation. Russell had previously worked in Kolkata during cholera outbreaks and so was qualified to observe the St Petersburg epidemic and to confirm its relationship to the Indian strain. A Scottish doctor, James Wylie, was head of medicine in the Russian army at the time, and he facilitated Barry and Russell's access to St Petersburg's military hospitals, where they examined patients in the throes of terrible suffering during twice-daily visits. Barry wrote, 'The sufferings of these athletic young men (grenadiers of the guards) have furnished me with the type of a disease, which I had certainly never seen before, which cannot be forgotten after having been observed.'[4] The doctors experimented with cures being pioneered in other parts of Europe but noted that the spread of the disease was accelerated by the season: a time of religious fasting (leaving people in weakened state), when the churches were filled with worshippers and the streets teeming with processions.[5] More generally, Barry and Russell

Scientists and Innovators

understood that the crisis was exacerbated by the state of poverty in which the majority of people lived, overheated dwellings, and the duration and frequency of religious fasts. With no little notion of British superiority, the doctors expressed the hope that, should the epidemic reach England, 'cleanly habits and a mild climate will mitigate its severity'.[6]

Barry and Russell described the panic caused by the spread of the cholera, with an estimated 20,000 seasonal workers fleeing the city in terror.[7] The doctors had hoped to take direct charge of a number of patients themselves, but found that this was impossible due to 'the violent excitement of the people against all foreigners, more particularly against medical men, whom they lately looked on as emissaries employed by their enemies to poison them'. A German doctor was said to have been killed 'by the mob', and several other medics were beaten as the public expressed its unhappiness at the apparent 'indiscriminate' removal of the sick to temporary hospitals.[8] Russell noted, 'It is extremely difficult to get at the truth of the facts which bear directly on the point, as they are often denied, frequently contradicted, and explained away'.[9] The scale of the task they faced was compounded by a raft of theories circulating about the spread of the disease and the kind of person most likely to contract it. Popular speculation linked cholera to sexual activity and the consumption of cucumbers and melons.[10] Barry and Russell described in detail how the epidemic was introduced to and spread through a prison, factories, certain small villages, the foundling hospital, the cadet school at Kronstadt, and individual ships and vessels.[11] They also described how, on a second outbreak at the foundling hospital, infected wet nurses were made to artificially express breastmilk in order to preserve their supply while they recovered from cholera.[12]

Tending to the sick was risky, and Barry placed himself in danger by attending to patients twice a day. By 27 July, of the 164 'medical men' working in St Petersburg, 25 had been infected and 9 had died of cholera.[13] But in a letter written within a month of his arrival in Russia, Barry shows how witnessing the outbreak first-hand improved his knowledge of the disease and helped to challenge his prior beliefs and refine his understanding about its behaviour.[14] The doctors' joint report closed by acknowledging the help

Scientists and Innovators

and assistance they received in Russia: 'The readiness with which every source of information was thrown open to us; the candour and good feeling with which all our inquiries were attended to; the kind treatment which we met with, both as British subjects and as individuals, in every rank, from the most exalted, to the humblest in the state.' After returning from Russia, Barry continued to work in public health. He was made deputy inspector of hospitals in Britain and in 1833–4 was appointed to commissions into the health of children working in factories and the condition of the working poor.[15] The four months he spent in Russia directed the course of the rest of his career, until his untimely death four years later at the age of fifty-five.

With advances in manufacturing and in communications and transport technologies as Alexander II sought to improve his empire's infrastructure, and as the Crimean War demanded the movement of troops and equipment, Irish engineers and industrialists found opportunities in Russia. This encompassed the full range of public works and private industry. Dublin-born engineer and property speculator Richard Turner (*c.* 1798–1881) is supposed to have visited Russia in 1848 in connection with the construction of greenhouses, but the only known evidence for the trip is a letter between two acquaintances speculating as to the success of his Russian project. Turner inherited his uncle's ironworks, becoming known for wrought-iron conservatories and for experimenting with casting the lightest iron structures of the age. He built the palm house at Kew Gardens, as well as many other private and public buildings around Ireland and Britain. It is not beyond the realm of possibility that his international fame may have prompted an invitation to Russia.[16] Charles O'Neill (1831–1894), a successful Manchester Irish calico printer, worked in Russia for twelve years from 1863. A chemist by training, he published a number of books on calico printing and dyeing and entered Manchester public life as a city councillor in 1885. He was a prominent member of the Irish diaspora in the city and in 1887 gave a well-attended lecture to the local branch of the Irish National League on the subject of life in Russia.[17] In 1905 Wexford-born engineer Arthur Rowe went to Yuryevets, at the confluence of the Volga and Unzha Rivers, to maintain specialist flour milling equipment. At the time the region was developing as a centre of manufacturing, taking advantage of its proximity to the great trading centre of Nizhny Novgorod. Rowe married a Greek woman, Julia Karageorgia, but in 1914 he abandoned her and their son to return briefly to Ireland before moving on to Canada, where he died. Arthur and Julia's child, Alexander Arturovich Rou, went on to become one of the most popular directors of films for Soviet children.

Ukrainian-born, Irish-resident engineer Charles H. Moberly was charged with conveying three shallow-draught steamers from Gravesend to the Volga port of Rybinsk in summer 1859. He later read a detailed account of his two-month journey and Russia's inland navigation to the Institute of Civil Engineers of Ireland.[18] Inland navigation was crucial prior to the development of the railways, with the road network being poor and susceptible to the spring thaw and autumn rains. The south-western reaches of the Russian Empire saw an influx of Irish military and railway engineers during the Crimean War, as the Civil Engineer Corps and Army Works Corps made essential improvements to the peninsula's transportation infrastructure. These works were completed under the supervision of a number of Irish engineers and through the labour of hundreds of Irish navvies. In August to November 1855 Carlow-born William Thomas Doyne (1823–1877) was the engineering superintendent in charge of the Army Works Corps in Crimea before going on to work on projects in Ceylon, New Zealand and Australia.[19] His story and those of others involved in the Crimean War effort are recounted in detail in David Murphy's *Ireland and the Crimean War* (2002) and so are not repeated here.

The upsurge in Irish professionals making their way to Russia during the Crimean War continued in the second half of the nineteenth century. Each of these contributed to scientific, geographical or socio-political knowledge of the Russian Empire in a period when Britain and Russia eyed each other suspiciously, jealously guarding their interests along the fragile, unstable and tentative Central Asian borders of their respective empires.

Son of the director of the Bank of Ireland, Edward Fitzgerald Law (1846–1908) was born in Co. Down and educated in Brighton and at

Scientists and Innovators

St Andrews. He had a varied and complicated career that involved two separate long periods in Russia. After three years in the British Army, in 1872 he left for Moscow, where he oversaw the erection of an overhead wire cableway at a private premises before becoming an agricultural machinery sales agent, a role that demanded extensive travel around the country. He also wrote occasionally for *The Daily Telegraph*. As the newspaper was banned in Russia, he reported anonymously, but articles identified as his pessimistically covered Russian social unrest, the state's reactionary response to radicals and reformers, the threat to Britain posed by Russia's interests in Central Asia, and anti-Semitism. Law had a Russian cousin who taught him about Russian life and introduced him to pastimes like skating and sledding. During his final year there he was acting consul at St Petersburg under the ambassadorship of his cousin, Lord Dufferin (see Chapter 16). In this capacity, he attended the trial of those accused of assassinating Alexander II. After ten years in Moscow he returned to Britain, turning down a position in the Belgian service in Africa to become manager of the Global Telephone Company in London (1883–4), publishing articles about Russian society and politics in the *Fortnightly Review* and advocating for better treatment of Jews by the Russian state. In 1885 he volunteered for duty in the Sudan and in the following year was recalled to Britain to work in army intelligence on the diplomatic crisis known as the Panjdeh Incident, when the Russian seizure of an Afghan border fort almost ignited another major conflict with Britain. Law then travelled to Manchuria for the Amur River Navigation Company. In January 1888 he found himself back in St Petersburg as commercial attaché to the British Embassy, with responsibility for Persian and Turkish matters. He left Russia for Greece in 1892, reporting on the country's financial situation and settling there with his Greek wife. Then followed a series of commercial diplomatic positions in Turkey and the Mediterranean before he left for India in 1900 to work in revenue and finance, resigning in 1905 and returning to Britain.[20]

Law was a curious and opportunistic person. Harnessing his military training and experience, he entered private industry in Russia at a time of increased mechanization in global agriculture, imperial expansion in Central

Scientists and Innovators

Asia, and in the wake of Russia's emancipation of the serfs. Aware of the wider geopolitical implications of Russian modernization and expansion, and armed with knowledge of provincial life gained through extensive travel, he attempted to raise British awareness of the tsar's ambitions. Law's talent for languages – he spoke French, German and Russian – helped him get to know the Russian peasantry during his travels around the empire as a military officer, a commercial traveller and a journalist. He was, apparently, fond of stating in his later years 'that Russia was indeed no part of Europe, but only the most Westerly of Asiatic States'.[21]

Around the same time as Law, another Irishman saw an opportunity to share information about a country that some thought was changing for the better after the abolition of serfdom. Newry-born Denis Caulfield Heron (1824–1881) visited St Petersburg and Moscow as a participant in the eighth International Statistical Congress at St Petersburg in August 1872. The lawyer and politician was educated at Trinity College Dublin, King's Inns and Lincoln's Inn before being appointed lecturer in political economy at Trinity College Dublin and, later, professor of political economy at Queen's College Galway. He resigned this post in 1859 to return to the bar, building his reputation by defending Fenians in the 1860s. He was later an MP and supported women's suffrage. He gave public lectures all over Ireland as a founding member of the Dublin Statistical Society (later the Statistical and Social Inquiry Society of Ireland).[22] After returning from the congress in St Petersburg he read a paper to the Statistical and Social Inquiry Society of Ireland, sharing information he acquired about Russia during the trip. His paper, later published in the Society's journal, is one of the most praiseworthy and blindly naïve Irish accounts of Romanov Russia. Caulfield evidently believed in the power of statistical information to inform social and economic change and found that Grand Duke Constantine shared his views, quoting his opening remarks to the assembly of international statisticians:

> [...] [that] the end of the science was to seek under what laws and what institutions, what physical and economical conditions, the happiness of mankind should be most assured, and also to discover the source of evils

Scientists and Innovators

> which arrested the progress of humanity. [...] [and] The regularity, the systematic order, and the uniformity of the observations over the entire extent of Russia, and over a population of 80,000,000 of inhabitants, furnished rich materials for the science.[23]

Heron's positivity may reflect the fact that Congress participants were provided with excellent accommodation and transportation, and permission to travel all over Russia as they wished. They were treated to four separate royal receptions; a 'magnificent' banquet hosted by the Imperial Iron Foundry Company; a fete at Kronstadt, where they were received by the Russian fleet; a public dinner in St Petersburg's Hall of Nobles, where Heron 'had the honour of proposing the toast of the Russian people'; and excursions around St Petersburg and Moscow. Heron reflected, 'In every part of Russia we met kindness, courtesy, and the warmest hospitality. Russian society is most agreeable.'

He attempted to obtain information about the condition of the peasantry while travelling between St Petersburg and Moscow and noted that his chief sources of information were French translations of government documents, personal enquiries, diplomatic reports and a friend from Astrakhan, a Mr Trirogoff. His account includes topics like the division of land after emancipation and the compensation paid to serf owners, as well as local government, Poland, the Caucasus, education, population, the army, livestock and national development. He was fulsome in his praise for the way in which 'the most conservative state in the world' achieved a peaceful transfer of millions of acres of land to the newly free peasants at what he termed 'a fair price, payable in instalments'. He paternalistically attributed the bloodlessness of this massive transfer of land to 'the character of the Russian peasantry – their quietness, their submission to authority, their devotion to their religion'. Overlooking the tsar's continuation of autocracy and the ongoing stifling of political opposition, he expressed admiration for Alexander II's charity in emancipating the serfs, for 'In the history of the world very few men have had the happiness to do so much good to mankind.'

Despite describing himself as 'a devoted student of history', Heron expressed a wish that Moscow and Warsaw could set aside their historical differences and suggested that this might be helped if 'all the books were burned, recounting the atrocities which, in the struggle for existence, in cruelty and terror, rival nationalities inflicted on each other, whenever they were victorious during the middle ages'. Continuing with this thread in his discussion of the emancipation of the serfs, Heron asserted: 'In reference to the land question, nowhere in Europe have the peasantry been so well treated as in Russia. In consequence, they are willing to let the historical bygones be bygones. The peasantry are grateful for the benefits they have received.'

Heron's Whiggish historical view of progress and prosperity saw him marvel at the extent of the Russian railway network, stretching from St Petersburg to Odesa, Krakow and Tbilisi, so that he thought, 'In a few years it will be as easy to ascend Mount Elbruz or Mount Ararat as it is to ascend any of the famous Swiss peaks'. He wished that Anglo-Russian relations might be settled to allow the development of the Amu Darya River navigation, to bring industry and economic development to the heart of Central Asia. Indeed, he was willing to overlook questions of democracy, reform and press freedom in favour of economic development, admitting that while 'Virtually all political power is concentrated in the Emperor and the Ministry at St Petersburgh [and] [...] The censorship of the press prevents all inquiry into the conduct of public officials. Nevertheless trade, commerce, agriculture, and manufactures flourish'. No matter about the ethnic groups subject to St Petersburg's rule, where Heron saw that 'the various nationalities of Circassia and Georgia, more than forty in number, have become peaceful and loyal subjects of the Emperor'. Heron's account concluded with the prediction that, whatever changes were to come in Russia, they would come about peacefully. The Irish who were present for the assassination of the tsar in 1881, and who both witnessed and participated in Russian radical politics, knew differently.

15
ADVENTURES BY LAND, SEA AND RAIL

Travel and exploration have been inextricably linked with European imperialism since the age of Christopher Columbus. The association reached its apex in the Victorian period, when those of means sponsored and organized private expeditions, often of limited commercial potential or scientific merit, to advance their own celebrity or notoriety. When these journeys took place within the Russian Empire, they depended on imperial infrastructure like railways, security and political structures, and a worldview that laid the globe at the feet of the powerful.

Born at Lissadell, Sligo, in 1843, Henry Gore-Booth was an explorer and adventurer cast in the classic Victorian mould. He expended vast sums of personal wealth and spent long periods away from his home, estate and family pursuing his favourite hobby – making hunting and fishing expeditions to northern seas and coasts. He and Arthur MacMurrough Kavanagh (discussed in Chapter 9) were friends and in the 1860s made three voyages to Norway together. During a visit to Lissadell, Kavanagh talked about navigation with Gore-Booth's manservant, Thomas Kilgallon, 'draw[ing] circles in describing the globe' by holding a pencil in his mouth.[1]

Adventures by Land, Sea and Rail

Gore-Booth was, however, best known for his expeditions to the Russian Arctic, undertaken towards the end of a period of frantic polar exploration bookended by the first British Arctic expeditions in 1818 and the Royal Naval Exhibition of 1891. Those Arctic expeditions included some of the most infamous misadventures in Western European history, from John Franklin's disastrous overland trek across Canada in 1819–22 that saw the death of 11 of a party of 20, the survivors existing on boiled leather and lichen, to the 1845 disappearance of the *Erebus* and *Terror* with 129 officers and crew under his leadership. Arctic exploration was of enormous significance in the Victorian period, and its influence on culture and politics in the period has been studied extensively.[2]

In 1879 Gore-Booth and the English Captain Albert Hastings Markham chartered the cutter *Isbjörn* – specially built for navigating ice – to explore the coast of Novaya Zemlya and sail to the Kara Sea via the Matochkin Strait, a narrow fjord dividing the north and south islands of Novaya Zemlya. Markham, who had been part of the British Arctic Expedition of 1875–6, wrote that while the primary purpose of the voyage was 'the pursuit of walruses, bears, and seals', he accepted Gore-Booth's invitation to join the expedition for the opportunity to conduct 'the more important work of the examination of the edge of the pack ice, at a late season of the year, in the northern part of what is now generally known as the Barents Sea.'[3] They reached a latitude of 78° – a few degrees shy of the 83° record set by the British Arctic Expedition of 1875–6 – and confirmed that Franz Josef Land could be reached by steamer in the months of August and September, while collecting natural history specimens and taking sea temperatures and soundings in the Kara and Barents Seas.[4] Markham published his account of the voyage in a paper read at the Royal Geographical Society (RGS) in November 1879, shortly after his return to England, and in a book he dedicated to Gore-Booth as funder of the expedition.[5] The preface to the book was written by his cousin Clements Markham, Secretary of the RGS, and it praised the extensive natural history collections made during the expedition, catalogued in thirty pages of appendices by eminent scientists like the botanist Sir Joseph Dalton Hooker.[6] Markham, a vocal supporter

Adventures by Land, Sea and Rail

of exploration and a person whose entire life was devoted to the service of the Royal Navy, outlined the expedition's importance in jingoistic terms:

> To my mind England, as a great maritime nation, should not be content with the unimportant role which she has of late years played in the grand work of geographical discovery, but, calling to remembrance the brave deeds performed by our forefathers, she should equip expeditions, not only for the exploration of that region culminating at the North Pole, but also for the complete discovery of the whole terrestrial globe![7]

His focus was threefold – commercial potential, scientific data and, above all, the glory of Britain. Indeed, he hoped that the *Isbjörn* expedition would contribute 'towards securing the resumption, by Englishmen, of the glorious work of north polar discovery on an adequate scale'.[8] Gore-Booth was more restrained in his assessment of the voyage, stating in response to Markham's paper at the RGS: 'as a sporting trip the voyage was a failure, but if it had assisted in any way towards furthering the objects of the Society, he was fully rewarded for the expense and trouble.'[9] Despite his assumed modesty, Gore-Booth was elected Fellow of the RGS in 1879 for the information the voyage furnished on the state of the sea ice between Novaya Zemlya and Spitzbergen.[10]

While those aboard the *Isbjörn* were experienced sailors, the voyage – like most polar expeditions – had its hardships. Markham was dissatisfied with the Norwegian sailors for storing drinking water in spirit barrels, giving it 'a groggy flavour'; later, replenishing the stock in the Matochkin Strait, they used salt barrels, causing all on board to experience 'an intolerable thirst' for weeks.[11]

In 1881 Gore-Booth embarked on a second voyage to the Russian Arctic, this time to join two other private vessels in searching for the missing *Eira*, which was owned by his friend, Leigh Smith. Gore-Booth purchased the *Kara* especially for this expedition. The search was widely publicized, with reports in high-circulation magazines like *The Illustrated London News*.[12] The search party found Smith and his crew in the Matochkin Strait in 1882, having survived the preceding winter in makeshift tents made from materials salvaged from their wrecked vessel.[13]

Gore-Booth brought his Catholic butler, Thomas Kilgallon, on every one of his voyages because, in the latter's own words, he 'knew all things in connection with his [Gore-Booth's] boating, fishing and shooting'.[14] Kilgallon accepted the role because he 'liked seeing the world'.[15] He spent his entire working life with the Gore-Booth family, having first entered their employ at the age of eleven.[16] He married Isabella Drury in 1878 and was frequently obliged to leave her and their children – Augusta (b. 1884), Isabella (b. 1882), Mary and Michael (b. 1879) – to go on expedition.[17] Kilgallon was evidently more than a butler and made himself extremely useful on expedition. He spoke a little Norwegian – possibly picked up during the three voyages along the Norwegian coast in the 1860s – and was therefore able to report to Gore-Booth and Markham the reluctance of the nine Norwegian crewmen to overwinter in the Russian Arctic aboard the *Isbjörn*. Indeed, Markham noted that 'In addition to the natural difficulties, we also had to overcome the objections of our crew to pushing onwards, and I think the latter was by far the hardest, and certainly the most disagreeable work of the two.'[18] In honour of his service, Markham and Gore-Booth named Kilgallon Shoal 'after our faithful and hard-working attendant'.[19]

While these expeditions are an interesting Irish chapter in the long history of Arctic exploration, they reveal little about human relationships and intercultural contact, save the unimportance of indigenous people in the eyes of people like Markham. Accounts of the expeditions portray the Arctic as uninhabited, touched only by long-gone whalers, hunters and glorified Western European explorers. One of the few human interactions the party recorded was on the *Isbjörn's* first approach to Novaya Zemlya on 10 June 1879, when they encountered a small boat carrying two Nenets (Samoyed) men, one woman and two children, and 'four wretched-looking dogs'. Markham described the people in terms commonly found in the literature of nineteenth-century exploration:

> The Samoyeds were clad in reindeer-skin coats with hoods, and sealskin trousers and boots. They were of short stature, bearing a strong resemblance to the Eskimos [...]. They appeared merry and good-tempered, and boarded us in a very unceremonious manner [...].

Adventures by Land, Sea and Rail

> They spoke a little Russian, so through the medium of our mate, who
> understood that language, we ascertained that they had passed the winter
> in a hut [...] the *Isbjörn* was the first vessel they had seen this year.[20]

Agreeable weather in the Kara Sea allowed the *Isbjörn* party to take long walks into the interior and along the coast, but the indigenous people do not figure as part of Gore-Booth and Markham's Arctic.[21]

Markham described Gore-Booth as 'a keen and successful sportsman [...] a practical geographer and an ardent admirer of nature'.[22] This may have been a generous assessment by a naval officer indebted to his wealthy patron. The landowner was the quintessential Victorian adventurer, keeping a bear he shot in the Arctic in 1881 on display in the dining room of Lissadell House. His six expeditions – three along the Norwegian coast, two to the Russian Arctic and one whaling expedition to Greenland – were vanity projects, freewheeling exercises in Victorian masculinity. They yielded little of scientific value and betrayed a vision of the Arctic as a space devoid of human life, erasing indigenous people from the record in an approach reflective of the Russian imperial state's disregard for their lives and unique cultures.

Dublin publisher Joseph Maunsell Hone and mountaineer Page Lawrence Dickinson took a different but no less reductive view of the ethnic minorities absorbed by Russian imperial expansion when they visited Persia and Georgia in 1909. Hone was active in the Irish literary revival, but disillusionment with the Free State's popular democracy led him to revise his nationalist views later in life.[23] Like other Irish visitors to the Russian Empire in the late nineteenth and early twentieth centuries, Hone's negative perceptions were grounded not in anti-imperialism, but in an Orientalist worldview. The Anglican pair's jointly authored travelogue juxtaposes the themes of industrialization and romantic nationalism, lauding the rapid economic growth of the cities of Baku and Batumi and creating a hierarchy of Transcaucasian ethnicities, privileging the plight of the Circassians and Georgians over others. This was no coincidence, as their struggles against the Russian imperial state had long been publicized and championed in Western Europe.

Adventures by Land, Sea and Rail

Their itinerary – Warsaw, Baku, across the Caspian Sea to Resht, Teheran, Tbilisi and Constantinople – was by then not a terribly unusual one, thanks in no small part to the spread of railways that allowed travellers to get from Berlin or Warsaw to Baku in a matter of days. The preface to their account of the tour admitted that routes through Persia were well-worn, and referred to their own voyage as 'of a modest kind indeed'.[24] Bizarrely, though, they also claimed that Warsaw was 'one of the few European capitals that the tourist has not yet wooed'.[25] The book's main selling point was their observations on the recent Persian Revolution of January 1909, but the latter part of the book emphasized the 'violent and [...] unscrupulous' hand of the Russian Empire in the Caucasus, where they found strong anti-Russian feeling.[26] Hone and Dickinson, like other writers of the age, conceptualized the Caucasus as the crossroads of three empires: the Russian, Persian and Ottoman. They described the region as 'one of the great highways of the world where all the proud races of ancient times passed, driving before them in turn innumerable vanquished tribes, who eventually found refuge in the mountain gorges'.[27]

Hone and Dickinson situated their experiences and impressions of Georgia in terms of local anti-imperialism and anti-Russian sentiment in the context of bans on the teaching of the Georgian language in schools (in effect from 1872).[28] From 1881 and the reign of Alexander III, the Russian Empire extended its grip over the country and responded viciously to nationalist movements there and elsewhere.[29] Hone and Dickinson's description of Russia's conquest of the Caucasus as 'violent and probably unscrupulous' was no understatement, but the generalization did little to enlighten Irish readers on the catalogue of imperial violence and oppression meted out against the peoples of the Caucasus over the centuries.[30] They noted the reverberations of the 1905 revolution in Baku, where 'the forces of anarchy and of authority still struggle on fairly even terms', the authorities betraying their nervousness in hyper-vigilance, arresting the travellers 'as spies' because they photographed a group of mounted Cossacks.[31]

Hone and Dickinson's understanding of Russian imperialism in the region hinged on fascination with the Circassians, a people whose long

Adventures by Land, Sea and Rail

history of suffering and oppression at the hands of the Russian imperial state was well publicized in Western Europe. They reported that they only found a satisfactory answer to their constant question 'Who are the Circassians?' by 'consult[ing] authorities' on their return to Ireland. They sought out the people portrayed in Western European literature and reportage from the mid-eighteenth century onwards – a symbolic population that existed only in the mind of Western Europeans. This is not to say that Circassians did not, or do not, exist. As Thomas McClean has shown, the Circassians were a potent symbol of imperial oppression in the nineteenth century, and 'Circassian' became a by-word for all of the peoples of the Caucasus.[32] Hone and Dickinson sought the embodiment of the Orientalist fantasy of Circassia. They admitted, 'Probably the Georgians whom we questioned were aware that the word "Circassian" conveys to the European romantic associations concerning beautiful girls in distress, and were, therefore, unwilling to let me know that they and the Circassians are different peoples.' Reinforcing their Orientalist perspective, captivated by a performance of Georgian dance, they suggested: 'The Georgians ought to send a troupe of their dancers to the capitals of Europe. The repertoire would be sure to delight [...]. It would be a way of attracting the attention of the West towards the circumstances of their nation, which is what the Georgians desire to do.' The Romance of the Circassian plight was emphasized by the charge of barbarity applied to the other peoples of the Caucasus, particularly those to the east, which Hone and Dickinson described as living in 'barren uplands [...] than which there can be no unfriendlier country in the world'.[33]

The pair proceeded on to Baku, which they considered historically important for its location 'on a high road from Europe to Asia'; they briefly set out its history in imperial terms, caught between Ottoman, Persian and Russian occupations. The travellers encountered the industrial port city at the height of its oil boom. An early hub for the oil industry, Baku was home to the world's first paraffin factory (1823), oil well (1846), oil refinery (1859) and kerosene factory (1863). During the boom – from the 1870s until 1914 – Baku's oil fields produced half of the world's oil, creating the first oil magnates. The city's economy and population exploded as labourers, entrepreneurs, businessmen and speculators flocked there in search of fortune. The boom created inequalities and generated particular kinds of crime; Hone and Dickinson detailed the kidnappings and muggings of 'prosperous citizens' and wealthy industrialists that they claimed took place in the city streets even in daylight, warning, 'A stranger must avoid being seen entering the banks.' Rich and poor lived cheek-by-jowl, and 'shoddy buildings in the European manner jostle shoulders with Oriental booths and tea-houses.' Hone and Dickinson portrayed the city as a Wild West of capitalism – in their words, 'a Mecca of adventurers' where 'violent primitive peoples' lived alongside 'every nationality west of Suez', producing 'social conditions as bizarre as it is possible to imagine'. They portrayed a city of opportunists, 'a city of gamblers', where 'passions are as crude and violent, nerves are as highly strung, as they were in any of the digging towns of California at the era of the great gold rush'. The oil wells formed a 'closely-huddled collection of wooden conical chimneys, which are continuously belching forth thick clouds of black smoke'. Similarly, they lauded the rapid industrialization and economic boom experienced in the Georgian port of Batumi as a boon of Russian rule: 'Batoum is a town which has prospered exceedingly since it was annexed to Russia. It had previously maintained for centuries the level of a dirty Turkish village. Now it has become the most important Russian port on the eastern side of the Black Sea.' Modern luxury hotels lined the boulevard along the harbour, but the city's sudden prosperity brought with it similar problems to Baku, labelled 'violence and nastiness'. The thread of modernization and Europeanization runs through the book, with the 'new European dignity' of Tbilisi and the loss of its 'Asiatic character' celebrated as the result of the dominance of Russian imperialism over Persia and Turkey.[34] For Hone and Dickinson, the Russian Empire was the most favourable of the three: non-Muslim and, in ways, European.

Their book received poor reviews. The *Geographical Journal* justifiably remarked that the authors 'cover no little-known ground in the empire' and the *Bulletin of the American Geographical Society* found the book 'somewhat

Adventures by Land, Sea and Rail

unsatisfactory [...] [it] adds little of interest that is not generally known and has not been more fully described elsewhere in a more authoritative and appealing way.'[35] The journey and the book appear opportunistic; indeed, Hone's knowledge of the publishing industry together with the enduring popularity of travel books may have misled the pair to believe that their observations would satisfy readers. Their presentation of life in the Caucasus hinged on long-held Orientalist stereotypes. Their criticisms of Russian imperialism were grounded in a belief that the Russian Empire was the more favourable of the three powers that struggled for centuries for supremacy in the region – a belief founded upon anti-Islamic prejudice.

Elizabeth Hawkins-Whitshead, known as Lizzie le Blond (Fig. 7), continued in the same vein as Gore-Booth and Markham when she wrote of her 1913 visit to Russia with barely a trace of human interaction. Born in Co. Wicklow in 1861, she became a travel writer and mountaineer, embarking on her first Alpine ascents at the age of twenty as a recovering consumptive and new mother. She pioneered winter climbing, guideless climbing and snow photography, and was the first president of the Ladies' Alpine Club. She published several books and many newspaper articles on mountaineering, some of which were reprinted in Irish papers, especially when they related to dramatic events like climbing accidents.[36] The *Irish Independent* noted her death in 1934 with a brief, four-line notice that referred to her as 'a pioneer of mountaineering for women', while the *Belfast News Letter* published a longer obituary that noted her achievements as 'a climber, writer, traveller, lecturer to troops during the Great War' – but dedicated over half of the piece to biographies of her father and three husbands.[37] However, one of the most important people in her life was her mountaineering guide, Joseph Imboden. The pair worked together on slopes all over Europe over a twenty-year period, and le Blond never failed to acknowledge the debt that she and other mountaineers owed to their guides. She dedicated *Adventures on the Roof of the World* (1904) to Imboden, and the book included a full chapter on guides and their work, highlighting acts of heroism and bravery.

Upper-middle-class women entered the socially elite sport of climbing in the second half of the nineteenth century. In general, they were educated,

Adventures by Land, Sea and Rail

confident and cultured, and advanced quickly in the sport; by 1875 almost every Alpine summit had been scaled by a woman as the middle classes flocked to the Alps by rail. Le Blond deplored mountaineering's increasing popularity, voicing concerns and criticisms akin to those heard today in relation to Mount Everest:

> There is no great mountain in the Alps so easy to ascend as Mont Blanc. There is not one on which there has been such a deplorable loss of life. The very facility with which Mont Blanc can be climbed has tempted hundreds of persons totally unused to and unfitted for mountaineering to go up it, while the tariff for the guides – £4 each – has called into existence a crowd of incapable and inexperienced men who are naturally unable, when the need for it arrives, to face conditions that masters of craft would have avoided by timely retreat. [38]

Le Blond stood out in this crowded arena as the first woman to climb guideless and, therefore, without men in the party – guides were always male – and as the first woman to make Norwegian ascents. The Alpine Club – founded in 1857 – was exclusively male until 1974, so in 1907 le Blond and like-minded others founded the Ladies' Alpine Club. Despite women's achievements in the sport, ascents described as 'suitable for ladies' were dismissed as easier, less challenging and less interesting.[39]

Le Blond was not the first woman mountaineer, but she was the only one of her generation to publish biographical accounts of her climbing activities. She published anthologies of amazing ascents by European mountaineers in the Alps, Caucasus and Dolomites since the mid-eighteenth century, including some of her own experiences. For example, *True Tales of Mountain Adventure* (1903) and *Adventures on the Roof of the World* (1904) included her own escapades, such as getting caught in an avalanche on the Hohberghorn in the Pennine Alps, ascending the Rothhorn twice in one day during difficult, snowy conditions, and climbing the Piz Scerscen (Bernina Range) twice in four days.[40] Le Blond was the most important woman writing about mountaineering in the late nineteenth and early twentieth centuries, but she never published under her own name – only as Mrs Fred Burnaby, Mrs Main or Mrs Aubrey le Blond, her three married

Adventures by Land, Sea and Rail

names.[41] Her *Adventures on the Roof of the World* was reviewed in the *Irish Examiner* as 'plainly and simply written, but nevertheless possessing great powers', but was somewhat damned with faint praise as a book that 'may be often relied on to fill the void of the half hour when there is nothing to do, or nothing to read'. Her books were, nonetheless, deservedly popular, relating the relatively short history of mountaineering for non-climbers in an accessible way, including explanations of technical, geographical and geological terminology. Her books were also attractively illustrated with photographs, many of which she had taken herself.

Le Blond had two connections to Russia. The first is a peripheral one, through her first husband, English-born Colonel Fred Burnaby. Burnaby was a British Army intelligence officer who made expeditions to Russia and Asia Minor. He was also an adventurer and an avid balloonist. He visited Russia in December 1870, travelling through St Petersburg, Moscow, Kyiv and Odesa (and onwards to Constantinople and Spain). In February 1875 he set out on a year-long expedition to the Khanate of Khiva, which he claimed was inspired by news that the Russian authorities had forbidden any foreign visitors to travel through the region. In 1876 he published his popular, rollicking adventure tale *A Ride to Khiva*, which attracted particular attention for his feats of derring-do. He made both of his well-publicized visits to Russia before his marriage in 1879, but seven of the first eight chapters of le Blond's autobiography, *Day In, Day Out* (1928), deal with his adventures, travels and ascents in Russia, Turkey and Egypt.

Lizzie had her own Russian experience in 1913 while travelling overland from Korea via the Trans-Siberian Railway with her third husband, Aubrey le Blond. The Trans-Siberian was, arguably, one of the greatest feats of engineering and public works of the nineteenth century. Begun in 1891, by the time of its completion in 1916 it was the world's longest railroad, stretching over 6000 miles across 11 time zones and linking the eastern- and westernmost parts of the world's largest contiguous empire. It meant that the journey from Moscow to Vladivostok – one that previously took eleven months by road or six months by sea – could be completed in a couple of weeks. Thousands of labourers, exiles and convicts worked in the swamps and tundra constructing a line that would carry luxury cars for first-class passengers, featuring en-suite compartments, a library, electric lighting and a grand piano.

Lizzie's visit to Russia is recorded in two brief chapters of her memoir, *Day In, Day Out* (1928). It is not clear whether her recollections, published fifteen years later, are based on contemporary letters or diaries, but they do lack detail on the long rail journey and any kind of personal connection or interaction with Russian people. Aubrey left Moscow for home on the day the couple arrived in the city, while Lizzie remained behind for a fortnight's sightseeing. She hired a Russian-speaking Italian man to guide her around the Kremlin and its museum, as well as the city's main churches and museums; recalling the visit fifteen years later, she wondered whether the treasures that she saw during her visit survived the 1917 revolution.

She left Moscow after three days, travelling to St Petersburg by overnight train. She found that German was widely spoken in Peter the Great's planned city, helping her manage for the most part without the services of a guide. Her visit started out conventionally, taking in the Hermitage and Winter Palace, where she saw the Royal Apartments, including Alexander II's former quarters, 'the actual blotter on which he signed the Act emancipating the serfs', and the sofa to which he was carried after his assassination. She established a personal connection in the palace, too, by noting the display of two portraits of Johanna Elisabeth of Holstein-Gottorp, Princess of Zerbst – mother of Catherine the Great and cousin of one of Lizzie's own ancestors.

While le Blond's visit to Russia's two largest cities was pedestrian at best, she did have a minor brush with the law, of the sort impossible to corroborate and enough to give a little colour to her time there. She was arrested for taking a photograph of Peterhof Palace, which was forbidden; she was taken to a nearby police station but claimed that because her passport was with the hotel, as per regulations, she could not be charged. The police only asked her to promise not to take any more photographs and did not confiscate her plates or equipment. Doubtless, her position as a wealthy, white, Western European woman shielded her from experiencing

Adventures by Land, Sea and Rail

the full vigour of tsarist law enforcement. Despite the relative lightness of touch that she experienced, the closing words of the Russian chapters of her memoir emphasized the all-encompassing strength, reach and presence of the Russian state in the same terms as those employed by so many other foreign visitors. Travelling from St Petersburg to Berlin in a private train compartment, she reflected:

> I confess to having felt a certain relief when my passport, which had been examined and stamped, and stamped again, and taken from me and returned, was returned for the very last time at the Russian frontier. Slowly the train crossed the bridge, and we were in Germany. [42]

There was no good reason for her to have felt any threat whatever while in Russia. These retrospective impressions, published fifteen years after the fact, were informed by her fear of the Soviet state.

Le Blond wrote in 1903, 'There is no manlier sport in the world than mountaineering.' She saw her intrusion into this male-dominated sport not as an attempt to emulate men or male characteristics – rather, it was a harnessing of the positive characteristics she saw in extreme sports. She found that the scale of the challenges posed by climbing

> cultivates [a person's] presence of mind, it teaches him to be unselfish and thoughtful for others who may be with him. It takes him amongst the grandest scenery in the world, it shows him the forces of nature let loose in the blinding snowstorm, or the roaring avalanche. It lifts him above all the petty friction of daily life, and takes him to where the atmosphere is always pure, and the outlook calm and wide. [43]

The majority of women of her generation were consigned and confined to the 'petty friction of everyday life' by social norms, legal restrictions and family pressures. Le Blond found that bracing activity made her physically and mentally stronger and even helped her to overcome the early stages of tuberculosis. Having married at just eighteen and become a mother shortly afterwards, she quickly shed the skin of the debutante. She concealed her climbing wear underneath long skirts to avoid scandalizing the hordes of upper-class hillwalkers and climbers who swarmed to the Alps by rail. But in

Adventures by Land, Sea and Rail

True Tales of Mountain Adventure (1903), she was careful to mention that her male climbing companions dressed in waistcoats and wristwatches that had to be removed for more challenging ascents and weather conditions; vanity led male climbers to impractical dress choices.[44] She reflected:

> I am often asked why people climb, and it is a hard question to answer satisfactorily. There is something which makes one long to mountaineer more and more [...] it is always a struggle between the mountain and the climber, and though perseverance, skill, experience, and pluck must give the victory to the climber in the end, yet the fight may be a long one. [45]

She valued mountaineering for the way in which it built character, but curiously she does not seem to have embraced other forms of travel in the same way. Her trip to Moscow and St Petersburg falls at the more prosaic end of Irish accounts of Russia, and sits well within a tradition of Irish writing about Russia that failed to challenge imperial expansion or the subjugation of ethnic and religious minorities, and relied on well-worn familiar tropes to communicate the shallowness of their human interactions in the Russian Empire.

141

V

PRELUDE TO REVOLUTION

I think in Russia one seems so much nearer to history than at home, and I look upon Ivan the Terrible as a great deal more living than George IV, and half expected to meet Peter the Great himself at Moscow.

Hariot Blackwood, *My Russian and Turkish Journals* (1917), p. 90

In 1911 the jurist and author Ilya Grigoryevich Ystridde-Orshanski published *An Exile's Daughter*, a romantic thriller centring on the exploits of one Nellie Dubrovska. She and her English mother leave Russia when her Russian father is imprisoned there. Nine years later Nellie leaves England to return to Russia as a governess, where she has a number of love affairs and attempts to assassinate a governor-general before being killed, together with her lover, by Cossack guards. A review in the *Freeman's Journal* – Ireland's largest newspaper by circulation at the time – praised the book for its 'vivid sketches of Russian life' and its exposure of the 'cruelty and tyranny of the Russian government'.[1] The novel reflected the transnational currents through which Russian radical politics operated in the late nineteenth and early twentieth centuries, the complex personal circumstances that lay behind individual women's decisions to migrate, and the mobility of the governess as a frequently multi-lingual figure moving with relative ease through different cultures. Those themes are explored in this section through the lives and careers of three Irish women in Russia around the close of the nineteenth century. This was a turbulent period that opened with the nihilist and anarchist terror campaigns that took on the might of the Russian Empire – spanning one-sixth of the earth's surface, built on the enslavement and conscription of millions – and the reverberations of 1905, namely, Russia's humiliating defeat to Japan and the ensuing revolution of the same year. The revolution resulted in the institution of the *duma* (parliament) and constitutional reform, with Nicholas II desperate to uphold the monarchy in the face of increasing opposition and challenge to autocracy by the expanding middle class and industrial workers. It is in this period that the events of 1917 had their roots.[2]

The period was distinctive in the longer timeline of Hiberno-Russian contacts. It comes as a punctuation point between the international conflict of Crimea and the drama of October 1917, after which a rich web of connections was nurtured by radical politics and international interest in Soviet Russia. The transnational anarchist campaign was, in many ways, comparable with Irish Fenian activity in the US and the UK from the 1860s. Self-styled Professor Mezzeroff, an American chemicals expert of Scots-Russian descent, ran a bomb-making school for Fenians in Brooklyn. He gave a series of public lectures in 1883 in which he claimed that with a thousand volunteer bomb-making tutors, he could arm the entire population of the island and win Irish independence. He also lauded Ireland's suitability for dynamite warfare, as he thought the then still-extensive peat bogs would provide the perfect medium for transporting delicate and unstable nitro-glycerine.[3]

In the last decades of the nineteenth century contacts between Ireland and Russia came to be defined by international political movements. Irish and Russian radicals found each other within easier reach, thanks to rapidly improving communications technologies and the formalization of transnational political movements. Indeed, the association of Russia with radical politics was so strong across the English-speaking world that a flurry of Russian-themed literary works with the word 'nihilist' in the title were published. For example, Oscar Wilde's *Vera; or, the Nihilists* (1883) interrogated Irish politics through a Russian theme, inspired by the case

Prelude to Revolution

of Vera Zasulich, who attempted to assassinate Fedor Fedorovich Trepov, governor-general of Moscow, in 1878.[4] Practical advances like improved steamship travel and railways attracted increasing numbers of visitors to Russia, and reports on events in the country were circulated globally via burgeoning media empires like Hearst, who employed Irish nationalist Michael Davitt to report on the Kishinev pogrom of 6 April 1903, in which 51 Jews were killed and 424 injured. His published articles created an international stir, prompting demonstrations in European and American cities and a petition to the tsar signed by 12,000 US citizens calling for justice for Jews in Russia. He travelled to St Petersburg in 1904 to report on the effects of the Russo-Japanese War, counting an aged Tolstoy among his interviewees, and returned again in 1905 to report on Bloody Sunday (the shooting dead of 130 unarmed demonstrators), interviewing people close to the revolutionary movement.[5] Other Irish journalists in Russia in the period included the polyglot Emile Dillon (1854–1933), who wrote for several publications under the penname E.B. Lanin and in 1887–1914 was Russian correspondent for the *Daily Telegraph*. He described his journalism as an attempt to reach readers

> who refuse to come down from their own lofty ethical plane to analyze the enormous forces which for centuries have been crushing out every moral sentiment and aspiration, every nascent germ of manhood that manifested itself in the Russian people, and to compare them with the marvellous resistance offered and with the upshot of the unequal struggle.[6]

Arthur Moore (1880–1962) reported from St Petersburg for *The Times* for several months in 1913–14. Irish American journalist Mary Boyle O'Reilly (1873–1939) – daughter of Fenian John Boyle O'Reilly and journalist Mary Murphy – reported from Russia in 1913 as foreign correspondent for the Newspaper Enterprise Association before going undercover in war-torn Belgium, France and Poland. She exposed the systemic anti-Semitism at work in the western Russian Empire by reporting on the infamous 1913 trial in which Jewish man Menahem Mendel Beilis was wrongly accused of the ritual murder of a thirteen-year-old boy in Kyiv – a trial that she described as 'Jew baiting, disguised as a legal program', and the tsar as 'the

Sketches of Russian people drawn by Martha Wilmot, 1803–8,
Royal Irish Academy MS 12 L 20 (i, ii, iii, iv)

Portrait of Yekaterina Vorontsova-Dashkova by Dmitry Grigoryevich Levitsky, 1784.
Oil on canvas, Hillwood Estate, Museum & Gardens, Washington

John Ladeveze Adlercron's Russian passport, 1807. National Library of Ireland

Nikolskaya Tower, Moscow, by Sir John Fiennes Twisleton Crampton, c. 1858–1860.
National Library of Ireland

'Prisoners for Siberia, Moscow' by Bayard Taylor, 1862/3. Library of Congress

Ethel Lilian Boole Voynich, 1955. Planeta Press

Hariot Georgina (née Rowan-Hamilton), Marchioness of Dufferin and Ava
by H. Walter Barnett, 1900–1910. National Portait Gallery

Depiction of the assassination of Tsar Alexander II in January 1881 published in the *Illustrated London News*, 2 April 1881. Mary Evans Picture Library

Margaretta Eagar with the eldest four Romanov children (l–r): Tatiana, Anastasiia, Olga, and Maria

Constance Markievicz, Woman of Zywotowka, 1902. By kind permission of the Lissadell Collection

Constance Markievicz in Ukrainian dress, 1902. The Deputy Keeper of the Records, Public Record Office of Northern Ireland and Sir Josslyn Gore-Booth, PRONI D 4131/K/4/1/32

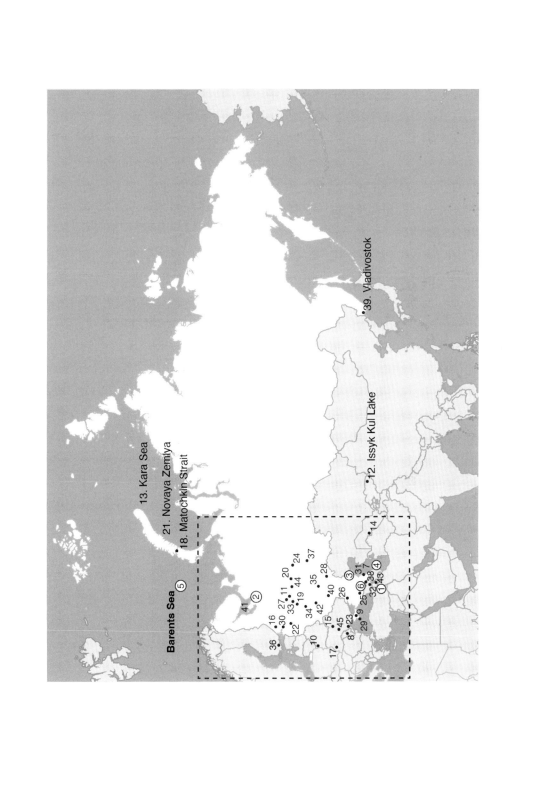

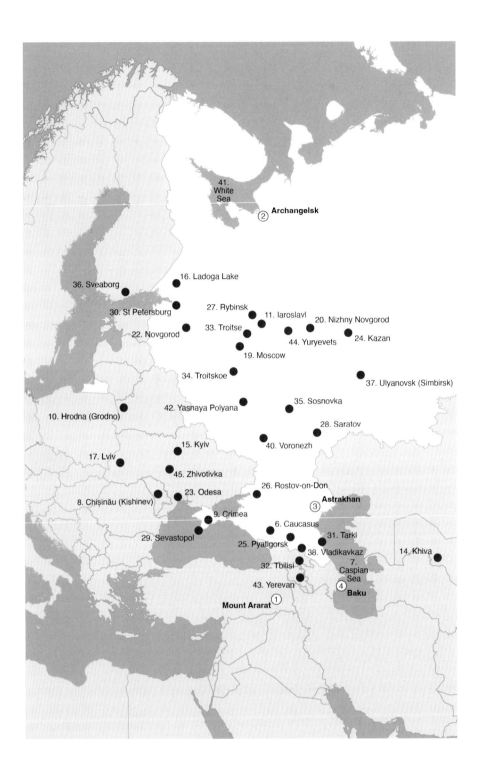

arch Jew-hater'.[7] Tyrone-born Francis McCullagh (1874–1956) reported from the battlefields of the Russo-Japanese War, returning to Siberia in 1918 with the British military mission but ultimately going undercover as a civilian to evade arrest.[8]

Irish experiences of Russia in this period are rich and varied. Lady Dufferin, spouse of one of the British Empire's most senior diplomats, was present in St Petersburg for the assassination of Alexander II in 1881. The Cork-born anarchist Ethel Lilian Boole Voynich travelled to Russia in 1887–9 before devoting herself to Russian anarchism, assisting the families of political prisoners, working as an editor and translator for radical émigré publications in London and smuggling prohibited texts from London to Ukraine. Margaretta Eagar was nanny to the four daughters of Nicholas II and Alexandra in 1899–1904, described in detail in her memoir, *Six Years at the Russian Court* (1906), and Constance Markievicz visited Ukraine under Russian rule, recording her impressions with her paintbrush.

Boole and Eagar represent a significant but understudied portion of the Irish diaspora – highly mobile and educated women who found work overseas as nannies and governesses. In many ways, these women's lives and careers encapsulate the limited options open to Irish women of their generation. While Russia was not a common choice of destination, Boole's and Eagar's decisions to never again live in Ireland reflect the choices of the majority of Irish women migrants of the period. The turbulent circumstances of Russian political life – as well as the transnational nature of radical politics – exerted real influences over these women's lives and mirror the transnational currents through which Russian radical politics operated. When taken together, these women's stories reflect the complex personal circumstances that lay behind individual decisions to migrate and the mobility inherent in occupations dominated by women – nannying, translating, teaching – as (frequently) multi-lingual figures able to navigate different cultures and circumstances.

These women's lives and careers have been neglected by historians, partly because they defy simplistic categorization and partly because of the contemporaneous tendency to view women who moved outside of

Prelude to Revolution

perceived norms as eccentric. Reviewing their lived experiences against wider socio-political contexts illuminates the rich networks of which they were part and the ways in which their lives and options were influenced and sometimes dictated by global events. Dufferin's, Eagar's and Voynich's lives overlapped in fascinating ways, not least as Voynich's Russian anarchist and nihilist counterparts struck at the heart of the system around which Dufferin's entire life was structured. I have often wondered whether Lord Dufferin would have described Voynich in the same icily misogynistic terms that he used to paint the portrait of a female nihilist he saw on trial in Russia, as 'a bosomless, sexless creature of the true Nihilistic type with a huge forehead, small intelligent eyes, and a hideous face'.[9]

16

A FRIGHT WITH THE BEAR:
LADY DUFFERIN AND THE
ASSASSINATION OF ALEXANDER II

In March 1880 Hariot Georgina Hamilton-Temple, Marchioness of Dufferin and Ava (Fig. 9), accompanied her husband on a bear hunt in the outskirts of St Petersburg. At the time he was Britain's representative in Russia, a career diplomat whose star was in the ascendant. Shortly after the bear-hunting expedition the high-profile couple received a telegraph from Queen Victoria, asking how Lady Dufferin was faring after her 'fright with the bear'. Lady Dufferin learned that several British newspapers had reprinted a fabricated story that originated in *Sankt-Peterburgskie Vedomosti* (*St Petersburg News*), alleging that her husband had slaughtered one of the animals at her very feet.[1] Lady Dufferin would, however, experience a 'fright with the bear' of a very different nature almost exactly a year later, when news of the assassination of Alexander II reached their St Petersburg residence.

In October 1862 the nineteen-year-old Co. Down woman was thrust into the international spotlight when she married Frederick Hamilton-Blackwood (later 1st Marquess of Dufferin and Ava). She quickly found herself fulfilling the many duties of the wife of a senior diplomat in Turkey and Russia, governor-general in Canada and viceroy in India. Privately, it was said to be a 'good-humoured and affectionate marriage' that produced six sons and three daughters – sadly, of the nine, Dufferin would outlive all but two.[2] Despite these devastating losses, Dufferin remained a strong, intrepid, shrewd and decisive woman. She published her entertaining journals and letters in three volumes: *Our Viceregal Life in India* (1889), *My Canadian Journal* (1891) and *My Russian and Turkish Journals* (1916). Her husband's biography was published three years after his death, drawing on personal papers provided by Dufferin herself.[3] The Dufferin embassy to St Petersburg was followed in 1895–8 by another Irishman, Sir Nicholas O'Conor of Roscommon, who had previously served in Berlin, Madrid, Rio de Janeiro, Paris, Seoul and Beijing.

Throughout her career, Dufferin exemplified the dynamism and pro-imperialism increasingly demanded of vice-regal wives in the late nineteenth century.[4] As a diplomatic spouse, Dufferin was keenly aware of global politics and international relations, formed meaningful relationships in all of the places where she and her husband were posted, and embraced her role and all that was expected of her. In Canada, she endured difficult cross-country sled journeys and rough accommodations that were far from what she was used to. After four years in India she was disappointed when her husband was recalled to London and described her leave-taking on the steps of their residence in 1888 with no small degree of sadness: 'We parted almost in tears [...]. Nor will I attempt to describe the complex feelings which fill our minds as we step down from this great position and look back upon all the cares, all the pleasures, all the interests, and all the friends we leave behind.'[5] Her regret on that occasion was matched by the expressions of gratitude extended to her for the initiatives she led during her time there.[6]

Dufferin left a particular legacy through her National Association for Supplying Female Medical Aid to the Women of India, better known as the Dufferin Fund. The purpose of the Fund was to relieve the suffering, by illness and childbearing, of Indian women – in Dufferin's own words,

A Fright with the Bear: Lady Dufferin and the Assassination of Alexander II

'to promote Female Medical Tuition, Medical Relief, and the establishment of Hospitals for Women all over the country'.[7] This would be achieved through the recruitment of women doctors, nurses and midwives who would provide care while respecting patients' religious beliefs and cultural preferences. Dufferin made use of existing and developing female professional and voluntary networks to advance her project; for example, in November 1885 she met with two English female medical missionaries in India and visited a female medical school at Agra.[8] By the time Dufferin left India in 1888 the scheme had been adopted in every province, and for decades afterwards hospitals bearing her name could be found scattered around the countries now known as Myanmar, India and Pakistan. Her work inspired Rudyard Kipling's 'The Song of the Women' (a piece that now reads as nauseatingly paternalistic at best). By 1907 the Fund had 12 provincial branches, 140 local and district associations and 260 hospital wards and dispensaries officered by women who delivered care to over 2 million women and children. It employed 48 female doctors with British qualifications, 90 assistant surgeons and 311 hospital assistants with Indian qualifications. The initiative left another important legacy by helping British and Irish women enter the medical profession. Zenana hospitals provided an important source of employment for these women, who had few other opportunities to practise medicine. For example, the first woman to both train and qualify at the Royal College of Surgeons in Ireland, Dr Mary Josephine Hannan, worked at the Dufferin Hospitals in Ulwar and Shikarpur in the 1890s.[9] The Fund doubtlessly saved lives and achieved its stated aim of alleviating the suffering of Indian women through childbirth and illness, but it was not immune from criticism. Campaigners highlighted the Fund's focus on zenana women – those who lived in seclusion for religious reasons – while non-zenana women continued to be deprived of care, particularly lower-caste and working-class Indian women who could not observe purdah due to the economic necessity of working outside the home.[10]

Dufferin's emerging public profile as a philanthropist was prefaced by periods in Canada and in Russia. There, she was effectively trained for her

A Fright with the Bear: Lady Dufferin and the Assassination of Alexander II

much more high-profile role as vicereine in India. She much more readily embraced life in India than in Russia, where political unrest appears to have inhibited her willingness to acquaint herself intimately with the language and culture. Maneesha Lal has suggested that the idea of the Dufferin Fund was thrust upon Dufferin as the brainchild of Queen Victoria[11] – this would help to explain the great differences in how Dufferin approached her role in both places. Indeed, her letters to her mother reveal her appreciation for the extent of the undertaking and her trepidation on the occasion of Fund's public launch: 'I don't in the least mind the work, but I sometimes shudder over the publicity and wish it were a quieter little affair.'[12] Dufferin's ability and willingness to set aside her own wishes for the benefit of her husband's career subtly conveys the ways in which the social was the political for diplomatic wives; Melanie Oppenheimer has shown how Dufferin passed onto her daughters her sense of responsibility and duty to Britain and the empire.[13] From the late nineteenth century through the post–World War II period a new understanding of selfhood emerged that prioritized fulfilment and self-actualization. Wives of professional men increasingly aspired to an 'authentic selfhood' defined by their own activities, rather than those of their husbands.[14] We are reminded, too, however, that overseas travel and residence offered many women the opportunity to be involved in international affairs under the guise of philanthropy or other acceptable activity.[15] It is also important to remember the political differences between the Dufferins' roles in India and Russia – the world of difference between viceregal paternalism and power in India, and the relative limitations of the embassy in St Petersburg. In any case, Dufferin's Russian letters convey an image of domestic comfort in the midst of political unrest likely calculated to soothe any concerns on behalf of the recipient, her mother.

As an embassy family, the Dufferins' needs were well catered for in St Petersburg. The household staff included a Swiss butler, an English-speaking Russian housemaid, a German-speaking Russian housemaid, a Russian *chasseur* (attendant), a Russian porter, a footman, a polyglot under-butler, a French cook, five *mujiks* (servants), a maid, a valet and two laundry-maids.[16] Lady Dufferin's letters relate her efforts to attend to the education of her children and the pleasurable familiarity in her husband's report that the royal village of Tsarsoke Selo had 'the air of green dullness, such as Irish demesnes so often wear'.[17] In contrast to these pictures of ease, familiarity and domestic routine, some of the most pervasive strains of Orientalism informed Dufferin's descriptions of Moscow. The city had long been contrasted with St Petersburg in a simplistic binary – St Petersburg as European, Moscow as Oriental. In May 1880, on her first visit to Moscow, she conveyed her awe in a letter to her mother:

> Though I have sent you my journal for so many years, I never sat down to write it before in a state of bewilderment as to what I should, and what I should not, tell you. I never had to describe anything which had previously been incorporated in a 'Murray' [guidebook] – and I never started on an expedition so saturated with the essences of historical, archaeological, and all the other 'logical' knowledge which that good man puts at one's finger-ends. In fact, hitherto I have only had to think of my personal adventures and of the country, not the things in it; so to-day, when I find myself expected to describe 'Moscow', I feel almost helpless. However, here goes.[18]

These words show that she was determined to experience Moscow as something entirely different to anything she had seen before; as an exotic, bewildering place. Her desire to experience the Oriental in Moscow was validated when her husband, 'who has travelled so much in the East', told her that 'he never saw a more beautiful Oriental city'.[19] Lord Dufferin himself described Moscow as possessing 'historical associations as well as an auto-ethnic vitality, instead of the European varnish which is the chief characteristic of St Petersburg'.[20] Lady Dufferin attempted to experience 'barbaric' Russia in the vicinity of St Petersburg, but with rather less success, by going on a bear-hunting expedition with her husband.[21]

Despite her Oriental dreams, the experiences that helped to define Dufferin's time in Russia were the anarchist terror campaign and the assassination of Alexander II. In 1878 Russia emerged victorious but bloodied from yet another war with the Ottoman Empire, and public opinion soured at the paltry gains made. The tsar's reformist agenda – emancipation of the serfs, modernization of infrastructure, the introduction of elected local government and easing of censorship – went too far for some, and not far enough for others. Throughout his reign the revolutionary movement grew in tandem with increasing industrialization, creating a massive proletariat receptive to radical messaging.[22]

Within weeks of her arrival in Russia on 14 April 1879, Dufferin heard a 'fearful' report of an attempt on the life of the tsar – the first of several – but he escaped unharmed. She related breathlessly how the 'news flew round the town' of how the attacker saluted the emperor before firing the first shot, which grazed a policeman's face; the emperor was bundled into a nearby caleche and driven home. The would-be assassin had reportedly taken poison after his arrest but was administered an effective antidote. In a show of solidarity with the Russian royal family, 'All the houses put out flags, and we had the Russian and English ones flying on ours.' Later that month Dufferin noted the extent of 'anti-revolutionary measures', with every householder hiring extra guards, every owner of firearms obliged to declare them, and many 'arrests, and measures taken to discover the Nihilists'. The matter formed 'our whole conversation here'. The threat continued through the winter of 1879–80, when a number of people were killed by a gas explosion at the Winter Palace on 17 February. It was intended to target the tsar and some guests, but a planned dinner party had been delayed and so the group avoided injury. The force of the explosion was sufficient to break some windows, but not loud enough, apparently, to wake the sleeping empress. Nevertheless, five carpenters were arrested, and one escaped. The following day Dufferin visited the site of the explosion, finding 'all are much agitated, and there is a feeling of horror everywhere' as another attack was expected two days later, on the tsar's silver jubilee. It was reported that some of the palace servants had been supplementing their income by renting their rooms to 'homeless vagabonds', among whom were suspected nihilists.[23]

On 13 March 1881, after a member of *Narodnaya Volya* (People's Will) flung a bomb under Alexander II's carriage, Dufferin described sitting by her window, watching for her husband's return and seeing soldiers 'going about in every direction, and sleighs bringing all the people who have just heard [the news] to the Palace' (Fig. 10). She recorded the assassination and funeral in great detail, as well as the 'horrid stories and melancholy forebodings [...] despairing talk'. She understood the threat in comparative terms, fretting that while St Petersburg and Paris had similar populations, the latter spent 11 million francs annually on policing but the former only 2 million.[24]

It is no coincidence that Dufferin published her *Russian and Turkish Journals* in spring 1917, between the February and October Revolutions. The letters on which the book was based had been written almost forty years previously, and profits from its sale were to go towards war charities. She had experienced the political unrest that was present in Russia from the 1880s but misinterpreted the Russian people's sacrifices for World War I and was possessed of a misguided optimism about the future of the country and its people. In the preface to the book, she stated: 'When we were in Russia a dark cloud of Anarchism hung over her chief cities, unrest and discontent were spoken of on all sides; while now the enthusiastic patriotism of her people, their self-sacrifice, their dogged perseverance, and their serious and reverent attitude towards life, fill us with admiration.'[25] Dogged indeed were the people of St Petersburg, living through food and labour shortages caused by the war – the same food shortages that would spark revolution in February 1917.[26] The city's palaces were converted to hospitals, as discovered by Limerick-born Florence Barrington (1894–1968), who volunteered from late 1916 with the Voluntary Ambulance Division in the city's Anglo-Russian Hospital.[27] The global perspective that had so enriched Dufferin's experiences overseas, and made her so open to learning about Indian life in particular, was to her detriment in this instance. Historian Dominic Lieven has pointed out that Russia lacked the sustained civilian mobilization required for the war effort because the state lacked the requisite level of legitimacy and support at the individual, family and village levels.[28] Roger Reese's social history of the Imperial Russian Army shows the dysfunction and brutalizing effects of a force made up of conscripted peasants, the majority of whom by 1917 had less than six months' service due to the attrition rate.[29] The war exacted a devastating human toll touching on every facet of Russian life. With her Anglican philanthropist's eye set on alleviating the suffering of those directly impacted by the war, Dufferin lost sight of the circumstances of life in St Petersburg and was unable to understand the war's effects on the city outside of the dominant British patriotic narrative of unity in adversity and of war as ennobling.[30] This narrative would itself be challenged in the immediate aftermath of the war, as British dominions and colonies – including Canada and India, where Dufferin's husband had represented the crown – would come to question the blood sacrifice.[31] In Russia, the social turbulence and widespread discontent that had been building for years reached fever pitch during World War I, and spilled over into revolution in 1917.

17

'Our Englishwoman': Ethel Lilian Boole Voynich's Underground Activism

Born in Co. Cork in 1864, Ethel Lilian Boole was the youngest of five daughters of the mathematicians Mary Everest and George Boole. Today, George Boole's algebra powers everything from cash machines and library catalogues to smartphones. He was Mary's mathematics tutor prior to their marriage, and they enjoyed a very happy relationship. Sadly, George died of a respiratory infection at the age of just forty-nine. Ethel was not yet a year old. Mary moved to London to support her five young daughters by working as a university librarian and mathematics tutor and by letting rooms to students. The continuous procession of students, bohemians and intellectuals who streamed through the family home must have left an impression on Ethel's young mind before her mother, requiring help in raising her daughters, sent Ethel to live with an abusive uncle in Lancashire. She spent two miserable years at the home of Charles Boole, who used her passion for music to torture her, forcing her to play piano for hours on end while he banged on the keys and pulled grimacing faces. He would falsely accuse her of stealing from his family and lock her in her room for hours, threatening various means of forcing a confession from her. Eventually, he told her mother that she was a bad influence on his own children and sent her back to London, where she had a breakdown shortly afterwards.[1] Ethel may have drawn on these dreadful episodes for her 1901 novel, *Jack Raymond*, in which a boy is tortured by a sadistic uncle. The poverty, abuse and instability of her early life exerted powerful negative emotional effects on the teenager.

Although she had left Ireland as a young child, it continued to have an important influence over her. In 1879 she passed a happy summer there with her great-uncle John Ryall, a classical scholar. It was then that she first read about the Italian revolutionary Giuseppe Mazzini.[2] From then, the fifteen-year-old preferred to be called Lily and would only wear black, in mourning for the state of the world.[3] The radical politics that would shortly become the centre of her life were under discussion in Ireland, too. In 1885 the *Dublin University Review* published an article by Trinity academic and self-described Presbyterian nationalist Frederick James Gregg that challenged Irish and British readers to reflect carefully on any knee-jerk response to Russian nihilism:

> Remember, when you shrink from this terrible thing, Russian Nihilism, that your boasted English liberty was not obtained by merely sitting still and waiting for it, but by the shedding of much blood [...] Think over the history of the gradual growth of your liberties, and you must of necessity sympathize with those who are setting out on a pilgrimage whose roughest part your fathers trod many long years ago.[4]

In 1882 Lily took up a three-year music scholarship at Berlin's Hochschule der Musik. The capital of the newly unified German states was rapidly expanding and modernizing, and was in the throes of a construction boom and population surge. Tenement housing and unsanitary conditions prevailed, with open sewage flowing down the streets.[5] Atheism and socialism flourished in the context of demographic change, commercialization and urban inward migration, particularly among the bourgeoisie and intellectuals.[6] It was against this backdrop that

Lily became a convinced atheist and political radical before returning to London in 1885.

In 1955 Lily's biographer, Soviet literary critic Evgeniya Taratuta, received from her a retrospective manuscript detailing her time in Russia seventy years previously. The opening line states: 'The assassination of Alexander II in March 1881, when I was not yet 17 years old, made a huge impression on me.'[7] Lily became curious to know the truth of reports of repressive conditions in Imperial Russia. She planned to visit Russia using remaining funds from her Berlin scholarship and by teaching music while there. The British anarchist, suffragist and founding Fabian socialist Charlotte Wilson initiated Lily into London's lively radical community, including the exiles Petr Kropotkin and Sergey Kravchinsky, commonly known as Stepnyak, whose book *Underground Russia* (1883) had been 'a revelation' to Lily.[8] From late 1886 Lily, together with her sister Lucy, took Russian lessons from Stepnyak in preparation for her Russian journey. Stepnyak was a central figure in the Ukrainian revolutionary movement who had fled to London after assassinating the head of the Russian secret police, General Nikolai Mezentsov, in 1878. Charlotte Wilson played such an important role in Lily's entry into radical politics that Lily modelled Gemma, the female protagonist of her bestselling novel *The Gadfly*, on her.[9]

Lily departed for Russia in April 1887, travelling via Warsaw. There, on Easter Sunday, she saw the citadel in the city's main square, home to political prisoners including her future husband, the Polish nationalist and *Narodnaya Volya* member Wilfrid Voynich. He would later make the romantic but unlikely claim that he had seen her striking figure – with a halo of golden hair, dressed entirely in black – from his cell window while he was awaiting transportation to Siberia.

The two years Lily spent in Russia left a deep impression and formed part of the basis of her later novel, *Olive Latham*. She lived for a short time in the two-storey neoclassical Venevitinovo Palace near Voronezh on the River Don, teaching English and piano to the children of the family. Tsar Alexander III was godfather to one of the children, and she later recalled, 'We could not stand each other.'[10] (Dublin-born Viscount

Garnet Wolseley [1833–1913] was presented to the tsar while visiting Moscow for his coronation in May 1883; his description of the emperor was more positive.[11]) After leaving her employment, Lily returned north by steamboat up the Volga to Nizhny Novgorod and its famous fair; it was during this journey that her lifelong interest in folksong was born. After staying two weeks in Moscow she moved to St Petersburg, where she worked as a teacher of English and music and helped the families of political prisoners. She lived with Stepnyak's sister-in-law, Praskovya Karaulova, a doctor whose husband Vasily was an imprisoned radical. The Karaulov home was noted by the police as the haunt of 'politically unreliable persons including the music teacher Ethel Boole'.[12] Lily carried a food parcel to the prison for Vasily every day but was never permitted to meet him. She spent the summer of 1888 in Pskov with Praskovya, who provided medical treatment to the impoverished. Immediately on Vasily's transportation to Siberia, Lily returned to London, smuggling secret manuscripts for delivery to Stepnyak: a public appeal for reform addressed to the tsar by Russian socialist and literary critic Maria Tsebrikova, which she requested Lily help have printed in London.[13] Lily was cautious about her activities and associations in Russia, aware of the risk of arrest and imprisonment. She participated in just one protest during her time there, a student demonstration at the funeral of the satirist Mikhail Saltykov-Shchedrin in May 1889, shortly before returning to London.

Research by Evgeniya Taratuta in the 1950s revealed that Lily was inducted into Stepnyak's extended family circle during her time in Russia. From London in June 1889 Stepnyak wrote a letter to his old friend Anna Mikhailovna Epstein, exiled in Vienna. The letter details the connections between Stepnyak's relatives and a particular 'Englishwoman':

> We await from day to day the arrival of Sasha [Fanin] whom a sweet little Englishwoman, who has become very friendly with the two Fanin sisters, is bringing to us, by all accounts. We taught her Russian here and directed her to Petersburg [...] She is a musician and gave us lessons [...] We hope to hear a lot of news, social and family, from our Englishwoman when she arrives.[14]

'Our Englishwoman': Ethel Lilian Boole Voynich's Underground Activism

Sasha Fanin was Stepnyak's wife's sister, and Lily was friendly with her. This letter shows the connections Lily already had with Russian radicals before travelling there, proves that she learned the language from Stepnyak and shows her role in helping political émigrés to maintain connections with home, as international travel was much riskier for them. Stepnyak was careful not to name Lily directly in case his letter was intercepted by the authorities and led the police to her door. Stepnyak's diary also contains references to visits from 'our Englishwoman' or 'Bulochka' – an affectionate derivative of the name Boole.[15] The network needed to protect Lily's position as someone who could traverse Europe without being intercepted or arousing suspicion.

Lily's return to London in summer 1889 closely coincided with the establishment of an organization called the Society of Friends of Russian Freedom (SFRF) in London in November 1889; an American sister organization was formed in 1891.[16] The Society quickly gained a high public profile in Ireland and Britain – its committee included sitting MPs and public figures like George Bernard Shaw and William Morris – and its newspaper, *Free Russia*, achieved an estimated circulation of 5000 readers monthly.[17] The *Belfast News Letter* editorialized in 1891 that 'The saddest reading I know of is contained in *Free Russia* [...] Those who do not know the inner working of Russian Government, the barbarities and cruelties, taxations, and the indignities that are heaped upon the subjects of the Czar, find it difficult to understand how his Majesty can allow the present despotism to last for a week.'[18] But within five years of its establishment the SFRF was under regular attack in the British and Russian press, accused of conspiring 'dynamite plots.'[19]

Lily became an active member of the Society, sitting on its executive committee and serving as sub-editor of *Free Russia* in 1892–3. The newspaper contains no articles credited to her pen, but her linguistic talent and her skill as a translator were crucial to the functioning of the Russian revolutionary organizations stretching from Britain to Ukraine. It was often the case that women were responsible for interpreting speeches and translating what historian Susan Hinely calls 'the mass of revolutionary literature that poured in and out of late Victorian London'.[20] While Lily seems to have preferred to stay out of the spotlight, the newspaper gives glimpses into the services she provided to the SFRF. On 1 March 1893 the Society held an 'Anglo-Russian Gathering' in Holborn, with musical performances and displays of Russian art and crafts; *Free Russia* reported that Lily performed a piano solo as part of the evening. She also investigated on behalf of the Society the Kražiai massacre of 22 November 1893, when a regiment of Don Cossacks attacked a group of Lithuanians protesting the closure of a Catholic church. Women like Lily facilitated the Society's fundraising events by selling books and stewarding; in February 1894 Lily, together with six other women, was thanked for her 'invaluable assistance' at a public lecture organized by the Society.[21]

Lily published English translations of three of Stepnyak's pamphlets, collected in a little volume titled *Nihilism As It Is*. As the English reforming politician Robert Spence Watson stated in its preface, the book was of value for providing 'a clearer view of one of the greatest struggles for progress and freedom which Europe has seen'.[22] In this respect, translators like Lily performed an important role as conduits for international anti-state discourse.[23] Stepnyak's main concern was to raise awareness in Western Europe about the conditions of life in the Russian Empire by publishing books, giving public lectures and making Russian and Ukrainian publications available in English.[24] He obviously valued Lily's work in this respect and wrote introductions for two of her anthologies, *Stories from Garshin* (1893) and *The Humour of Russia* (1895), praising her 'exceptional knowledge of the Russian language' that enabled her to translate humorous tales and idiomatic language. The latter collection included one of Stepnyak's own short stories and the first translation of Dostoyevsky's story 'The Crocodile' into any language.[25] Responding to international criticism of the state of the Russian creative arts, Stepnyak's introduction to *Stories from Garshin* argued that the problem since the 1840s was not confined to Russia but was evident across Europe and was symptomatic of reactionary, autocratic governments: 'When the flower of a generation is ruthlessly decimated, the best, the most ardent spirits, finding an early grave in the mines of Siberia, or in the gloomy subterranean cells of the fortresses, there is little scope for the development of national genius.'[26]

London was an important meeting-place for radicals, bohemians and intellectuals, and Stepnyak drew exiled revolutionaries into his orbit. His St John's Wood home was a hub for political émigrés and progressives in the creative arts. After returning from Russia Lily's circle widened to include such well-known socialists as Eleanor Marx, Friedrich Engels, George Bernard Shaw and William Morris.[27] It was through Stepnyak that Lily met her future husband, the Lithuanian-born exile Mikhail Wilfrid Voynich. He has been described as a colourful figure; he trained as an apothecary's assistant in Moscow before getting involved with the Polish Social Revolutionary Party, fundraising and disseminating illegal literature.[28] He was arrested in October 1885 and exiled to Siberia, but made a daring escape in summer 1890, slowly making his way to London.[29] In Siberia, Wilfrid is said to have met the Karaulovs, whom Lily knew in St Petersburg. Privy to Wilfrid's escape plan, they told him to contact Stepnyak and Lily when he reached London. After a gruelling journey by caravan through Mongolia and China, Wilfrid was found wandering around London by a Jewish student who understood Russian; the bedraggled traveller held a note bearing Stepnyak's and Lily's names.

Wilfrid joined Lily in working closely with Stepnyak on the Fund of the Free Russian Press, set up in 1892 with the purpose of printing and disseminating banned revolutionary literature in Russia; he ran its London bookstore and managed the organization.[30] Soon, Wilfrid and Lily moved in together, and she adopted his surname, styling herself 'E.L.V.'; they formally married in 1902 in the registry office in the parish of St Giles, London. *Free Russia* listed 'Mrs Wilfrid Voynich' as a member of its executive committee from late 1892.[31] In 1891 Voynich established the Russian Free Press Fund with a view to publishing titles banned by the Russian censor, and in 1893 he founded the magazine, *Letuchie Listki* (*Fly Sheets*); it was discontinued in 1899. This, and other presses run by exiled radicals, made significant contributions to the Russian revolutionary movement in the late nineteenth and early twentieth centuries.[32]

Lily's underground activities extended beyond translation and organizing. She used her relative privilege as a middle-class Western European woman to traverse the continent unsuspected, carrying sensitive documents and trafficking suppressed anarchist literature. In 1894 she made a dangerous mission to Lviv in Ukraine to make new revolutionary contacts and organize the smuggling of illegal publications into Russia. The infamous Valuev Circular of 1863 and Ems Ukaz of 1876 together completely outlawed publications in the Ukrainian language in an attempt to repress Ukrainian nationalist and separatist sentiment. It was around this time that Wilfrid broke with the Society of Friends of Russian Freedom to form his own organization, the League of Book Carriers. Lily's resignation and move to the general committee after just a year as a member of the SFRF executive committee was noted in *Free Russia* and 'a note of thanks was accorded for her valuable services as sub-editor'. She continued to participate in Society activities and sat on the general committee until January 1895.[33] She may have resigned in preparation for a move to Italy, where she researched her novel *The Gadfly*.

Despite their differences, Lily and Wilfrid must have been devastated when Stepnyak died in December 1895 after being hit by a train. They distanced themselves from their old networks. Wilfrid opened a rare book store – an ideal front for smuggling and disseminating illegal publications – and Lily became an active member of the Polish Relief Fund.[34] Wilfrid's love of medieval manuscripts purportedly led to his discovery in 1912 of the still-controversial cryptic document known as the 'Voynich manuscript'.

Lily was not the only Irish woman of her generation to undertake a secret mission to Russia. Maud Gonne delivered a batch of documents to St Petersburg in 1888 on behalf of a very different cause. In the summer of the previous year Gonne went to France to recuperate from tuberculosis, and while there she fell in love with journalist and right-wing political activist Lucien Millevoye, who was determined to return the province of Alsace-Lorraine to France – it had been claimed by Germany in 1871 after the Franco-Prussian War. A few months later Gonne came into a sizeable inheritance that gave her complete independence and travelled to Russia. She arrived in St Petersburg in January 1888 and befriended Princess Catherine Radziwill, who had recently returned from a residence in Berlin. Radziwill's memoir relates how Gonne had in her possession some papers that had come from Alsatian opponents to German rule, which she gave to Konstantin Pobedonostsev (the lay head of the Russian Orthodox Church), who in turn passed them on to Alexander III. The documents related to the struggle of small Balkan states for freedom from the Ottoman Empire; much was at stake because of the fragility of the complex alliances across the region. To avoid war, Bismarck was moved to declare the papers forgeries.[35]

In 1897 Lily published *The Gadfly*, a novel that gained particular currency among Russian socialists. The novel tells the story of English Catholic Arthur Burton who travels to Pisa in 1833 to train as a priest, grieving his recently deceased mother and with the grudging financial support of his Protestant stepbrother. Achieving a political coming-of-age against the backdrop of the Italian Risorgimento, Arthur is reacquainted with a childhood friend, the anti-clerical revolutionary Gemma Warren, who has been entrusted by Young Italy with smuggling prohibited literature via her family's mercantile connections in Bordeaux. As Arthur's involvement with Gemma and Young Italy deepens, Padre Montanelli, his religious mentor in Pisa (and, as Arthur later discovers, his biological father), attempts to steer him from his radical course. Arrested and held for a month in desperate conditions with daily interrogations, Arthur is released to find that a confessor in Pisa betrayed his confidence about the smuggling of books. Shunned by his Young Italy comrades and reeling from the revelation that Padre Montanelli is his father, Arthur renounces Catholicism, fakes his own death, flees to South America, assumes the identity of Felice Rivarez and authors a regular radical newspaper column as 'The Gadfly'. He returns to Italy in 1846 after a thirteen-year exile to find revolution in the air and Gemma the widow of a former rival. Gemma briefly entertains the notion that Rivarez is her childhood friend returned and agrees to accompany him on a mission to receive an arms shipment. Before the mission can be completed, the imperial might of the Austro-Hungarian police effects his capture.

The story reaches its climax as Rivarez files the bars of his prison cell window through the night, collapsing in the course of his attempted escape with an agonizing nervous attack resulting from old injuries. His recapture leaves Gemma and his other comrades bereft. Padre Montanelli, now a Cardinal, must sanction Rivarez's court-martial, and in a tortured final interview, the imprisoned Rivarez reveals his true identity to his biological father. After his death by firing squad, Gemma returns to her subversive activities and Padre Montanelli dies of a broken heart.

Lily began writing the novel in 1889 and carried out extensive research in Italian archives in 1895, producing a work so detailed that it remains the chief source of common images of the Italian Risorgimento.[36] In the main, though, the novel's richness derives from Lily's harnessing of her own life experiences. It can be understood as a melodramatic fictionalization of the international revolutionary culture of which she herself was part.[37] The context in which she wrote the book is also significant: at a time when she and Wilfrid experienced serious financial difficulty, to the point that they at times went hungry; a time when she worked herself to ill-health and exhaustion; a time when she travelled to Ukraine on a top-secret mission and to Italy to research her novel; and when she was still working actively on translations of Russian radical publications. Finally, it is worth noting that Stepnyak spent time in Italy in the late 1870s (prior to his arrival in London), where he was involved with the anarchist Benevento Insurrection of 1878. As Stepnyak was one of the great idols of Lily's life, it is likely that she was also inspired by his involvement in the successor to the Young Italy movement. Despite all of these indications, Lily denied any resemblance between the novel's plot or characters and her own life, telling *The New York Times* in 1898 that 'Arthur, the hero of *The Gadfly*, is an entirely imaginary person. Both the plot and the characters of the book are purely fictitious.'[38]

Lily's supposed affair with Ukrainian-born Sigmund Rosenblum, also known as Sidney Reilly or the 'Ace of Spies', has attained legendary status, but the facts remain uncertain. As alleged in Robin Bruce Lockhart's 1967 book *Reilly: Ace of Spies*, Lily and Reilly ran away to Italy together, where he abandoned her before she returned to Wilfrid in London; she wrote

The Gadfly based on Reilly's life story as he revealed it to her during their affair. But Reilly's biographer, Andrew Cook, argues that Reilly fabricated this story in 1918–19, when he had to explain how he had been recruited to British intelligence agencies, and that in fact he was inspired by *The Gadfly's* Arthur Burton – not the other way around. Pamela Blevins argues that Lily had begun writing *The Gadfly* in 1889 and that the novel was almost finished by the time she met Reilly.[39]

The Gadfly was an international literary phenomenon that quickly gained importance among the radical left and the labour movement. Millions of copies have sold worldwide. It was translated into Russian within a year of its publication and by the mid-twentieth century was available in thirty languages. The first stage adaptation was made by Lily's friend and SFRF associate George Bernard Shaw in 1898, and three Soviet screen adaptations were made: a silent film by Georgian director Kote Marjanishvili in 1928; a second film in 1955 with a score by Dmitry Shostakovich; and a three-part TV miniseries released in 1980. In his memoir, socialist Peadar O'Donnell recalled the book's popularity among political prisoners during the Irish revolutionary period (not least for the memorable horror of the execution scene).[40] After Lily's death, the Soviet state organ *Pravda* published a memorial referring to the *The Gadfly* as 'one of the favourite books of everyone who fights for human happiness, against the reactionary forces of violence and oppression.'[41]

Lily published other novels, but none had the same impact as *The Gadfly*. *Jack Raymond* (1901; Russian transl. 1902) and *Olive Latham* were both anti-clerical; the latter was also partly based on her experiences with the Karaulovs in St Petersburg, telling the story of the English fiancée of a dying revolutionary left to rot in a Russian prison (1904; Russian transl. 1906). She must have drawn on her visit to Russia of twenty years previously in painting the experiences of a serious, studious young English woman in Russian radical circles, enriched with sensitive descriptions of Russian land- and townscapes, and the anxiety of the protagonist's repeated failed attempts to visit her loved one in prison. After Olive's fiancé's death in prison, she returns to England and assists Karol, an exiled radical, in editing a censored Polish newsletter – an undertaking that the character's father refers to as 'the world's real work'.[42] *An Interrupted Friendship* (1910) was a sequel to *The Gadfly* and was published in Russian translation in 1926 under the title *The Gadfly in Exile* (*Ovod v Izgnanii*). Twenty years would pass before Lily made the series a trilogy.

During World War I Wilfrid left London for New York, where he continued dealing in rare books, but Lily remained in Britain, volunteering with the Quakers and only joining Wilfrid across the Atlantic in 1921. While the pair had completed their disassociation from radicalism, Wilfrid nonetheless attracted the attention of the American Bureau of Information (later the FBI) following rumours that he was in possession of a US military cipher – fuelled, no doubt, by his trading in rare books and manuscripts. Lily and Wilfrid are recorded in ship manifests as having visited the UK and Europe several times in the 1920s and 1930s, possibly in connection with his book dealing business.

From the 1920s Lily devoted herself to music: teaching, publishing a translation of *Chopin's Letters* (1931) and composing cantatas. Her translation of Chopin's letters shows that she never lost her earlier interest in folksong as she attempted in the preface to trace the folk origins of many of Chopin's works and the influence of Adam Mickiewicz's ballads on his compositions. The book also contains echoes of her earlier political activism in her remark that 'It is a little surprising to find a Polish patriot not merely keeping but proudly treasuring a diamond ring given him by the Tzar.'[43]

During World War II Lily wrote and published her final novel, the completion of *The Gadfly* trilogy, entitled *Put Off Thy Shoes* (1945). It was a thematic return to *The Gadfly* and accounted for its heroine Gemma Warren's forebears' lives in Cornwall. She may have been prompted to recall her early passions by the political context of 1940s America. The war brought an alliance between the US and the USSR, providing a brief reprieve for American communists, who before and after the war found the US a cold house. The American Communist Party's support for the war effort helped to swell their ranks, with women making up 50 per cent of the membership by 1943.[44] During this time Lily could not have been oblivious to the work of Elizabeth Gurley Flynn, the New York-born daughter of Irish immigrants who pursued intersectional feminist goals on an American national stage as part of the Communist Party's National Committee.

Remarkably – almost unbelievably – Lily claimed to have been completely unaware of the cult status *The Gadfly* had attained in the USSR until 1955, when a Soviet delegation arrived at the New York apartment that she had shared with her companion, Anne Nill, since Wilfrid's death in 1930. The delegation, led by the USSR's representative to the United Nations, informed her of *The Gadfly's* undying popularity in communist countries. Afterwards, she received from the Soviet authorities a $15,000 payment in lieu of royalties, which the USSR did not usually pay to writers – surely an astonishing development for the author, sixty years after the book was first published. As late as 1979 a collection of twelve commemorative black-and-white photographic postcards celebrating Lily's life was published in Moscow, with a short biography by Taratuta (Fig. 8).

Lily's return to musical composition in her later life sums up the transnational basis of her revolutionary politics. One of those compositions, *An Epitaph in the Form of a Ballad*, was dedicated to the memory of Irish nationalist and anti-imperialist Roger Casement. Lily later stated that she wrote the first draft of the cantata immediately upon hearing of the execution of the leaders of the 1916 Easter Rising. She also offered financial support to Casement's sister, Agnes Newman, via George Gavan Duffy.[45] Having made *The Gadfly* a trilogy, and perhaps inspired by the brief wartime alliance between the US and USSR, Lily completed the cantata in 1948. The composition united Irish and African independence movements, as well as historical radical movements in Italy, Poland and Russia, and was informed by her background in revolutionary politics. It can be no coincidence that the piece was completed on the centenary of the 1848 revolutions across Europe, events that inspired her first and most enduringly important work.

18

AN OCCUPATION WITHOUT BORDERS: MARGARETTA EAGAR, NANNY TO OTMA

Margaretta Eagar (Fig. 11) is remembered as nanny to the four daughters of Nicholas II and Alexandra in 1899–1904, collectively remembered as OTMA, the single autograph that Olga, Tatiana, Maria and Anastasiya chose for themselves. Here, Eagar's life and career are interpreted as encapsulating late nineteenth- and early twentieth-century patterns of Irish women's migration. While Russia was not a common destination, her decision to migrate and the fact that she never returned to Ireland – moving on to London after Russia – were choices made by thousands of Irish women of her generation. Eagar was typical of the majority of Irish woman migrants of the period. In the years 1891–1905 between 52.6 per cent and 54.7 per cent of all emigrants from Irish ports were female.[1] Like most of these women, Eagar was unmarried; in 1887–1900, only 16 per cent of all Irish who relocated to the US were married.[2] Together with the high average marriage age, the rate of emigration indicates the poor prospects and the low social status that women had in Ireland; the country had one of the highest average ages of first marriage in Europe, increasing from 26 for women and 30 for men in 1861, to a peak of 29.1 for women and 34.9 for men in 1925–6.[3] While Eagar's life and career are often presented simply as a curious tale, her story reveals hidden dimensions and complexities in the phenomenon of Irish women's emigration, which – uniquely in global terms – was on par with Irish men's emigration in the period.

Eagar's background was fairly unremarkable – she was born in Limerick in 1863, the fifth of the eleven children of a Church of Ireland prison governor and his musically talented wife. She was well-educated and could speak French. Having trained as a nurse in Belfast, she worked as a matron in a girls' orphanage. In 1897–8 a friend of one of her sisters, Emily Loch, visited Russia as lady-in-waiting to the daughter of Princess Christian of Schleswig-Holstein; the latter was a cousin of Empress Alexandra, with whom Loch developed a friendship during the empress's many visits to the Hesse family in Germany.[4] Learning that the empress needed a nanny to attend to her growing family, Loch presented her with a letter recommending Eagar for the role. Her glowing report of Eagar's domestic skills and childcare experience secured the offer, and Eagar undertook additional childcare training in London before travelling to St Petersburg in late 1898.[5] The valuable connection provided by Loch exemplifies the traditions of women's domestic work, whereby personal recommendations were invaluable for both employer and employee. Loch evidently had the trust of Eagar and the empress. While many British and Irish women became live-in governesses out of financial necessity, it appears that Eagar embraced this offer as an opportunity – both to live overseas and to build her reputation by working in the imperial household.[6] Her 'important post' was known and celebrated in her own time, publicized in Irish regional newspapers alongside that of Agnes Ffolliott, governess to Carol II of Romania.[7] Anglo-Indian traveller and educator Anna Leonowens (1834–1914) also achieved celebrity and not a little infamy on publishing her memoirs *The English Governess at the Siamese Court* (2 vols, 1870) and *Romance of the Harem* (1873), which later inspired Margaret Langdon's fictionalized account, *Anna and the King of Siam* (1945), and Rodgers and Hammerstein's musical, *The King and I* (1951).

Eagar's memoir, *Six Years at the Russian Court* (1906), details the opulence of life in Russia's highest society. While the imperial family home was at Tsarskoe Selo, Eagar was familiar with St Petersburg's Winter Palace, its 1500 rooms decorated with cabinets filled with jewels, Fabergé eggs and artwork by Rembrandt and Rubens, and the ballroom with capacity for 5000 guests. She also witnessed the tremendous feasts given throughout the year to mark events like the annual opening of the St Petersburg season in early January, when provincial nobles flocked to the city to pass the winter in high company. On one such occasion the imperial hosts served over 1000 chickens, 350 large lobsters and several thousand gallons of soup in addition to cold meats, jellies, sweets, fruit and wine – sharp contrasts with Eagar's descriptions of the harsh realities of peasant life and a child mortality rate of 35 per cent.[8]

Nannying and governessing were at heart transnational occupations, with thousands of Irish, British, French and German women filling the plentiful and occasionally prestigious roles available internationally.[9] Historian Olga Solodyankina argues that foreign governesses (and, I would add, nurses or nannies) embodied important channels of 'cross-cultural communication' in Russia, where they were among the first foreigners hired specifically to inculcate Western European mores into the children of Russian noble families, including the imperial family and non-Russian families living in Russia.[10] Indeed, the widespread negative stereotyping of foreign governesses functioned transnationally, as nineteenth-century nationalism's emphasis on distinct national characteristics created fertile ground for the reception and perpetuation of stereotypes, leading Russian families to prefer British ('English') nannies for their reputation for bringing order to the lives of small children.[11] Georgiana Bloomfield, wife of Irish-born ambassador to Russia John Bloomfield (see Chapter 10), noted in 1845 that English nurses were greatly preferred in Russia and were 'generally bribed to enter their service'.[12] However, the social status of the foreign nanny declined as she became a more common figure in Russia. For their part, most foreign nannies and governesses were attracted to Russia for the relatively good rates of pay.[13]

An Occupation without Borders: Margaretta Eagar, Nanny to OTMA

There are no statistics on the number of Irish governesses or nannies in Russia – officials did not usually make distinctions between English, Welsh, Scottish and Irish – but there are some indications that Eagar was not alone in choosing this path. Paul I's youngest son, Mikhail (b. 1798) had a nurse named Sarah Kennedy who may have been Irish. British nannies and governesses became a more common feature of Russian aristocratic families during the reigns of Alexander I and Nicholas I, and Irish women must have been among their number.[14] Historian Harvey Pitcher noted that between the Napoleonic Wars and the Russian Revolution, 'the English governess gradually became established as a familiar institution in upper-class Russian society', reaching a peak in the 1860s with 'the great foreign expansion of the English governess'.[15] Anthony Cross found that by the 1840s 'the British governess in Russia was a relatively familiar figure', and Ulrike Lentz goes so far as to say that foreign governesses were 'ubiquitous' on Russian noble estates.[16] In 1855 the *Kerry Evening Post* published a warning that it was 'intimated from high quarters' that 'English governesses' should quit Russia because the negative economic effects of the Crimean War would induce many Russian families to send their daughters to work, creating a competitive employment market.[17] In 1877 the *Ballinrobe Chronicle* published an extract of a letter purportedly from a young English woman teaching German, English and music to a Russian family of three children. With positive remarks about her situation and the respect afforded governesses in Russian families, the letter appears intended to encourage others to follow in her footsteps, but cautioned that 'Russia is no longer the "gold mine" for governesses that it was twenty years ago.'[18] The popularity of governessing, nannying and companioning abroad as a career choice for Irish women is reflected in a warning published in the *Kerry Evening Post* in 1899, cautioning young women against accepting 'a situation in Russia [...] without having previously received satisfactory information regarding it [...] from Mr Richard Wylie, one of the oldest and most esteemed of the English residents in St Petersburg'.[19] In 1910 another Irish writer noted that 'quite a number of Irish governesses will be found' in Warsaw and Tbilisi, but that these 'daughters of small farmers and shopkeepers in the West of

Ireland, arrive in answer to advertisements, and, being usually unsuited to the positions to which they aspire, their passage home has to be defrayed by the Consular authorities'.[20] One scholar estimates that there were around 1500 Western European governesses in the vicinity of St Petersburg, but the demand for foreign governesses dwindled in the last decades of the nineteenth century, as growing Russian nationalism generated a preference for native governesses.[21]

Margaret Lynch-Brennan's research shows that domestic service was an important source of paid employment for Irish women in the US, and that from 1840–1930 Irish-born women dominated domestic service in American east coast cities.[22] Eagar was different to the 'Irish Bridget', as these domestic servants were commonly known, in that she was Protestant, middle-class and in her thirties when she travelled to Russia, and as a nanny she did not perform housework. Nevertheless, her experiences form an enlightening supplement to the growing scholarship on the experiences of nineteenth- and twentieth-century Irish women in domestic service roles worldwide. It is important to remember that Eagar's life in the Russian imperial palace at Tsarskoe Selo was a very insular one. With appearances to maintain, and respectability being of the utmost importance, she was not free to socialize or to mix with whomever she pleased.[23] Her life with the Romanovs must often have been lonely, even if Nicholas and Alexandra redecorated their home, Alexander Palace at Tsarsoke Selo, in an English country style that would have felt familiar to Eagar.[24]

When Eagar arrived at the imperial household, there were two little girls to take care of: Olga (b. 1895) and Tatiana (b. 1897). Three more children were born during her time with the family – Maria in 1899, Anastasiya in 1901 and Alexei in 1904, two months before Eagar's departure. She was in charge of the girls' health and wellbeing, but also taught them basic literacy until masters of languages and music took over. Eagar spoke English and French with the princesses; French was still necessary in Russian high society and was spoken widely at court. While Eagar's memoir details many interactions with Nicholas and Alexandra, and she wrote about them with a great deal of respect, it is unlikely that she got to know them

An Occupation without Borders: Margaretta Eagar, Nanny to OTMA

on a personal level. She and Empress Alexandra probably communicated in English, which the empress spoke fluently; both she and the German-born empress spoke Russian only poorly. Eagar regarded the children very highly, writing of them with warmth and affection; she described the girls as pretty but also as possessing great depth of character.

Eagar provided the four Russian royal princesses with stability amid the constant movement of imperial family life: the seasonal removal of the court between St Petersburg and Moscow, regular trips to the Crimea and Poland and family holidays to Copenhagen and Germany. These journeys gave Eagar opportunities to become a little better acquainted with the southern and western reaches of the Russian Empire and with the rural poor. She found similarities between them and their Irish counterparts, particularly with respect to folk traditions and beliefs.

While her memoir sheds little light on the circumstances of life in Russia, the influence of external events, particularly the Russo-Japanese War, made themselves felt in terms of the options open to her and the choices she made. Furthermore, her memoir and the articles she published in popular magazines helped shape ideas about Russia in Britain and Ireland, even if they were not the first intimate glimpses that Irish readers were offered of life in the imperial family. In 1887 Scottish-born Ermengarde Greville-Nugent (née Ogilvy), living in Co. Westmeath with her Irish husband, published her translation of a first-hand account of the death of 21-year-old tsarevich Alexander from cerebro-spinal meningitis in Nice in 1865, offering it to Irish readers as 'so touching a narrative, and one which throws so much light on the inner life of that sorrow-stricken family'.[25] Eagar published articles about her life in the imperial household in the Christian weekly *The Quiver*, the British periodical *The Girl's Own Paper and Woman's Magazine*, and in the New Zealand daily *Star*, and her memoir was serialized in seven issues of the popular magazine *Leisure Hour* before publication in book form, illustrated with photographs of the Russian imperial family.[26] *Leisure Hour* foregrounded the intimate look inside palace life by advertising the first installation of the series on the magazine's front cover, illustrated by a portrait of the infant Alexei Nikolaevich, heir to the throne, cradled by his father, Nicholas II.

An Occupation without Borders: Margaretta Eagar, Nanny to OTMA

Russia's anarchists had passed the peak of their terror campaign by the time Eagar arrived in Russia, but the Irishwoman was aware of the dangers they continued to pose, particularly to the children of the tsar. However, the war with Japan – a matter of negative public opinion in Russia itself – cast a darker shadow. In the preface to her memoir, Eagar states that she was motivated to publish the book by the magnitude of the untruths relating to Russia and the Romanovs published in the British press, to which she sought to provide a corrective. This negative press was partly the result of the breakdown in Anglo-Russian relations that arose from Britain's alliance with Japan during the war. These political circumstances may have precipitated Eagar's sudden departure from the royal household in September 1904. It is not known whether her constant and enthusiastic rebuttals of anti-Japanese rhetoric caused upset in the palace, or whether it was unseemly, from a public perspective, to have a British citizen at the heart of Russian imperial family life at such a delicate time. In any case, the shadow cast by international events over Eagar's departure from Russia recalls Martha Wilmot's hasty departure in winter 1808 under a cloud of suspicion as a potential enemy of the state (Chapter 6). A moment of international unity brought warmth to this chilly atmosphere when Queen Victoria died in 1901 after sixty-three years on the throne. The outpouring of grief across the British Empire found an echo in St Petersburg, with Eagar describing people in mourning dress crowding into the churches. The grief in the royal palace must have been palpable, as the tsar's little daughters were Victoria's great-granddaughters.

Eagar's position as a self-appointed defender of the tsar motivated her to include a chapter in her memoir titled 'The True Story of Kishineff', addressing a recent pogrom in Chișinău, then part of the southern reaches of the Russian Empire. The pogrom, in which 51 were murdered and 424 injured, took place on 6 April 1903. Irish nationalist and journalist Michael Davitt travelled to the city to report on the violence for Hearst's London bureau, the first of three visits he made to Russia. The pogrom prompted international outrage, with demonstrations in European and American cities and a petition to the tsar signed by 12,000 people. Arrests numbered

800, of whom 100 were charged with murder or another serious crime.[27] It is difficult to see how the horrific events could be justified in any way, and Eagar's brief account described some of the atrocities, but she insisted that 'neither the Emperor nor the Russian government was to blame in the matter' because the city's governor had been bribed to ignore the violence and prevent any official intervention.[28]

Eagar's abrupt departure from Russia was a matter of public attention. She felt pressured to respond to the sensational claims made against her in British newspapers, speculating that she had been caught stealing papers from the tsar's study. She was now under suspicion by both the Russian state and the British press. The publicity must have been unbearable. She published a brief letter in *The Times*, refuting all allegations and stating that she had left her post on good terms, in receipt of a cash sum and a full pension. Her memoir simply stated, 'Shortly after the birth of the Czarovich [tsarevich] I left Russia owing to private and personal reasons. I was very sorry and grieved to say good-bye to the dear children whom I love so well.'[29] She left their employ before Rasputin entered the palace as healer to the haemophiliac heir, Alexei. Indeed, there is a possibility that she may have been dismissed as part of the family's determination to keep the child's haemophilia secret.

Eagar is proudly remembered in her native Limerick, and her story has appeared periodically in Irish national newspapers, presented as a surprising anecdote.[30] However, I see her legacy as twofold, and of some importance. Firstly, she is an excellent case study in the role of nannying as a career option for Irish women migrants in the late nineteenth and early twentieth centuries. Worldwide, thousands of other Irish women of her generation made a respectable living as nannies, but their stories remain largely untold. Women like Eagar – and, in the mid-twentieth century, women like Kathy McKeon, who at nineteen became nanny to former US first lady Jackie Kennedy's children – may well have worked for exceptional families, but their relationships with the children they cared for transcended social class, and their positions at the intimate core of the families they worked for made them unofficial ambassadors for Ireland.[31]

An Occupation without Borders: Margaretta Eagar, Nanny to OTMA

The families for whom they worked formed their impressions of Ireland from their relationships with their Irish nannies.

Secondly, Eagar's memoir and the articles she published in popular women's and girls' magazines were instrumental in shaping the enduring memories of princesses Olga, Tatiana, Maria and Anastasiya as small children, when in fact they were aged between seventeen and twenty-two years of age when they were executed following the Russian revolution. Eagar's intimate memoir, beaded with charming personal details, wove an almost relatable portrait of a young family that appears to presage their tragic fate. For example, she related an anecdote about a prophecy relating to the end of the Romanov family – a curse arising from the accidental deaths in 1904 of three mariners aboard a ship bearing the name of the deceased Alexander III. Brought to life with photographic portraits, the memoir's appeal lies in the celebrity of its supporting cast; its significance lies in the ways in which it enhanced the later tragedy of their deaths by emphasizing their youth. Secluded at Tsarskoe Selo from the outbreak of World War I in 1914, the two elder girls, Olga and Tatiana, never made their official debuts – they never were known publicly as young women. In the words of historian Robert Massie, 'The passage of time and the shortness of their lives have blurred the qualities of the four daughters of the last tsar.'[32] Olga, Tatiana, Maria and Anastasiya are entombed in Eagar's words, twelve years prematurely.

19
IRISH NATIONALISTS AND RUSSIAN IMPERIALISM

Constance Markievicz (*née* Gore-Booth) and Shane Leslie were well-known Irish nationalists from two of Ireland's wealthiest landowning families. While they espoused different forms of nationalism, both were prominent in the Gaelic Revival. Yet they both enjoyed hospitality on Russian estates that benefited from the oppression of Russian and Ukrainian rural labourers and servants. Their interactions with the economic and social structures that underpinned the Russian Empire show the importance of class as a means of identification that superseded national borders, and indicate the fear the 1917 revolutions sparked among the landed elite across Europe as one of the most radical challenges to the social order in the continent's history.

Constance Gore-Booth (1868–1927) met Polish aristocrat Casimir Dunin Markievicz (1874–1932) in Paris in 1899. Both were keen artists and moved in bohemian circles. She had previously studied at London's famous Slade School of Art, and he was a teacher of painting. They married in 1900 and moved to Dublin, where they became immersed in the city's lively bohemian and theatre circles, and Constance quickly rose to prominence.[1]

Irish Nationalists and Russian Imperialism

In 1902 the couple travelled to Eastern Europe to visit his family at Zhyvotivka (or, in Polish, Zywotowka), leaving their baby daughter, Maeve, with her grandmother at Lissadell. The Markievicz family held extensive lands in the western reaches of the Russian Empire, in present-day Ukraine. At the time the region was known as 'Little Russia' and was mostly under Russian control, with the westernmost region part of the Austro-Hungarian Empire. Caught between two imperial powers and denied political autonomy, the Ukrainian people were subject to tsarist oppression from the late eighteenth century. Any resistance was swiftly quashed, such as the trial and exile of the leaders of the Kyiv-based nationalist Brotherhood of Saints Cyril and Methodius in 1847. The Valuev Circular of 1863 and Ems Ukaz of 1876 banned education and publishing in the Ukrainian language; nationalists and separatists were forced underground by state surveillance and repression.[2] The region became increasingly impoverished as the nineteenth century wore on, while landowners made great profits from the grain produced by the rich, black earth.

With at least seven published, substantive, book-length accounts dedicated to her life, Constance Markievicz is probably the best-known woman in Irish history.[3] Despite this, her visit to the Markievicz family estate in Ukraine in 1902 is one of the least understood chapters of her life. No authenticated written record of the visit survives, possibly due to the couple's frequent relocations (Paris – Dublin – Paris – Ukraine – Dublin in the space of a few short years) and the long periods Constance spent on the run later. In 1934 the writer Sean O'Faolain published Constance's biography, in which he quoted unattributed remarks about Ukraine she was said to have made in a letter to a friend:

> I am delighted with the country – I am almost sorry we are going to live in Ireland. Yet there are tiresome things about it as well. The peasants are miserable. Yesterday we went for a long drive and passed a man lying drunk in the ditch by the roadside. I wanted to get out and help him. But the horses galloped past and Casimir said he would be all right. So there was nothing to be done.[4]

O'Faolain stated that Constance 'lost her heart' to Ukraine, partly because she 'found so much there to remind her of Ireland, the same easy-going way of life, the same haphazard method of getting things done'. Yet the Russian imperial yoke was so inexorable that she reportedly told a friend that, by comparison, 'she could not really see that Ireland suffered from any political grievances'.[5]

The patterns of life on the Zhyvotivka estate were familiar to Constance, who was from one of Ireland's wealthiest families and had a privileged upbringing at Lissadell. She responded to the rural landscape and people of Ukraine with her paintbrush in an impressionistic style that reflects her immersion in the Parisian arts scene. The hazy, dreamlike quality of her portrayals of rural Ukraine reflects a romantic, idealized vision. In one piece (Fig. 12), a woman walks alone on a mud road lined by fields, carrying a sack over one shoulder – the weight of the burden indicated by her slightly bent posture and her use of both arms – with the town and its white-painted church receding behind her. The subject's shawl, full-length skirts and loosely tied hair would not have been out of place in Constance's native Sligo. Another work portrays a woman at rest from her labour in the fields, her cheeks flushed from exertion. A kettle and cloth bundle sit by her lap draped in a long white apron. A third painting is a landscape depicting golden cornfields on gently rolling hills, a stray thistle interrupting the foreground.

More intriguingly, photographs taken at Zhyvotivka show Constance posing as a peasant woman (Fig. 13). Gail Baylis has shown how later, Constance carefully managed and curated her image for posterity by commissioning photographic portraits that emphasized her nationalist credentials and military ability.[6] The Zhyvotivka photographs must be considered an early expression of Constance's wider concern with crafting her public image, but they also speak to her life as an artist and bohemian who had spent long periods in Paris and London. The portraits betray a romanticization of rural life, with Constance role-playing the peasant woman going barefoot about her daily labour – but with a snow-white lace-trimmed apron and floral crown upon her head, accessories that were certainly were worn by local women only on special occasions. In her youth she got to know her father's tenants well; their relative poverty may have taken on a romantic hue through the smog and overcrowding of Paris and London. In light of Constance's later nationalist activism, the Zhyvotivka photographs demonstrate her nascent appreciation of distinct national and cultural identities.

Constance and Casimir's marriage ended in 1911, but Casimir's relationship with the Russian imperial state remained important in the formation of Constance's political thought. Lauren Arrington suggests in her joint biography of the couple that conversations with Constance about Irish independence prompted Casimir to consider the position of Poland and Ukraine in relation to Russia.[7] At the outbreak of World War I Casimir was working in Warsaw's Polish Theatre; under the threat of German invasion, the theatre went on tour to Kyiv, and Casimir went home to Zhyvotivka, where he passed his days peacefully, hunting and painting, until Nicholas II promised Poland freedom in return for allegiance to Russia. Casimir decided to join the Imperial Russian Army, a decision Arrington finds 'typical of his social class'; his politics never extended to anti-imperialism, despite his sympathy for the Dublin working class and for women's suffrage. He fought in the Carpathian campaign in winter 1914–15, sustaining an injury that left him partially deaf. He was decorated with the St George Cross for bravery and returned to Zhyvotivka in spring 1915. Shortly afterwards, reports circulated in the Russian press of Constance's exploits in the 1916 Rising. The Russian newspaper *Russkoye Slovo* covered the Rising and noted that Constance 'lived in Russia for a long time, at her husband's homestead [...] where according to the local Polish, she enjoyed universal esteem'. Casimir gave an interview to the paper in which he emphasized his proximity to the executed leaders of the Rising and referred to himself as 'a Russian subject interested in art only', separating himself from Polish nationalism.[8]

The complex history and politics of the Russian Empire remained on Constance's radar. In 1918 she wrote a series of letters to her sister Eva from Holloway Prison, where she was incarcerated for her alleged involvement in a 'German plot' to instigate insurrection in Ireland. Constance opened one of her letters with an enquiry about the whereabouts and wellbeing of Casimir's son Stanislas ('Staskou'). In October 1915 Stanislas had been sent from Dublin to Petrograd for training because his father wanted him to complete his military service. With fluent English, Stanislas was made war correspondent and interpreter with the Russian Volunteer Fleet in Arkhangelsk.[9] In summer 1918 Constance asked Eva to find out 'through any and all Russian agents' what had become of him because 'Russia must be an awful place to be in.'[10]

Her opinion of Russia as an 'awful place' was informed by the events of 1917. Constance's and Casimir's perspectives on the Russian Empire and the 1917 revolutions reflected their differing political views on Irish and Polish nationalism and class struggle as outlined by their biographer Lauren Arrington. As part of Europe's landowning elite, Casimir understood the effects radical social and political change in the Russian Empire would have on his own social standing and financial security. In 1916 he published a pamphlet, *Irlandiya*, that simultaneously argued for Irish and for Polish sovereignty. It included the line, 'May the sun of Russian freedom, illuminating the whole world, warm even this distant island, the victim of the historical errors of the cultured English people.'[11] Just months later, in June 1917, the Ukrainian nationalist Central Rada declared Ukraine an autonomous land within a federated Russia, a move received by Petrograd's provisional government as a betrayal of the revolution. This was followed that autumn by the Rada's call for the seizure of land from the nobility and the church, placing Casimir on the wrong side of Ukrainian politics.[12] In September 1919 Constance admitted to her sister Eva that she had been wondering 'on whose side Casi is' in the Russian Civil War and Bolshevik invasion of Ukraine, and later speculated, 'he might just as easily be a Bolshevik as anything else. Fine ideas always attracted him, and he would be quite capable of being enthused into thoroughly enjoying wearing a big beard and waving a red flag. He was always torn in two between his artistic appreciation of the rich and princely people and just as strong appreciation of the wrongs of people and the beauty of self-sacrifice.'[13] She avoided corresponding with him directly, knowing that in 'the old Russia' even corresponding with 'a rebel like me' would have 'got them all on a black list'.[14]

In 1918–19, from her Holloway prison cell, Constance followed events in Russia and read founding Bolshevik party member Maxim Litvinov's book, *The Bolshevik Revolution* (1919). Expressing solidarity with the Red Army, she wrote to her sister Eva during the White Army offensive on Ukraine in 1919: 'I rejoice in the bad weather when I think of Denikin sticking in the mud of the Ukraine. [...] maybe Lenin will win through after all. God speed him – and poor Russia.'[15] She both anticipated and feared an international domino effect of revolutions, at once delighted by the triumph of workers' strikes in Britain and concerned about the impact of unrest on the wider population, particularly in terms of food supplies. Responding to reports of the successes of Communist Party government in Russia from 1920 from the socialist and republican activist Nora Connolly (daughter of James Connolly), Constance expressed concern about the Red Terror and its parallels with the aftermath of the French Revolution. She drew historic parallels between the devastating humanitarian effects of the Allied blockade on Russia and the scorched earth tactics used in Ireland by the Tudors and Cromwell.[16]

Constance's visit to Zhyvotivka is an important moment in terms of understanding the development of her thought on imperialism and cultural sovereignty. The posed photographs and her landscape paintings allow us to see Ukraine through her eyes – a peaceful rural idyll. There is no indication of the rich and vibrant cultural life of cities like Lviv or Kyiv; no hint at the efforts of Ukrainian radicals to oppose Nicholas II's brutal and reactionary oppression of dissenters; no critique of the circumstances of peasant life or the landowning class's abuse of rural peasant labour. This reflects her own relationship to Irish nationalism and republicanism as the daughter of one of the wealthiest landowners in the country – albeit a philanthropic one – particularly in the years before her rise to prominence in Irish nationalist politics and before her conversion to Catholicism in 1917.[17] It also reflects Casimir's complicated position as a titled landowner beholden to the Russian imperial state.

Irish Nationalists and Russian Imperialism

Like Constance Markievicz, the writer and Irish nationalist Shane Leslie (1885–1971) grew up in extraordinarily privileged circumstances. Despite his family's extensive wealth and social capital, Shane had an unhappy childhood. He hated Eton, which he attended before completing his education at the Sorbonne and Cambridge, and suffered several nervous breakdowns. As a young man, Leslie converted to Catholicism, studied the Irish language, and changed his name from John Randolph to Shane. He turned his back on his aristocratic heritage and financial birthright when he took a vow of celibacy (which he would later break, and ended up marrying twice), renouncing his right of succession to the vast family estates in favour of his brother Norman. If Leslie wavered in his early vow of celibacy, his dedication to cultural nationalism was lifelong. He was active in the Gaelic League and the Irish language movement, and published poetry inspired by the Gaelic revival.[18] In October 1907, having just graduated from Cambridge, he travelled to Russia as the guest of Count Alexander Konstantinovich von Benckendorff, Imperial Russia's last ambassador to the Court of St James. He published a retrospective account of the trip in his memoir, *The Film of Memory* (1938). He reflected, 'Many pilgrims have found their way since to Moscow, but generally to visit the Mecca of the Soviet. [...] It is now something to remember and almost to boast: to have travelled through Imperial Russia before Lenin or Stalin were heard of.' Arriving in Moscow by rail from Berlin, his first impressions were of

> White snow-clad plains [...] little villages each with a church dome painted blue or green while the orthodox cross glistened in the sunlight. [...] It was like a city of dreams under the vividness of colouring and the clearness of atmosphere. Even the street crows looked a dazzling jet against the crystal snows. There were moujiks and priests in plenty in the streets and a struggling line of convicts in chains with half their heads shaved.[19]

After spending a day seeing the main sights of Moscow, he took a night train to the Benckendorff estate at Sosnovka, 300 miles to the south-east. The drive offered the opportunity to indulge in the now exhausted literary device of the comically disorganized Russian journey:

Irish Nationalists and Russian Imperialism

> At midnight there was a crash and the train left the line without rolling down the bank. The neighbouring community immediately rushed out of their houses not to give material assistance but to enjoy the conversation of the travellers. [...] There was nothing to be done but to make delicious tea out of the hot water. Russians always took a samovar or tea-strainer in their baggage. Political discussion, not being permitted in public, depended then on such accidents.[20]

He eventually arrived at a station fifty miles from Sosnovka and hired a coach to take him to his destination:

> A post-boy swathed in sheepskins drove the ponies out into the starry night. We drove and drove and drove into the Russian forest [...]. After several hours we lost our way and I was left frozen to the troitska [*troika*, carriage or sleigh] while my driver threw stones at windows to waken sleepers and inquire his road. I composed myself to the despair of dereliction [...] until to my relief we were hailed by a party of horsemen [...] sent by Count Benckendorff to search the steppes for me.[21]

He remained at Sosnovka until December, wolf-hunting, shooting duck and sledge-driving. He described the wolf-hunt as 'enthralling', facilitated by 'a peasant, who had been bitten by a wolf in childhood and could therefore speak the wolf-language', who was sent to howl in the forest on the preceding night to locate a pack for the benefit of the hunt.[22]

The climax of Leslie's short account is his visit to 79-year-old Leo Tolstoy. (Journalist and Irish nationalist Michael Davitt had also visited Tolstoy, in 1904 and 1905.) The writer was one of Leslie's heroes, 'The great lodestone to the intellectual world [...] the most attractive and noble figure in Europe'.[23] Leslie stayed at the writer's house at Yasnaya Polyana for a night, sleeping 'in a room full of desks which was devoted to the village children'.[24] His arrival on 2 December was recorded by Dushan Makovitsky, Tolstoy's doctor: 'At 5.30 p.m. Mr Leslie arrived, an aristocrat and Irish patriot of 22 years of age, to see the simple life. L.N. [Lev Nikolayevich] spoke with him in the study about serious issues.'[25] On first meeting, Tolstoy sought the measure of his young Irish visitor with three questions: whether he was Christian, whether he was 'pure towards women' and whether he was vegetarian.[26] The short visit 'passed like a dream', and Leslie became particularly friendly with Sophia Tolstoy who, in Leslie's words, was 'swathed in peasants' dress for his [Tolstoy's] sake, but hinted to me that she had lived luxurious days in her youth. Everything had been sacrificed to Tolstoy's ideas.'[27] She arranged a gift for Leslie of a signed photograph of her husband.[28] Leslie took notes of Tolstoy's philosophy and opinions as they conversed in French, some of which he published in the memoir, including the remark, 'What you desire for Ireland you must desire for the whole world.'[29] He noted these without comment, along with Tolstoy's view that 'Every man, even men of letters, were bound to carry out some labour in the fields or workshop.'[30]

Leslie spent some time in St Petersburg before returning to London. There, he quickly 'found [him]self on the edge of trouble' by attending an illegal meeting of students at the university, which was broken up by the police. That night he left by train for Vilnius, where he was 'anxious to express Irish sympathies in patriotic circles.'[31] At the time, the territory now known as Lithuania was part of the Russian Empire and had been since the partition of Poland–Lithuania over a century earlier. Lithuanian uprisings in 1830–1 and 1863–4 resulted in harsher tsarist repression and Russification policies, including the prohibition of the Lithuanian language in schools, attacks on Catholic churches and a ban on the Lithuanian press. Leslie reflected, 'Poland under Russian rule suggested analogies with Ireland. I was shown Polish schools where language and religion were kept alive despite the heavy hand of Muscovy. I was advised not to approach the statue of a Russian Empress which required the attentions of a sentry by day and night for fear of a patriot's bomb.'[32] (He referred to Lithuania as Poland – this was common at the time.) After his return to Ireland, he collected signatures of over 5500 Irish schoolchildren for sending to schools in Lithuania, to show their solidarity for cultural nationalists seeking language rights. He took pleasure in revealing a family connection to the region via a love affair many generations past on his grandmother's side, resulting in 'a distant infusion of Polish blood' that he thought explained his 'frenzy of enthusiasm for the Polish cause.'[33]

Irish Nationalists and Russian Imperialism

Despite Leslie's political sympathy for Lithuania, a curious incident at the close of his account of his visit to the Russian Empire demonstrates that he was unable to appreciate the intersection of the social, economic and gendered factors that contribute to poverty. Stating that he stayed in 'odd hotels' there, he related how one night, he was awoken by a knock on his door. A 'gentleman with long ringlets and a greasy demeanour was bowing and scraping [...] pointing to a girl in Polish dress [...] a fanciful native costume'. Leslie turned the pair away, returning to sleep despite the 'sound of wailing in the corridor'.[34] Leslie relates the story as a triumph of his superior wit over a boorish pimp, his sympathy for the political position of Lithuania stopping short of any empathy or concern for the girl, whose age is unknown. His class and social position made him deaf to her cries, and his description of the man seethes with anti-Semitism.

Markievicz and Leslie are both remembered, albeit in different ways, as Irish nationalists from unlikely backgrounds, with their origins in two of Ireland's wealthiest families. After returning to Ireland from Ukraine Markievicz became active in Irish republican circles, and she remains one of the best-known figures of the Irish revolutionary period. Leslie is less popularly known, and his writings, in their Gaelic revival register, have not retained an enduring appeal. He reflected in 1938, 'I have not since crossed the Russian boundaries where changes have been considerable and as yet inestimable. Russia has been used as a social laboratory for the rest of the world. Violent experiments and reactions: rainbows in test-tubes: precipitate of bloodshed: and a slow final deposit that only the historians in the year 2000 will be able to gauge.'[35] His retrospective observations overlooked Irish communists' support for the national struggle and reflected the demonization of socialism and communism in 1930s Ireland.

Conclusions:
Imagining Russia, Imagining Ireland, from Peter the Great to Nicholas II

Eighteenth- and nineteenth-century Irish encounters with Russia were ad hoc, the result of individual curiosity, professional necessity or personal relationships. They reflect the multitude of reasons for travel: missionary work, reporting, fleeing persecution, seeking employment, education, pleasure. Delving into individual lives and motivations, then placing them into collective contexts reveals wider patterns and the functions of exchanges and connections, be they political ideas, imperial state structures, human networks, transport infrastructure, communications technology, or even the spread of pathogens.

The over-representation of diplomats and diplomatic spouses in the story speaks to the mutual dependence of the educated Irish upper and middle classes and the British imperial administration. This administration was densely populated by the Irish – titled or middle-class, military or mandarin – who relied on the worldwide machine of imperial bureaucracy, diplomacy and enforcement for employment opportunities. Others followed

Conclusions: Imagining Russia, Imagining Ireland, from Peter the Great to Nicholas II

the definitive global events of the age, whether reporting on Russia's clashes with Britain and Japan, or manning the frontlines of those conflicts. Fashion also played its part, with Ireland's wealthiest seeking adventure and novelty in the peaks of the Caucasus or on the dusty plains of the Steppe. The time-pressed made express tours of St Petersburg and Moscow, taking advantage of improvements in travel and communications technology. Innovators, engineers and scientists travelled to Russia to exchange ideas and share their expertise.

Irish experiences in Russia during World War I have not been included in this book – the wealth of military, naval, journalistic, nursing and other medical professionals who made their way from Ireland during that time would require a separate study. Nurses like Limerick-born Florence Barrington – a descendant of William Hartigan Barrington, who travelled to Russia in 1837 (see Chapter 8) – volunteered with the Voluntary Ambulance Division behind Russian lines. She worked in the Anglo-Russian Hospital in Petrograd from late 1916 in the same palace in which an unsuccessful attempt had previously been made on the life of Rasputin. Florence kept a diary describing the difficulties of everyday life for the Russian people and detailing a journey she made by rail from Petrograd to Odesa and onwards to the Russian border with Romania, where she worked at a British hospital until September 1917. She gave a lecture in Dublin on her return, describing her experiences and exhibiting Russian tablecloths, ikons, medals, birch bark shoes, and a model of the new mosque in Petrograd.[1] At the same time, Antarctic explorer Tom Crean participated in Allied anti-Bolshevik missions from 1917 until his retirement from the Royal Navy in 1920, drawing on his extensive experience in the southern oceans.[2] In 1918 Longford native Sir Frederick O'Connor went on a secret Allied diplomatic mission to Siberia where he was, in his own words, 'plunged into a most extraordinary medley of international politics, intrigues, and rivalries'.[3]

Towards the close of the nineteenth century, transnational radicalism sparked a new wave of Irish–Russian connections and gave voice to those opposed to imperialism and authoritarianism. Those radical political

Conclusions: Imagining Russia, Imagining Ireland, from Peter the Great to Nicholas II

connections endured into the 1930s. The 1920s saw a flowering of Irish interest in the new socialist republic, with those active in the Irish struggle for independence broadly sympathetic to anti-imperialist and socialist ideals. The Irish Friends of Soviet Russia organized and facilitated visits to Russia, including a six-week-long group excursion in 1930. The organization counted among its members prominent figures from the founding generation of the Irish political left, including the republicans and women's rights activists Hanna Sheehy-Skeffington, Charlotte Despard and Rosamond Jacob. The lively connections of this period are detailed in Emmet O'Connor's book, *Reds and the Green: Ireland, Russia and the Communist Internationals, 1919–43* (2004).

The richness of over two centuries of Irish–Russian connections were all but forgotten by the mid-twentieth century, overshadowed by the revolutionary legacies of Irish republicanism and Soviet Bolshevism. The favourable atmosphere of 1920s Ireland towards relations with Moscow gave way in the late 1930s under the weight of the conservative Catholic state and society, the fledgling Irish Republic less amenable to or tolerant of the suggestion of diplomatic relations with the USSR. Ireland had no formal diplomatic relations with the USSR until 1974, when the first Irish embassy opened in Moscow.

However, the earlier radical sympathies of the Irish state's founders and their eagerness to gain recognition for the Irish Free State came back to haunt its conservative, Catholic leadership in the 1940s. In 1920 Éamon de Valera was in New York, fundraising and campaigning for international recognition of the Free State. He befriended a Soviet representative, Ludwig Karlovich Martens, who was likewise fundraising for the civil war in Russia. Aware of the success of the Irish campaign, Martens approached de Valera, seeking a loan of $20,000 and offering four pieces of diamond, topaz and platinum jewellery as collateral.[4] In January 1922 Harry Boland and Seán Nunan travelled from New York to Dublin carrying the jewels, which ended up being hidden in a chimney in Boland's aunt's house in Fairview. The Boland family secreted the jewels until 1938, after de Valera had been returned as Taoiseach in the previous year. The Taoiseach tried

Conclusions: Imagining Russia, Imagining Ireland, from Peter the Great to Nicholas II

to keep the story quiet – the optics of an arch-Catholic social conservative striking deals with communists would not have been good – but the story broke, and the public and their representatives demanded answers.[5] A letter-writer to the *Irish Times* raged:

> Communism is abhorred in this country, and the disclosure of the fact
> (after 28 years' silence) that their money was used to help to establish and
> propagate that evil doctrine must cause feelings of great pain and anger
> in this country. [...] Will he [de Valera] dare to assert that it was the wish
> or desire of the people he was representing that he should help in laying
> the foundations of Communism?[6]

The fledgling nation was impoverished, emigration was endemic, and the greatest single source of GDP was remittances from Irish migrants abroad. Dáil Deputies questioned whether the Russian jewels could be sold or placed on public display and the proceeds donated to charity.[7] Minister for Finance Patrick McGilligan was of the view that the gems were a potential source of revenue for the exchequer and ordered an independent valuation.[8] The jewels proved to be worth a fraction of their stated value, as little as £1,600.[9] Under political pressure, and in the absence of bilateral diplomatic channels, de Valera instructed Frederick Boland, Secretary General of the Department of External Affairs, to prevail upon John Dulanty, Irish High Commissioner in London, to negotiate with Russian ambassador to the UK Georgy Zaroubin for the return of the jewels and the repayment of the cash loan. After much back-and-forth the loan was repaid in full, without interest, and the jewels returned to Russia in September 1949.[10] This bizarre episode bares the hypocrisies underpinning the harsh, even oppressive social context of mid-twentieth century Ireland; the legacies of the circumstances of poverty and conflict in which the state was founded; and the role of the diaspora and international networks in Irish independence.

Indeed, the social conservatism and stifling religiosity of mid-century Ireland – a cold house for social progressives, those with leftist or socialist sympathies and those who did not 'fit in' or conform to a stringent social code – is reflected in the numbers of young people who entered religious

190

orders. In 1950 95 per cent of the population self-identified as Roman Catholic, and the country was home to 13,360 nuns – not including the hundreds who were working as missionaries abroad.[11] The astonishing prevalence of religious life as a professional choice shaped Irish encounters globally. In 1937 – incidentally, the year in which de Valera was returned as Taoiseach and the Free State effectively became a Republic, with its own constitution – the Jesuit Bishop of Shanghai invited the Irish Missionary Sisters of St Columban, who had been in China for twenty years, to provide education for exiled White Russians there. The foundation was made in January 1938, with the Irish Sisters modifying their religious services to accommodate Orthodox rites and reporting back to Ireland via mission magazines on the pupils' delight at hearing 'the Irish Sisters sing the ancient Russian responses to the traditional Russian chant'. They established a club for Russian girls, catechism classes for English-speaking children, branches of the Legion of Mary and Girl Guides, a kindergarten, elementary and high schools, and music and drama classes. In 1947 the pupils gave a concert including one song in the Irish language. But with the Communist takeover of Shanghai in May 1949, Russians started leaving the city for the US and Canada. The schools closed, and the Sisters' work was suspended as they moved on to other places.[12] The shift from politically radical Irish–Russian connections to the spiritual imperialism of mission work by white Irish nuns in Asia could not more explicitly or bluntly encapsulate the social contexts of mid-twentieth century Ireland. Another Irish connection to those exiled Russian noble families existed in the person of Kathleen Ffrench – daughter of Monivea landowner and diplomat Robert Ffrench and Russian noblewoman Sofia Alexandrovna Kindiakova – who died in Harbin in 1938, having lost her Simbirsk estate during the 1917 revolution.[13]

Empire was both the most important context for, and the most significant complicating factor in, Irish relationships with Romanov Russia. On one hand, Irish pro-imperialists were unrelenting in their criticisms of Russia as an example of unenlightened empire. The British Empire, in their view, spread civilization and improvement, while the Russian Empire preserved peoples, cultures and the economy in a state

Conclusions: Imagining Russia, Imagining Ireland, from Peter the Great to Nicholas II

of backwardness. But Irish people were also implicated in Russian imperialism, with high-ranking officers of the Irish military diaspora leading attacks and marches into occupied territories. For example, Peter de Lacy played a leading role in the War of the Polish Succession that ultimately increased Russian control over Polish affairs. In 1733 he led 30,000 Russian troops into Poland and, later that year, laid siege to Gdansk with 12,000 troops.[14] These actions contributed to the erasure of the Polish state in the following decades. He also led the Russian capture of Azov in 1736, a key imperial strategic goal and just one chapter in the long and ongoing history of Russian aggression and expansion into the Crimea. George Browne functioned at the highest levels of Catherine the Great's imperial administration as governor of Riga, implementing her reforms intended to reduce the legal rights of Baltic Germans; an attempt was made on his life in 1784, during the peasant uprising that followed the introduction of a poll tax.[15] Until the emancipation of the serfs in 1861, those Irish who lived on or visited Russia's vast estates were implicated in and benefited from feudalism, enjoying levels of comfort and ease that depended on the subjugation of the majority of the Russian people. Thereafter, the elite continued to benefit from enduring structural inequalities.

Overall, these understudied episodes in Irish history reveal the ways in which people forged connections across cultures in the past. When appraised as a group, the individual case studies included in this book reveal surprising connections that were underpinned in no small part by wider diaspora networks. Many of these individuals were connected by only a few degrees of separation, often without their knowledge. For example, the Jacobite soldier Anthony O'Hara seems to have known Jenny O'Reilly Vyazemskaya, whose in-laws knew Princess Dashkova, the great friend and mentor of the Wilmot sisters; and John Field knew and influenced Chopin, whose letters were later edited by Lily Voynich.

Similarly, the individuals studied in this book experienced events of great significance from completely different vantage points. Lily Voynich became interested in Russian anarchism after reading about the assassination of Alexander II, while Lady Dufferin was in St Petersburg on that very day and recorded her consternation in a letter to her mother. Unpicking these very different, yet intertwined, experiences raises interesting questions about the positioning of Irish history and its strong association with Atlantic and British imperial histories. Yet as the lives and careers studied in this book demonstrate, Irish diaspora networks remained influential even in locations where their numbers were much smaller. The stories told in this book also demonstrate the adaptability and flexibility of identities. The Irish military diaspora, for example, took advantage of ethno-religious networks while also functioning within shared European culture mediated through the French and German languages. Mobility took other forms aside from migration, with Irish people travelling to the reaches of the Russian Empire for love, friendship or adventure. Their individual stories reflect the broader social, political and economic circumstances of the age in which they lived, their lives imprinted by the effects of war and imperialism.

Appendix
Chronology of Accounts of
Romanov Russia by Irish Authors

This list includes only contemporaneously published eyewitness accounts (not individual newspaper articles or posthumously published editions). For a more comprehensive list of sources, see the author's website: www. historianka.com.

1768 George Macartney, *An Account of Russia in the Year MDCCLXVII* (London: privately printed).

1813 [Eleanor Cavanagh] 'Two Original and Curious Letters from an Irish Girl, in Russia, to her Friends in Ireland', *The Universal Magazine* 140:19, 441–8.

1822 James Prior, *A Voyage to St Petersburg in 1814: With Remarks on the Imperial Russian Navy* (London: R. Phillips and Co.).

1832 David Barry and William Russell, *Official Reports Made to Government by Drs Russell and Barry on the Disease called Cholera Spasmodica, as Observed during their Mission to Russia in 1831* (London: Winchester and Varnham).

1835 Robert Walsh, 'Reminiscences of Russia', *The Amulet: A Christian and Literary Remembrancer* 10, 145–80.

1836 Rayford Ramble, *Travelling Opinions and Sketches, in Russia and Poland* (Dublin: John Cumming).

1838 Charles Vane [Marquess of Londonderry], *Recollections of a Tour in the North of Europe in 1836–1837* (2 vols, London: Richard Bentley).

1840 Martha Bradford [Wilmot] (ed.), *Memoirs of the Princess Daschkaw, Lady of Honour to Catherine II, Empress of All the Russias, Written by Herself, Comprising Letters of the Empress, and Other Correspondence* (2 vols, London: Henry Colburn). Includes letters by Martha and Katherine Wilmot, and Eleanor Cavanagh, written during their residences in Russia in 1803–8.

1846 Richard Southwell Bourke, *St Petersburg and Moscow: A Visit to the Court of the Czar* (2 vols, London: Henry Colburn).

1846 Gore Ouseley, *Biographical Notices of Persian Poets with Critical and Explanatory Remarks. To which is Prefixed a Memoir of Sir Gore Ouseley by J. Reynolds* (London: Oriental Translation Fund).

1854 Philip O'Flaherty, *The Young Soldier* (Belfast: Shepherd and Aitchison).

1855 Philip O'Flaherty, *Sketches of the War: Being a Second Series of Letters* (Edinburgh: Shepherd and Elliot).

1857 Selina Bunbury, *Russia After the War: The Narrative of a Visit to That Country in 1856* (2 vols, London: Hurst and Blackett).

1858 William Howard Russell, *The British Expedition to the Crimea* (London: G. Routledge and Co.).

1863 Samuel Roberts Graves, *A Yachting Cruise in the Baltic* (London: Longman, Green, Longman and Roberts).

1867 George Bell, *Rough Notes by an Old Soldier* (London: Day and Son).

1867 John Ross Browne, *The Land of Thor* (New York: Harper and Brothers).

1870 [Anon.] *Sketches of Travel in Russia, Turkey, Greece, &c, &c, in 1869* (Dublin: Webb and Jennings).

1873 Denis Caulfield Heron, 'A Visit to Russia', *Journal of the Statistical and Social Inquiry Society of Ireland* 6, 181–202.

1873 James Creagh, *A Scamper to Sebastopol and Jerusalem in 1867* (London: Richard Bentley).

1877 James Bryce, *Transcaucasia and Ararat: Being Notes of a Vacation Tour in the Autumn of 1876* (London: Macmillan and Co.).

1877–8 James Bryce, 'Armenia and Mount Ararat', *Proceedings of the Royal Geographical Society* 22:3, 169–86.

1882 Edmond O'Donovan, *The Merv Oasis: Travels and Adventures East of the Caspian during the Years 1879, 80, 81, Including Five Months' Residence among the Tekkés of Merv* (London: Smith, Elder and Co.).

1892 E.B. Lanin [Emile Joseph Dillon], *Russian Characteristics, Reprinted, with Revisions, from the 'Fortnightly Review'* (London: Chapman and Hall).

1893 James O'Malley, *The Life of James O'Malley* (Montreal: Desaulnier's Printing Co.).

1895 Margaret Kerwin, 'One Woman's Story', *Ours: The Green Howards Gazette* 3:25 (April 1895), 94–6.

1897 Sr Mary Aloysius [Catherine Doyle], *Memories of the Crimea* (London: Burns and Oates).

1900 Matthew Horace Hayes, *Among Horses in Russia* (London: R.A. Everett and Co.).

1903 Michael Davitt, *Within the Pale: the True Story of Anti-Semitic Persecution in Russia* (New York: Barnes).

1903 George Lynch, *The Path of Empire* (London: Duckworth and Co.).

1905 Margaretta Eagar, 'The Russian Court in Summer', *The Star*, (30 Sept. 1905).

1906 Margaretta Eagar, 'Christmas at the Court of the Tsar', *The Quiver* (Jan. 1906), 26–30.

1906 Margaretta Eagar, *Six Years at the Russian Court* (New York: Charles L. Bowman).

1906 Francis McCullagh, *With the Cossacks, Being the Story of an Irishman who Rode with the Cossacks throughout the Russo-Japanese War* (London: Eveleigh Nash).

1908 Samuel Gamble Bayne, *Quicksteps through Scandinavia, with a Retreat from Moscow* (London: Harper and Brothers).

1909 Margaretta Eagar, 'Further Glimpses of the Tsaritsa's Little Girls', *The Girl's Own Paper and Woman's Magazine* 30, 366–7.

1909 Margaretta Eagar, 'More about the Little Grand Duchesses of Russia', *The Girl's Own Paper and Woman's Magazine* 30, 535.

1910 Joseph M. Hone and Page L. Dickinson, *Persia in Revolution: With Notes of Travel in the Caucasus* (London: T. Fisher Unwin).

1917 Hariot G. Blackwood [Lady Dufferin], *My Russian and Turkish Journals* (New York: Charles Scribner's Sons). Details residence in Russia of 1879–81.

1918 Emile Joseph Dillon, *The Eclipse of Russia* (London: J.M. Dent and Sons).

1929 Emile Joseph Dillon, *Russia Today and Yesterday* (London: J.M. Dent and Sons).

1923 Garnet Joseph Wolseley, *The Letters of Lord and Lady Wolseley* (London: William Heinemann). Letters relating to his visit to Russia in 1883 are at pp. 95–106.

1928 Mrs Aubrey [Lizzie] Le Blond, *Day In, Day Out* (London: J. Lane). Details visit made in 1913.

Chronology of Accounts of Romanov Russia by Irish Authors

1931 O'Connor, Frederick, *On the Frontier and Beyond: A Record of Thirty Years' Service* (London: John Murray, 1931). Records Allied diplomatic mission of 1918 (pp. 252–71).

1938 Shane Leslie, *The Film of Memory* (London: Michael Joseph). Details visit made in 1907.

NOTES

INTRODUCTION

1 Edmund Spenser, *A View of the Present State of Ireland* (1598), available at https://celt. ucc.ie/published/E500000-001.html.

2 Felicity Stout, "'The Strange and Wonderfull Discoverie of Russia": Richard Hakluyt and Censorship' in Daniel Carey and Claire Jowitt (eds), *Richard Hakluyt and Travel Writing in Early Modern Europe* (Farnham: Ashgate, 2012), p. 155.

3 See David Beers Quinn, *The Elizabethans and the Irish* (Ithaca NY: Cornell University Press, 1966); Nicholas Canny, *Making Ireland British, 1580–1650* (Oxford: Oxford University Press, 2001); Patricia Palmer, *Language and Conquest in Early Modern Ireland: English Renaissance Literature and Elizabethan Imperial Expansion* (Cambridge: Cambridge University Press, 2001).

4 Thomas Campbell, *A Philosophical Survey of the South of Ireland, in a Series of Letters to John Watkinson, MD* (Dublin: W. Whitestone, 1778), p. 142.

5 John Sheehan, 'Silver and Gold Hoards: Status, Wealth and Trade in the Viking Age', *Archaeology Ireland* 9:3 (1995), 20.

6 Tomás Ó Fiaich, 'The Schottenklöster in Southern Germany: die bewegung der Iroschottischen klöster in Sud-Deutschland [The Movement of Iro-Scottish Monasteries in South Germany]', *Seanchas Ardmhacha* 18:2 (2001), 35; Diarmuid Ó Riain, '*Monachi Peregrini*: The Mobile Monks of the Irish Benedictine Houses in Medieval Germany and Austria' in Olivier Delouis, Maria Mossakovska-Gaubert and Annick Peters-Custot (eds), *Les mobilités monastiques en Orient et en Occident de l'Antiquité tardive au Moyen Âge [Monastic Mobilities in the East and West from Late Antiquity to the Middle Ages]* (Rome: Publications de l'École française de Rome, 2019), pp. 337–52.

7 Chester S.L. Dunning and David R.C. Hudson, 'The Transportation of Irish Swordsmen to Sweden and Russia and Plantation in Ulster (1609–1613)', *Archivium*

Notes XXIII–XXV

Hibernicum 66 (2013), 422–53; Chester S.L. Dunning, 'Scottish and Irish Soldiers in Early Seventeenth-Century Russia: The Case of George Learmonth and the Belaia Garrison', *Journal of Irish and Scottish Studies* 7:2 (2014), 23–42, available at https://www.abdn.ac.uk/riiss/content-images/JISSv7.2online.pdf.

8 Regional and city censuses were made from the seventeenth century onwards, but these often counted only taxable, male heads of households. The first and only imperial census was made in 1897, but it did not record nationality, only native language and religion. See Lee Schwartz, 'A History of Russian and Soviet Censuses' in Ralph S. Clem (ed.), *Research Guide to the Russian and Soviet Censuses* (Ithaca: Cornell University Press, 1986), pp. 48–69.

9 See Barry McLoughlin, *Left to the Wolves: Irish Victims of Stalinist Terror* (Dublin: Irish Academic Press, 2007) and Emmet O'Connor, *Reds and the Green: Ireland, Russia and the Communist Internationals, 1919–43* (Dublin: UCD Press, 2004).

10 See Leonard G. Friesen (ed.), *Minority Report: Mennonite Identities in Imperial Russia and Soviet Ukraine Reconsidered, 1789–1945* (Toronto: University of Toronto Press, 2018).

11 His most notable works include: Anthony G. Cross (ed.), *Russia under Western Eyes, 1517–1825* (London: Elek Books, 1971), *Britain and Russia: Contacts and Comparisons, 1700–1800* (Newtonville: Oriental Research Partners, 1979), *By the Banks of the Neva: Chapters from the Lives and Careers of the British in Eighteenth Century Russia* (Cambridge: Cambridge University Press, 1997); Anthony G. Cross and G.S. Smith (eds), *Eighteenth-Century Russian Literature, Culture and Thought: A Bibliography of English-Language Scholarship and Translations* (Newtonville: Oriental Research Partners, 1984).

12 Jacqueline Cromarty, *Scots in Russia, 1661–1934: Eleven Scots Who Visited Russia* (Edinburgh: Scotland's Cultural Heritage, 1987); David Dobson, *Scots in Poland, Russia and the Baltic States* (Baltimore: Clearfield, 2000); Steve Murdoch, 'Soldiers, Sailors, Jacobite Spy: Russo-Jacobite Relations 1688–1750', *Slavonica* 3:1 (1996–7), 7–27; Rebecca Wills, *The Jacobites and Russia 1715–1750* (East Linton: Tuckwell Press, 2002).

13 Tatiana V. Artemieva, Peter Jones and Michael Mikeshin (eds), *The Philosophical Age: Almanac 15: Scotland and Russia in the Enlightenment* (St Petersburg: Center for the History of Ideas, 2001), available at http://ideashistory.org.ru/pdfs/a15.pdf.

14 Paul Dukes (ed.), *Journal of Irish and Scottish Studies* 3:2 (2014): *The Patrick Gordon Diary*, available at https://www.abdn.ac.uk/riiss/content-images/JISSv3.2_OpenAccess.pdf.

15 Niall Whelehan (ed.), *Transnational Perspectives on Modern Irish History* (London: Routledge, 2015); Patrick Fitzgerald and Brian Lambkin, *Migration in Irish History, 1607–2007* (Basingstoke: Palgrave Macmillan, 2008); Raphaël Ingelbien, *Irish Cultures of Travel: Writing on the Continent, 1829–1914* (London: Palgrave Macmillan, 2016).

16 Thomas O'Connor (ed.), *The Irish in Europe, 1580–1815* (Dublin: Four Courts Press, 2001); Thomas O'Connor and Mary Ann Lyons (eds), *Irish Migrants in Europe after Kinsale, 1602–1820* (Dublin: Four Courts Press, 2003); Thomas O'Connor and Mary

XXVI–XXIX *Notes*

Ann Lyons (eds), *Irish Communities in Early Modern Europe* (Dublin: Four Courts Press, 2006); David Worthington (ed.), *British and Irish Emigrants and Exiles in Europe, 1603–1688* (Leiden: Brill, 2010); David Worthington, *British and Irish Experiences and Impressions of Central Europe, c. 1560–1688* (Farnham: Ashgate, 2012).

17 Patrick O'Meara, 'Irishmen in Eighteenth-Century Russian Service', *Irish Slavonic Studies* 5 (1984), 13–25; Marcus Wheeler, 'Did Peter the Great Visit Ireland?', *Irish Slavonic Studies* 5 (1984), 11–12; Anthony G. Cross, 'Catherine the Great "All the Way from Russia to Emancipate Ireland"', *Irish Slavonic Studies* 10 (1989), 89–92.

18 Valentine O'Hara, *Anthony O'Hara Knight of Malta: Memoir of a Russian Diehard* (London: Richards, 1938); Peter Roebuck (ed.), *Macartney of Lisanoure: Essays in Biography* (Belfast: Ulster Historical Foundation, 1983); David Branson, *John Field and Chopin* (New York: St Martin's Press, 1972); Patrick Pigott, *The Life and Music of John Field* (London: Faber and Faber, 1973); Aleksandr A. Nikolaev, *John Field*, transl. Harold M. Cardello, (New York: Musical Scope Publishers, 1973).

19 Róisín Healy, *Poland in the Irish Nationalist Imagination, 1722–1922: Anti-Colonialism within Europe* (Basingstoke: Palgrave Macmillan, 2017); Thomas McLean, *The Other East and Nineteenth-Century British Literature: Imagining Poland and the Russian Empire* (Basingstoke: Palgrave Macmillan, 2012).

20 Tim Wilson, 'The Experiences of Southern Ireland and Prussian Poland Compared, 1918–23', *Irish Studies in International Affairs* 13 (2002), 61–86.

21 William Tighe to Elizabeth Tighe [c.1780] (PRONI: D2685/4/3).

22 Marshall T. Poe, *'A People Born to Slavery': Russia in Early Modern European Ethnography, 1476–1748* (Ithaca: Cornell University Press, 2000), p. 128.

23 Wilmot's reading list included Adam Olearius' influential *Voyages and Travels of the Ambassadors from the Duke of Holstein to the Great Duke of Muscovy, and the King of Persia* (1633); Jane Vigor's *Letters from a Lady Who Resided Some Years in Russia* (1775); Elizabeth, Lady Craven's *A Journey through the Crimea to Constantinople* (1789); Maria Guthrie's *A Tour Performed in the Years 1795–6, through The Taurida, or Crimea* [etc.] (1802); histories and natural histories by William Tooke, Gerhard Friedrich Müller, Voltaire and Matthew Guthrie; and the travels of William Coxe (1784), William Richardson (1784) and Chappe d'Auteroche (1768). Katherine Wilmot (1806) 'Journal' (RIA: MS 12L34). Some of these books may have been part of Dashkova's library; see Alexander Woronzoff-Dashkoff, 'Princess E.R. Dashkova's Moscow Library', *SEER* 72:1 (1994), 62–3.

24 James Bryce, *Transcaucasia and Ararat: Being Notes of a Vacation Tour in the Autumn of 1876* ([1877] 4th ed., London: Macmillan and Co., 1896), pp. 36, 195–6.

25 Joseph Lennon, *Irish Orientalism: A Literary and Intellectual History* (Syracuse NY: Syracuse University Press, 2004), p. 64.

26 Colin McKelvie, 'Early English Books in Armagh Public Library: A Short-Title Catalogue of Books Printed before 1641', *Irish Booklore* 3:2 (1977), 91–103.

27 1872 Catalogue Online at www.tcd.ie.

28 *Memoirs of the Life of Prince Menzikoff* (Dublin: G. Risk, G. Ewing and W. Smith, 1727); John Mottley, *The History of the Life of Peter I. Emperor of Russia* (3 vols, Dublin:

Notes XXX–XXXIV

G. Risk, G. Ewing and W. Smith, 1740); *Memoirs of the Life of John-Daniel Mentzel* (Dublin: M. Rhames, 1744); William Coxe, *Travels into Poland, Russia, Sweden, and Denmark* (3 vols, Dublin: Byrne and Co., 1784); [Peter Henry Bruce], *Memoirs of Peter Henry Bruce … in the Services of Prussia, Russia, and Great Britain* (Dublin: Byrne and Co., 1783).

29 For more on Connor, see Róisín Healy, 'The View from the Margins: Ireland and Poland-Lithuania, 1698–1798' in Richard Unger (ed.), *Britain and Poland-Lithuania: Contact and Comparison from the Middle Ages to 1795* (Leiden: Brill, 2008), pp. 355–73, and Liam Chambers, 'Medicine and Miracles in the Late Seventeenth Century: Bernard Connor's *Evangelium Medici* (1697)' in James Kelly and Fiona Clark (eds), *Ireland and Medicine in the Seventeenth and Eighteenth Centuries* (Farnham: Ashgate, 2016), pp. 53–72.

30 R.H. Dalitz and G.C. Stone, 'Doctor Bernard Connor: Physician to King Jan III Sobieski and Author of the History of Poland (1698)', *Oxford Slavonic Papers* 14 (1981), 14–35.

31 Bernard Connor, *The History of Poland* (2 vols, London: Brown and Roper, 1698), vol. II, p. 187.

32 Dalitz and Stone, 'Doctor Bernard Connor'. See also Henryk Głębocki, *A Disastrous Matter: The Polish Question in the Russian Political Thought and Discourse of the Great Reform Age, 1856–1866* (Krakow: Jagiellonian University Press, 2016).

33 Connor, *The History of Poland*, vol. I, p. v.

34 Robert Bell, *History of Russia* (3 vols, London: Longman and Co., 1836–8), vol. I, p. 1.

35 Sara Dickinson, *Breaking Ground: Travel and National Culture in Russia from Peter I to the Era of Pushkin* (Amsterdam: Rodopi, 2006), pp. 35–6.

36 Healy, *Poland in the Irish Nationalist Imagination*, p. 2.

37 John Ross Browne, *The Land of Thor* (New York: Harper and Brothers, 1867), p. 193.

38 Gerard Keown, *First of the Small Nations: The Beginnings of Irish Foreign Policy in the Interwar Years, 1919–1932* (Oxford: Oxford University Press), p. 8.

39 Quoted in Janet M. Hartley, *The Volga: A History of Russia's Greatest River* (New Haven and London: Yale University Press, 2021), p. 6.

40 Mark Bassin, 'Inventing Siberia: Visions of the Russian East in the Early Nineteenth Century', *American Historical Review* 26:3 (1991), 768; Susan Layton, *Russian Literature and Empire: Conquest of the Caucasus from Pushkin to Tolstoy* (Cambridge: Cambridge University Press, 1994).

41 Healy, *Poland in the Irish Nationalist Imagination*, pp. 33–5, 49, 55–7; Colin Brooks, 'British Political Culture and the Dismemberment of States: Britain and the First Partition of Poland 1762–1772', *Parliaments, Estates and Representation* 13:1 (1993), 51–64.

42 Healy, *Poland in the Irish Nationalist Imagination*, p. 1.

43 Christopher Woods, 'Wyse, Sir Thomas' in *DIB*.

44 Healy, *Poland in the Irish Nationalist Imagination*, pp. 78–88.

45 Larry Wolff, *Inventing Eastern Europe: The Map of Civilization on the Mind of the Enlightenment* (Stanford: Stanford University Press, 1994).

XXXIV–XXXVIII Notes

46 John Ladeveze Adlercron, Journal of a Tour, 1805 (NLI: MS 3756); Joseph M. Hone and Page L. Dickinson, *Persia in Revolution: With Notes of Travel in the Caucasus* (London: T. Fisher Unwin, 1910), p. 163; Mrs Aubrey le Blond, *Day In, Day Out* (London: J. Lane, 1928), pp. 165–177.

47 Katherine Wilmot to Alicia Wilmot, 4 Aug. 1805 (RIA: MS 12L30, p. 10); Katherine Wilmot to Anna Maria Chetwood, 16 June 1807 (RIA: MS 12L30, p. 159).

48 Michelle Lamarche Marrese, 'Princess Dashkova and the Politics of Language in Eighteenth-Century Russia' in Derek Offord, Lara Ryazanova-Clarke, Vladislav Rjéoutski and Gesine Argent (eds), *French and Russian in Imperial Russia: Language Attitudes and Identity* (Edinburgh: Edinburgh University Press, 2015), pp. 31–47.

49 George Forbes,'Correspondence with Lord Harrington, 1733–4' in *Historic Manuscripts Commission Report 2* (London: H.M. Stationery Office, 1871), p. 216.

50 Martha Wilmot to her mother [Martha Wilmot, *née* Moore], 31 July 1803 (RIA: MS 12L24, p. 61).

51 Lucy Ward, *The Empress and the English Doctor* (London: Oneworld Publications, 2022), p. 183.

52 Letters concerning Empress Catherine, Quin Family Collection, *c.* 1781–3 (NAI: MSS 999/392/5/51–55, 999/392/5/62).

53 [Anon.], 'Istoricheskaya galeria. Field' ['Historical Gallery. Field'] in *Syn otechestva* [*Son of the Fatherland*] 15 (1834), pp. 504–15.

54 Terry de Valera, *John Field, His Life and Work and His Influence on Chopin* (Dublin, 1994), p. 10.

55 Martha Wilmot, 27 Jan. 1808, in Catherine Wilmot and Martha Wilmot, *The Russian Journals of Martha and Catherine Wilmot*, ed. Harford Montgomery Hyde and Edith Stewart (London: Macmillan, 1934), p. 320; Gore Ouseley, *Biographical Notices of Persian Poets with Critical and Explanatory Remarks. To which is Prefixed a Memoir of Sir Gore Ouseley by J. Reynolds* (London: Oriental Translation Fund, 1846), p. ccxii.

56 Alfred Webb, *Compendium of Irish Biography* (Dublin: H.M. Gill, 1878), p. 176.

57 'T.','John Field', *Khudozhestvennaya gazeta na 1837* [*Arts Gazette for 1837*] 1 (Jan. 1837), 14–16.

58 Patrick Piggott, *The Life and Music of John Field* (London: Faber and Faber, 1973), p. 4.

59 Tad Szulc, *Chopin in Paris: The Life and Times of the Romantic Composer* (New York: Scribner, 1998), p. 90.

60 E.L. Voynich (transl., ed.), *Chopin's Letters* (New York: Alfred A. Knopf, 1931), p. 154.

61 Iu.D. Levin, 'Russian Responses to the Poetry of Ossian' in Anthony G. Cross (ed.), *Great Britain and Russia in the Eighteenth Century: Contacts and Comparisons* (Newtonville: Oriental Research Partners, 1979), pp. 49–64.

62 Martha Wilmot to Alicia Wilmot, 17 Mar. 1805 (RIA: MS 12L24, p. 261).

63 Thomas Moore,'Air – The Bells of St Petersburgh' in *The Works of Thomas Moore* (Paris: Galignani, 1823), p. 232.

Notes XXXVIII–XLI

64 Gabriella Imposti, 'The Reception of Thomas Moore in Russia during the Romantic Age' in Francesca Benatti, Seán Ryder and Justin Tonra (eds), *Thomas Moore: Texts, Context, Hypertext* (Oxford: Peter Lang, 2013), p. 136; Eoin MacWhite, 'Thomas Moore and Poland', *Proceedings of the Royal Irish Academy 72C* (1972), 49–62.

65 Thomas Moore, *Memoirs, Journal, and Correspondence of Thomas Moore*, ed. John Russell (New York: D. Appleton, 1857), vol. VI, p. 5.

66 MacWhite, 'Thomas Moore and Poland'.

67 Ivan Turgenev to Petr Vyazemsky, 16 Oct. 1823, in V.I. Saitov (ed.), *Ostafyevsky arkhiv knyazey Vyazemskikh tom 2: perepiska Knyazya P.A. Vyazemskago s A.I. Turgenevem, 1820–1823* [*Ostafyevo Archive of the Princes Vyazemsky vol. 2: Letters of Prince P.A. Vyazemsky to A.I. Turgenev, 1820–1823*] (St Petersburg: Stasyulevich, 1899), p. 361.

68 *The Literary Gazette and Journal of the Belles Lettres, Arts, Sciences, etc.*, no. 1212 (11 Apr. 1840).

69 Anthony G. Cross, 'Early British Acquaintance with Russian Popular Song and Music (the Letters and Journals of the Wilmot Sisters)', *SEER* 66:1 (1988), 21–34, here 32.

70 For example, *FJ*, 7, 14 Aug. 1823; 28 July 1825.

71 *FJ*, 10, 15 Oct. 1821; Arthur Prudden Coleman, 'John Bowring and the Poetry of the Slavs', *Proceedings of the American Philosophical Society* 84:3 (1941), 432.

72 Advertisement issued in London, *c.* 1810–12 (NLI: EPH E514).

73 *FJ*: 19 Apr. 1834, 22 Apr. 1834, 7 Dec. 1836, 5 Feb. 1840, 6 Feb. 1840, 21 Sept. 1839, 12 Feb. 1840, 22 Feb. 1840.

74 *FJ*, 4 Apr. 1821.

75 *FJ*, 21 Sept. 1839.

76 *FJ*: 4 Apr. 1821, 15 Oct. 1821, 10 Oct. 1821, 21 Sept. 1839, 12 Nov. 1839.

77 James Orr, *Poems* (Belfast: Smyth and Lyons, 1804).

78 Thomas McLean, 'Arms and the Circassian Woman: Frances Browne's "The Star of Atteghei"', *Victorian Poetry* 41:3 (2003), 295–318; McLean, *The Other East*, pp. 135–53.

79 Charles Lysaght, 'Leslie, John Randolph ('Shane')' in *DIB*; signed photograph of Tolstoy, Shane Leslie Papers, Georgetown University: Box 34, folder 19.

80 Robert Service, *The Last of the Tsars: Nicholas II and the Russian Revolution* (London: Pan Macmillan, 2017), p. 113.

81 Liam Ó Rinn to Petr Kropotkin, 18 Feb. 1912, transcription by The Kropotkin Papers, available at kropotkinpapers.org; Diarmuid Breathnach and Máire Ní Mhurchú, 'Ó Rinn, Liam (1886–1943)' at ainm.ie.

82 Catherine Wynne, *Lady Butler: War Artist and Traveller, 1846–1933* (Dublin: Four Courts Press, 2019).

83 Ruth Devine, 'Kirkwood, Harriet (*née* Jameson)' in *DIB*.

84 Linde Lunney, 'Dunlevy, Mairéad' in *DIB*.

85 Rockwell Kent (1882–1971), *Dan Ward's Stack, Ireland* (1926/7), Hermitage Museum: GE-9924.

SECTION 1

1. Chester S.L. Dunning and David R.C. Hudson, 'The Transportation of Irish Swordsmen to Sweden and Russia and Plantation in Ulster (1609–1613)', *Archivium Hibernicum* 66 (2013), 452n; Chester S.L. Dunning, 'Scottish and Irish Soldiers in Early Seventeenth-Century Russia: The Case of George Learmonth and the Belaia Garrison', *Journal of Irish and Scottish Studies* 7:2 (2014), 23–42. See also Yaroslav Fedoruk, 'An Unrealized Project of the Irish Colonization of Ukraine (1655)', *Journal of Ukrainian Studies* 33–34 (2008–2009), 117–33.

2. Denis J.B. Shaw argues that Russia was less isolated in the pre-Petrine period than is usually portrayed, in 'Mapmaking, Science and State Building in Russia before Peter the Great', *Journal of Historical Geography* 31 (2005), 409–29.

3. George Macartney, *An Account of Russia in the Year MDCCLXVII* (London: privately printed, 1768), p. 77.

CHAPTER 1

1. Thomas Bartlett and Keith Jeffery (eds), *A Military History of Ireland* (Cambridge: Cambridge University Press, 1996), especially Thomas Bartlett and Keith Jeffery, 'An Irish Military Tradition?', pp. 1–25, and Harman Murtagh, 'Irish Soldiers Abroad, 1600–1800', pp. 294–314.

2. Aleksandr B. Kamenskii, *The Russian Empire in the Eighteenth Century: Searching for a Place in the World*, transl., ed. David Griffiths (New York: Armonk, 1997), p. 67.

3. Patrick J. O'Meara, 'Field Marshal Peter Lacy: an Irishman in Eighteenth-Century Russia' in Tatiana V. Artemieva, Peter Jones and Michael Mikeshin (eds), *The Philosophical Age: Almanac 15: Scotland and Russia in the Enlightenment* (St Petersburg: Center for the History of Ideas, 2001), p. 85, available at http://ideashistory.org.ru/pdfs/a15.pdf.

4. Priscilla Roosevelt, *Life on the Russian Country Estate: A Social and Cultural History* (New Haven: Yale University Press, 1995), p. 28.

5. P.J. Wallis and R.V. Wallis (eds), *Eighteenth Century Medics* (2nd ed., Newcastle-Upon-Tyne: Project for Historical Bibliography, 1988), p. 551; A.G. Cross, *By the Banks of the Neva: Chapters from the Lives and Careers of the British in Eighteenth Century Russia* (Cambridge: Cambridge University Press, 1997), p. 129.

6. Royal College of Physicians in Ireland: Index to the Kirkpatrick Archive, p. 29; Wallis and Wallis (eds), *Eighteenth Century Medics*, p. 160.

7. John McAuliffe Curtin, 'James Quinlan, Formerly Surgeon-General to the Czar of Russia, 1826', *Irish Journal of Medical Science*, 6th ser., 493 (1967), 7–15.

8. W.P. Courtney, rev. Elizabeth Baigent, 'Prior, Sir James' in *ODNB*; James Prior, *A Voyage to St Petersburg in 1814, with Remarks on the Imperial Russian Navy* (London: Sir Richard Phillips and Co., 1822).

9. Steve Murdoch, 'Soldiers, Sailors, Jacobite Spy: Russo-Jacobite Relations 1688–1750', *Slavonica* 3:1 (1996–7), 7–27; Paul Dukes (ed.), *Journal of Irish and Scottish Studies* 3:2 (2014): *The Patrick Gordon Diary*, available at https://www.abdn.ac.uk/riiss/content-images/JISSv3.2_OpenAccess.pdf.

Notes 6–8

10 The figure of 3000 Scots is cited in Dunning, 'Scottish and Irish Soldiers in Early Seventeenth-Century Russia', 23.

11 See Rebecca Wills, *The Jacobites and Russia 1715–1750* (East Linton: Tuckwell Press, 2002).

12 Minute of a meeting of the Lords Committee containing news of the Pretender and his links with the Tsar's physician Dr Robert Erskine, 11 May 1717 (National Archives: PRO: State Papers 35/9, ff. 8v–9).

13 Report to Peter I from F.P. Veselovsky, enclosing a copy of the British reply to his memorial, 12 Feb. 1720 (Arkhiv vneshnei politiki Rossiiskoi Federatsii [Archive of Foreign Policy of the Russian Federation]: F. 'Snosheniya Rossii s Anglii', op. 35/1, d. 491, ll. 46–53). English translation available in Simon Dixon *et al.* (transl., ed.), *Britain and Russia in the age of Peter the Great: Historical Documents* (London: School of Slavonic and East European Studies, 1998), pp. 211–14.

14 Pedigree of O'Rourke, with Descent from Brian O'Brian … , 1944 (GO MS 175: NLI microfilm p8305, p. 214).

15 Wills, *The Jacobites and Russia*, pp. 173–4.

16 Dmitrii N. Bantysh-Kamenskii, *Biografii rossiyskikh generalissimusov i general-feldmarshalov* [*Biographies of Russian Generals and General-Fieldmarshals*] (4 vols, St Petersburg: v Tipografii Tretyago Departmenta Ministerstva Gosudarstvennikh Imushestv, 1840), vol. II, p. 204.

17 Wills, *The Jacobites and Russia*, p. 56.

18 *Belfast News Letter*, 5 June 1739, 30 June 1739.

19 Wills, *The Jacobites and Russia*, p. 205; Career of Peter de Lacy, 'Ofitserskiye skazki [Officers' Lives]' (Rossiiskii gosudarstvennyi voenno-istoricheskii arkhiv [Russian State Military History Archive, Moscow]: F. 490, op. 2, d. 50).

20 Edward de Lacy-Bellingari, *The Roll of the House of Lacy* (Baltimore: Waverly Press, 1928), p. 252; Descent of Count Patrick O'Brien de Lacy, Born O'Brien, of Grodno, from de Lacy, *c.* 1844 (GO MS 176: NLI microfilm p8306, p. 63).

21 de Lacy-Bellingari, *The Roll of the House of Lacy*, pp. 252, 268; Harman Murtagh, 'Lacy [de Lacy], Maurice' in *ODNB*.

22 Pedigree of O'Rourke, with Descent from Brian O'Brian..., 1844 (GO MS 175: NLI microfilm p8305, p. 214); George Dawe, 'Iosif O'Rowrke', no later than 1825. Hermitage Museum, St Petersburg. It has not been possible to reproduce the painting in this book due to the sanctions adopted against Russia following its illegal invasion of Ukraine.

23 Maryna Elinskaya, 'O'Rurki, Irlandskiya grafi, u Belarusi' ['O'Rourke, the Irish Earl, in Belarus'], *Belaruskie-Albaruthenica* 14 (2000): *Belarus'-Irlandiya: materiyali navukovaga seminara 'Belaruska-Irlandskiya gistarchna-kulturniya suvyazi'* [*Belarus-Ireland: Materials of the Research Seminar 'Belarussian-Irish Historical and Cultural Connections'*], 96.

24 Gráinne Henry, 'Women "Wild Geese", 1585–1625: Irish Women and Migration to European Armies in the Late Sixteenth and Early Seventeenth Centuries' in Patrick

O'Sullivan (ed.), *The Irish World Wide*, vol. IV: *Irish Women and Irish Migration* (Leicester: Leicester University Press, 1997), p. 33; Jerrold Casway, 'Irish Women Overseas, 1500–1800' in Margaret MacCurtain and Mary O'Dowd (eds), *Women in Early Modern Ireland* (Dublin: Wolfhound Press, 1991), p. 119.

25 Pedigree of O'Rourke..., 1944 (GO MS 175: NLI microfilm p8305, p. 214); Genealogy of O'Rourke, 1782 (GO MS 165: NLI microfilm p8302, p. 367); Letters, 1926, with Documentary Evidence, to Rev. Edward de Lacy..., 1926 (GO MS 8800: NLI microfilm p8396, p. 4).

26 Descent of Patrick Nicholas Stuart (GO MS 176: NLI microfilm p8306, p. 59); Nicholas J. Synott, 'Notes on the Family of de Lacy in Ireland', *Journal of the Royal Society of Antiquaries of Ireland* 49 (1919), facing 128; de Lacy-Bellingari, *The Roll of the House of Lacy*, pp. 219–20.

27 de Lacy-Bellingari, *The Roll of the House of Lacy*, p. 214; Maurice Hennessy, *The Wild Geese: Irish Soldiers in Exile* (London: Sidgwick and Jackson, 1973), p. 106.

28 de Lacy-Bellingari, *The Roll of the House of Lacy*, p. 214.

29 James Keith, Draft letter to Field Marshal Lacy, Jan. 1747, in *Ninth Report of the Royal Commission on Historic Manuscripts, part II* (London: HM Stationery Office, 1884), p. 227.

30 *Memoirs of Catherine the Great*, transl. Katharine Anthony (New York: Tudor Publishing, 1935), p. 91.

31 Pedigree of Browne of Camas (GO MS 176: NLI microfilm p8306, p. 159); Descent of Patrick Nicholas Stuart (GO MS 176: NLI microfilm p8306, p. 59); John Jordan, 'John Delap: An Irish Seaman in Russia', *The Irish Sword* 2 (1954), 56; J.G. Simms, 'The Irish on the Continent, 1691–1800', in T.W. Moody and W.E. Vaughan (eds), *A New History of Ireland IV: Eighteenth-Century Ireland 1691–1800* (Oxford University Press, 1986), pp. 642–4, here p. 644; Cross, *By the Banks of the Neva*, p. 151.

32 James McGurk, 'Wild Geese: The Irish in European Armies', in Patrick O'Sullivan (ed.), *The Irish World Wide*, vol. I: *Patterns of Migration* (Leicester: Leicester University Press, 1991), p. 51.

33 Patrick O'Meara, 'Irishmen in Eighteenth-Century Russian Service', *Irish Slavonic Studies* 5 (1984), 20.

34 Hennessy, *The Wild Geese*, pp. 107–8.

35 Joseph Fitzgerald Molloy, *The Russian Court in the Eighteenth Century*, 3rd ed. (2 vols, London: Hutchinson, 1906), vol. 1, pp. 18–19.

36 [Anon.], 'Account of the Genealogy of Count O'Rourke', *The Hibernian Magazine*, Mar. 1782.

37 Anthony O'Hara to Charles O'Hara, 8/19 Apr. 1796 (NLI: MS 20,297/4/18); Ekaterina Romanovna Dashkova, *The Memoirs of Princess Dashkova: Russia in the Time of Catherine the Great*, transl., ed. Kyril Fitzlyon (2nd ed., Durham NC: Duke University Press, 1995), p. 185.

38 On the women associated with the Irish military migration to the Continent, see: Casway, 'Irish Women Overseas, 1500–1800', pp. 112–32; Henry, 'Women "Wild Geese"',

Notes 10–16

pp. 23–40; Mary Ann Lyons, "*Digne de compassion*": Female Dependents of Irish Jacobite Soldiers in France, *c.* 1692–*c.* 1730', *Eighteenth-Century Ireland* 23 (2008), 55–75.

39 Casway, 'Irish Women Overseas', p. 119.

40 Ibid., pp. 121–3; Andrea Knox, 'Women of the Wild Geese: Irish Women, Exile and Identity in Spain, 1750–1775', *Immigrants and Minorities* 23:2–3 (2005), 149–59.

41 John P. le Donne, *Absolutism and the Ruling Class: The Formation of the Russian Political Order* (Oxford: Oxford University Press, 1991), pp. 46–7.

42 Elinskaya, 'O'Rurki, Irlandskiya grafi, u Belarusi' ['O'Rourke, the Irish Earl, in Belarus'], 97.

43 *Genealogisches Handbuch der Baltischen Ritterschaften* [*Genealogical Handbook of Baltic Knighthood*], teil 1, 1: Livland (Görlitz, 1929), p. 636.

44 Elinskaya, 'O'Rurki, Irlandskiya grafi, u Belarusi' ['O'Rourke, the Irish Earl, in Belarus'], 96.

45 Ben Hurst, 'A Russian Irish Man', *America*, 29 Oct. 1910.

CHAPTER 2

An earlier version of this section was published as part of my article, 'Irish Soldiers in Russia, 1690–1812: A Re-assessment', *The Irish Sword* 28 (2011), 43–58.

1 Valentine O'Hara, *Anthony O'Hara, Knight of Malta: Memoir of a Russian Diehard* (London: Richards, 1938), p. 27.

2 Anthony O'Hara to Charles O'Hara, 16/27 Dec. 1787 (NLI: MS 20,297/1/1) – spelling has been modernized.

3 O'Hara, *Anthony O'Hara*, p. 12.

4 Patrick M. Geoghegan, 'O'Hara, Charles' in *DIB*.

5 Anthony O'Hara to Charles O'Hara, 14 May 1799 (NLI: MS 20,297/6/23) – English translation by O'Hara, *Anthony O'Hara*, p. 72.

6 Anthony O'Hara to Charles O'Hara, 3/14 Apr. 1804 (NLI: MS 20,297/7/29).

7 Anthony O'Hara to Charles O'Hara, 4 Apr. 1810 (NLI: MS 20,297/8).

8 Anthony O'Hara to Charles Whitworth (copy), 16 Feb. 1794 (NLI: MS 20,297/2/8).

9 See Desmond Gregory, *Malta, Britain, and the European Powers, 1793–1815* (Cranbury NJ: Associated University Presses, 1996) and Dennis Angelo Castillo, *The Maltese Cross: A Strategic History of Malta* (Westport CT: Praeger, 2006).

10 Anthony O'Hara, *Reflections sur les articles énoncés dans le Traite d'Amiens rélativement a l'Ordre de Malthe* [Reflections on the articles stated in the Treaty of Amiens relating to the Order of Malta], 1802 (NLI: MS 20,297/8/30) – English translation by O'Hara, *Anthony O'Hara*, p. 195.

11 Anthony O'Hara to Charles O'Hara, 27 June 1791 (NLI: MS 20,297/1/3) – spelling has been modernized.

12 Anthony O'Hara to Charles O'Hara, 30 Nov./11 Dec. 1795 (NLI: MS 20,297/3/15); O'Hara, *Anthony O'Hara*, p. 150.

13 Anthony O'Hara to Charles O'Hara, 26 Sept./7 Oct. 1796 (NLI: MS 20,297/4/19); Anthony O'Hara to Charles O'Hara, 23 Mar./3 Apr. 1800 (NLI: MS 20,297/7/27).

14 Anthony O'Hara to Charles O'Hara, 30 Nov./11 Dec. 1795 (NLI: MS 20,297/3/15); O'Hara, *Anthony O'Hara*, p. 150.

15 John Hennig, 'Goethe's Friendship with Anthony O'Hara', *Modern Language Review* 39:2 (1944), 146–51.

16 See also Clare O'Halloran, *Golden Ages and Barbarous Nations: Antiquarian Debate and Cultural Politics in Ireland, c. 1750–1800* (Cork: Cork University Press, 2004).

CHAPTER 3

An earlier version of this section was published as part of my article, 'Irish Soldiers in Russia, 1690–1812: A Re-assessment', *The Irish Sword* 28 (2011), 43–58.

1 [Anon.], 'Account of the Genealogy of Count O'Rourke', *The Hibernian Magazine*, Mar. 1782.

2 Ibid.

3 O'Meara, 'Irishmen in Eighteenth-Century Russian Service', 20.

4 [Anon.], 'Account of the Genealogy of Count O'Rourke.'

5 John O'Rourke, *A Treatise on the Art of War: or, Rules for Conducting an Army in All the Various of Regular Campaigns* (London: T. Spilsbury, 1778), preface.

6 [Anon.], 'Account of the Genealogy of Count O'Rourke'.

7 Ibid.

8 *Belfast News Letter*, 12 Jan. 1802.

9 O'Rourke, *A Treatise*, pp. 229–30.

10 [Anon.], *The Case of Count John O'Rourke, Presented to His Majesty, in June, 1784, by His Excellency the Marquis of Carmarthen, Minister and Secretary of State* (London: n.p., 1784), p. 5.

11 [Anon.], 'Account of the Genealogy of Count O'Rourke.'

CHAPTER 4

An earlier version of this section was published as Angela Byrne, "No Longer to be Gazed at as a Distant Glimmering Star': Irish-Born British Diplomats' Accounts of Russia, 1733–1767' in Vanessa Alayrac-Fielding and Ellen R. Welch (eds), *Intermédiaires Culturels / Cultural Intermediaries* (Paris: Honoré Champion Éditeur, 2015), pp. 57–82.

1 Matthew P. Romaniello, *Enterprising Empires: Russia and Britain in Eighteenth-Century Eurasia* (Cambridge: Cambridge University Press, 2019) contains detailed analysis of the treaties negotiated by Forbes and Macartney.

2 J.M. Jigg, rev. R.D.E. Eagles, 'Gunning, Sir Robert, First Baronet' in *ODNB*; Robert Gunning, 'Dispatches' in *SIRIO*, vol. 19, pp. 276–510.

Notes   22–27

3   Diego Téllez Alarcia, 'Richard Wall: Light and Shade of an Irish Minister in Spain (1694–1777)', *Irish Studies Review* 11:2 (2003), 123–36.

4   John Glen King, 'The Present State of the Church of Russia 1767' in Macartney, *An Account of Russia*, pp. 187–230.

5   Kurt Burch, 'The "Properties" of the State System and Global Capitalism' in Stephen J. Rosow, Naeem Inayatullah and Mark Rupert (eds), *The Global Economy as Political Space* (Boulder CO: Lynne Rienner, 1994), p. 51.

6   Martin Malia, *Russia Under Western Eyes: From the Bronze Horseman to the Lenin Mausoleum* (Cambridge MA: Harvard University Press, 1999), p. 21.

7   Michael Bitter, 'George Forbes's "Account of Russia"', *SEER* 82:4 (2004), 892; 'Instructions for Our Right Trusty and Wellbeloved Councillor George, Lord Forbes' in *SIRIO*, vol. 66, pp. 577–82.

8   Bitter, 'George Forbes's "Account of Russia"', 887n; John Forbes, *Memoirs of the Earls of Granard* (London: Longmans, Green, Reader and Dyer, 1868), p. 121.

9   Forbes, *Memoirs*, p. 122.

10   George Forbes to Lord Harrington, 11 Aug. 1733 (OS), in *SIRIO*, vol. 76, p. 61.

11   Kamenskii, *The Russian Empire*; Stephen J. Lee, *Aspects of European History, 1494–1789*, 2nd ed. (London: Routledge, 2000); Joseph H. Shennan, *International Relations in Europe 1689–1789* (London: Routledge, 1995).

12   Hamish Scott, 'Diplomatic Culture in Old Regime Europe' in Hamish Scott and Brendan Simms (eds), *Cultures of Power in Europe During the Long Eighteenth Century* (Cambridge: Cambridge University Press, 2007), p. 69.

13   'English Ministers Abroad – Travellers and Tourists', *The Dublin University Magazine: A Literary and Political Journal* xiv (1839), 31–3.

14   Jennifer Mori, *The Culture of Diplomacy: Britain in Europe, c. 1750–1830* (Manchester: Manchester University Press, 2010), pp. 17–18.

15   David B. Horn, *The British Diplomatic Service, 1689–1789* (Oxford: Oxford University Press, 1961), p. 138.

16   Michael Roberts, 'Russia 1764–7' in Peter Roebuck (ed.), *Macartney of Lisanoure: Essays in Biography* (Belfast: Ulster Historical Foundation, 1983), p. 31.

17   Alfred Webb, *Compendium of Irish Biography* (Dublin: M.H. Gill and Son, 1878), p. 299.

18   Scott, 'Diplomatic Culture', p. 69.

19   Macartney, *An Account of Russia*, p. 48.

20   Ibid., pp. 52–5.

21   Ibid., pp. 51–2.

22   Ibid., pp. 69, 70, 168.

23   Hans Rogger, *National Consciousness in Eighteenth-Century Russia* (Massachusetts: Harvard University Press, 1960), pp. 43–4.

24   Bitter, 'George Forbes's "Account of Russia"', 891–4.

25   The misattribution is probably a result of the dating of Tyrawley's account (13 July 1764). It seems that Tyrawley composed his short account retrospectively, twenty years

after the fact. Nigel E. Saul, 'Lord Tyrawley's *A Succinct Account of Russia*', *SEER* 50 (1972), 436–41.

26 Macartney, *An Account of Russia*, pp. 139, 144, 145, 157; see also pp. 150, 168, 181.

27 Anthony G. Cross, '"A Sort of Connexion with that Country": John Robison's Contribution to Scoto-Russian Cultural Relations', *The Philosophical Age: Almanac 15: Scotland and Russia in the Enlightenment: Proceedings of the International Conference* (St Petersburg: Centre for History of Ideas, 2001), p. 55, available at http://ideashistory. org.ru/a15.html.

28 Scott, 'Diplomatic Culture', 61.

29 George Macartney to Lord Sandwich, 21 July 1765 (PRONI: MIC/227/1). Spelling has been modernized.

30 Roberts, 'Russia 1764–7', pp. 59–60.

31 Michael Roberts, *Macartney in Russia: English Historical Review*, supplement no. 7 (London: Longmans, Green and Co., 1974), p. 72; Cross, *By the Banks of the Neva*, p. 377; Mori, *The Culture of Diplomacy*, pp. 64–6.

32 Henry Shirley to Secretary Conway, 28 May 1767, in *SIRIO*, vol. 12, p. 301.

33 James Jefferies to Lord Stanhope, 9 Jan. 1718 (OS), in *SIRIO*, vol. 61, pp. 466–7.

34 James Jefferies to George Tilson, 22 Jan. 1719 (OS), in *SIRIO*, vol. 61, p. 480.

35 James Jefferies to Lord Stanhope, 6 Feb. 1719 (OS), in *SIRIO*, vol. 61, pp. 486–7.

36 James Jefferies to Lord Stanhope, 3 Apr. 1719 (OS), in *SIRIO*, vol. 61, pp. 513–15.

37 George Forbes, 'Account of Russia', 1733–4 (Castle Forbes, Co. Longford: PRONI microfilm, T/375/H/6/11/1–6 and MIC/568, pp. 1–2, 15, 51) – spelling has been modernized.

38 Macartney, *An Account of Russia*, pp. 63, 64, 83, 89, 90; 79–81; 101, 117; 132; 119; 63–4.

39 Forbes, 'Account of Russia', pp. 11–12, 25.

40 Macartney, *An Account of Russia*, p. 25.

41 William E.H. Lecky, *A History of Ireland in the Eighteenth Century* (Chicago: University of Chicago Press, 1972), p. 255.

42 Thomas Bartlett (ed.), *Macartney in Ireland, 1768–72: A Calendar of the Chief Secretaryship Papers of Sir George Macartney* (Belfast: PRONI, 1979), p. 341.

43 Peter Roebuck, 'Later Years 1780–1806', in Roebuck (ed.), *Macartney of Lisanoure*, pp. 296–300; Roland Thorne, 'Macartney, George, Earl Macartney' in *ODNB*.

44 Matthew Smith Anderson, *Europe in the Eighteenth Century 1713–1789* (London: Longman, 1987), p. 73.

45 Macartney, *An Account of Russia*, p. vi.

46 Ibid., p. 48.

47 Ibid., pp. 56–7.

48 Ibid., pp. 39–40.

49 Hendriette Kliemann-Geisinger, 'Mapping the North – Spatial Dimensions and Geographical Concepts of Northern Europe' in Karen Klitgaard Povlsen (ed.), *Northbound: Travels, Encounters, and Constructions 1700–1830* (Aarhus: Aarhus University Press, 2007), pp. 69–88; Janet M. Hartley, 'Is Russia Part of Europe?

Notes 34–40

Russian Perceptions of Europe in the Reign of Alexander I', *Cahiers du Monde Russe et Soviétique* 33:4 (1992), 369–85.

50 Macartney, *An Account of Russia*, p. 84.

51 John Barrow (ed.), *Some Account of the Public Life, and a Selection from the Unpublished Writings, of the Earl of Macartney* (London: Cadell and Davies, 1807), vol. 1, p. v.

SECTION 11

1 Amanda E. Herbert, *Female Alliances: Gender, Identity, and Friendship in Early Modern Britain* (New Haven: Yale University Press, 2014), p. 117.

2 Jeremy Black, *The British Abroad: The Grand Tour in the Eighteenth Century* (New York: St Martin's Press, 1992), pp. 56, 183.

3 'Senex' [Horatio Townsend], 'Recollections of a Trip to Spa', *Blackwood's Magazine*, Sept. 1827, 292–3.

4 George Macartney to the Earl of Sandwich, 1 Mar. 1765, in *SIRIO*, vol. 12, pp. 199–200.

5 Janet Todd, *Rebel Daughters: Ireland in Conflict 1798* (London: Viking, 2003), p. 326.

6 Eleanor Cavanagh to Henrietta Chetwood, 20 Aug. 1805 [copy made by Martha Wilmot] (RIA: MS 12L33, pp. 12–16).

7 Martha Wilmot, Journal, 1805 (RIA: MS 12L19, pp. 55–7).

8 Cormac Ó Gráda, 'Poverty, Population, and Agriculture, 1801–45' in W.E. Vaughan (ed.), *A New History of Ireland v: Ireland Under the Union, 1801–70* (Oxford: Oxford University Press, 1989), pp. 109–10; Christopher Woods, *Travellers' Accounts as Source-Material for Irish Historians* (Dublin: Four Courts Press, 2010), pp. 26–8.

9 Martha Wilmot to her mother Martha Wilmot (*née* Moore), 12 Feb. 1804 (RIA: MS 12L24, p. 165).

10 William Wilde, 'Failures of Crops, Years of Scarcity, Famines, etc.' in *The Census of Ireland for the Year 1851: Part V: Tables of Deaths, vol. I: Containing the Report, Table of Pestilences, and Analysis of the Tables of Deaths* (Dublin: Alexander Thom, 1856), p. 362; Christine Kinealy, Gerard Moran and Jason King (eds), *'Fallen Leaves of Humanity': Famines in Ireland before and after the Great Famine* (London: Routledge, 2018).

11 Martha Wilmot, Journal, 1803–5 (RIA: MS 12L18, p. 108).

12 Martha Wilmot, Journal, 1805–7 (RIA: MS 12L20, p. 187).

CHAPTER 5

1 France is suggested in both Vyacheslav V. Bondarenko, *Vyazemsky* (Moscow: Molodaya Gvardya, 2004), p. 18, and [A.G. Cross], 'A Russian in Georgian England: An Anonymous Still Unidentified' in *Von Wenigen. ot Hemnogikh* (St Petersburg: Izdatelstvo Pushkinskogo Doma, 2008), p. 86.

2 The *Listes des Seigneurs et Dames Venus aux Eaux Minérales de Spa* are available at http://swedhs.org/visiteurs/index.html.

3 Pis'ma Vyazemskogo, A.I. Vyazemskoi Evgenii Ivanovne (urozhd. O'Reili, po pervomu muzhu Kvin). Priloriani annotatsii Vyazemskogo P.P. [Vyazemsky Letters.

A.I. Vyazemsky to Evgeniya Ivanovna (*née* O'Reilly, m. Quinn). With annotations by P.P. Vyazemsky], 1784–6 (RGALI: F. 195, op. 1, d. 453).

4   *Listes de Visiteurs*, 7. Aug. 1783.

5   A.I. Vyazemsky, Puteviya zametki [Travel Notes] in 'F.I. Bulgakov (ed.), *Ostafyevsky arkhiv knyazya A.I. Vyazemskikh: Andrey Ivanovich Vyazemsky, Knyaz', 1754–1807* [*Ostafyevo Archive of Prince A.I. Vyazemsky: Andrey Ivanovich Vyazemsky, Prince, 1754–1807*] (St Petersburg: Izdatelstvo S.D. Sheremeteva, 1881), pp. 343–4.

6   Cross, 'A Russian in Georgian England', p. 87.

7   Vyazemsky, Puteviya zametki [Travel Notes], p. 344.

8   The portrait is a miniature, one of a pair made of Jenny and Andrey by Xavier de Maistre. They were moved from Ostafyevo to the State Tretyakov Gallery, Moscow, in 1930, where they remain. It has not been possible to reproduce the portrait in this book due to sanctions imposed on Russia following the illegal invasion of Ukraine.

9   'Vlestyashchii sin zlatogo veka: N.M. Karamzin i ego epokha' [Leading Son of the Golden Age: N.M. Karamzin and his Era] project website. Available at http://karamzin.rusarchives.ru/personalii/vyazemskaya-evgeniya-ivanovna.

10 Bondarenko, *Vyazemsky*, p. 20.

11 M.J. O'Reilly, 'The House of O'Reilly. Curious Records and Family Documents', 1868 (NLI: O'Reilly MSS: microfilm p1030–1).

12 *Ostafyevsky arkhiv knyazya A.I. Vyazemskikh* [*Ostafyevo Archive of Prince A.I. Vyazemsky*], pp. v–vi.

13 Priscilla Roosevelt, *Life on the Russian Country Estate: A Social and Cultural History* (New Haven: Yale University Press, 1995), p. 301.

14 For example, Pis'ma Vyazemskoi Evgenii Ivanovni (urozhd. O'Reili, po pervomu muzhu Kvin) Vyazemskomu A.I. [Letters of Evgeniya Ivanovna Vyazemsky (*née* O'Reilly, m. Quinn) to A.I. Vyazemsky], 1793–6 (RGALI: F. 195, op. 1, d. 488(2), l. 67).

15 Pis'ma Vyazemskoi Evgenii Ivanovni (urozhd. O'Reili, po pervomu braku Kvin) k muzhu Vyazemskomu Andreyu Ivanovichu [Letters of Evgeniya Ivanovna Vyazemsky (*née* O'Reilly, m. Quinn) to her husband Andrey Ivanovich Vyazemsky], 1784–88 (RGALI: F. 195, op. 1, d. 487(1), l. 40).

16 Bondarenko, *Vyazemsky*, p. 21.

17 Petr Vyazemsky to Ivan Turgenev, 14 Nov. 1828 in 'V.I. Saitov (ed.), *Ostafyevsky arkhiv knyazey Vyazemskikh tom 3: Perepiska Knyazya P.A. Vyazemskago s A.I. Turgenevem, 1824–1836* [*Ostafyevo Archive of the Princes Vyazemsky vol. 3: Letters of Prince P.A. Vyazemsky to A.I. Turgenev, 1824–1836*], (St Petersburg: Stasyulevich, 1899), pp. 181–3. Petr may have inferred the Bordeaux connection from the prominence of an Irish family by that name in the French city.

18 Donald Davie, 'The Poetry of Prince Vyazemsky (1792–1878)', *Hermathena* 86 (1955): 3–19, here 7–8.

19 Pis'ma Vyazemskoi Evgenii Ivanovni (urozhd. O'Reili, po pervomu muzhu Kvin) Vyazemskomu A.I. [Letters of Evgeniya Ivanovna Vyazemsky (*née* O'Reilly, m. Quinn) to A.I. Vyazemsky], 1793–6 (RGALI: F. 195, op. 1, d. 488(1), l. 26).

Notes 44–49

20 Pis'ma Vyazemskoi Evgenii Ivanovni (urozhd. O'Reili, po pervomu braku Kvin) k muzhu Vyazemskomu Andreyu Ivanovichu [Letters of Evgeniya Ivanovna Vyazemsky (*née* O'Reilly, m. Quinn) to her husband Andrey Ivanovich Vyazemsky], 1784–88 (RGALI: F. 195, op. 1, d. 487(2), l. 66).

21 John P. le Donne, 'Appointments to the Russian Senate', *Cahiers du Monde Russe* 16:1 (1975), 44.

22 Ekaterina Romanovna Dashkova, *The Memoirs of Princess Dashkova: Russia in the Time of Catherine the Great*, transl., ed. Kyril Fitzlyon, 2nd ed. (Durham NC: Duke University Press, 1995), pp. 206–7, 211–12.

CHAPTER 6

1 Letters from Arabella Denny to Princess Dashkova, 14–18 July 1780 and 23 Dec. 1780, in Ekaterina Romanovna Dashkova, *Memoirs of the Princess Daschkaw, Lady of Honour to Catherine II, Empress of all the Russias, Written by Herself, Comprising Letters of the Empress, and Other Correspondence*, transl., ed. Martha Bradford [*née* Wilmot] (2 vols, London: Henry Colburn, 1840), vol. II, pp. 137–44.

2 Ekaterina Romanovna Dashkova, 'Autobiographical Memoirs, in French, of Ekaterina Romanovna, Princess Dashkova (or Daschkaw), Transcribed, in 1805, During a Residence with the Princess, by Miss Martha Wilmot, Afterwards Mrs. Bradford, from the Original Draught', 1805 (BL: MS 31911, ff. 12–16).

3 Arthur Pollock to his father, 12 Oct. 1806, Apr. 1807 (Mountainstown House, Co. Meath: NLI microfilm p5308, Pollock Papers); Martha Wilmot, Journal, 1805–7 (RIA: MS 12L20, p. 255).

4 Dashkova, 'Autobiographical Memoirs', ff. 250–3, translated from the original French by the author.

5 Dashkova, *Memoirs*, vol. I, p. 152.

6 Mr 'de Worontzow' is named, and Mlle Kamensky is named as nanny to Dashkova's children, in *Memoirs*, vol. I, p. 152.

7 Mary Hamilton, Diary, Aug.–Oct. 1776 (Manchester University Library: GB 133 HAM/2/1).

8 Morgan's family (the Tisdalls) are recorded in Spa in 1768, 1772 and 1776 (*Listes de Visiteurs*); Dashkova, *Memoirs*, vol. I, pp. 158–9.

9 Roosevelt, *Life on the Russian Country Estate*, p. 338n; Katherine Wilmot to Anna Maria Chetwood, 1 Oct. 1805 (RIA: MS 12L30, p. 44).

10 Dashkova, *Memoirs*, vol. I, pp. 159–60, 174–5.

11 Ibid., vol. I, p. 189.

12 Ibid., vol. I, pp. 162–3.

13 Angela Byrne, 'Les voyageuses irlandaises à Spa au 18e siècle' [Female Travellers to Spa in the Eighteenth Century] in Daniel Droixhe with Muriel Collart (eds), *Spa, Carrefour de l'Europe des Lumières. Les Hôtes de la Cité Thermale au XVIIIe Siècle* [Spa, Crossroads of Enlightenment Europe. The Hosts of the Thermal City in the Eighteenth Century] (Paris: Hermann, 2013), pp. 67–87.

214

14 Elizabeth Eger, 'Paper Trails and Eloquent Objects: Bluestocking Friendship and Material Culture', *Parergon* 26:2 (2009), 109–38.

15 Herbert, *Female Alliances*, pp. 22–3.

16 Dashkova, 'Autobiographical Memoirs', ff. 263, 265.

17 The letter is reproduced in *Materialy dlia biografii knyagini E.R. Dashkovoi [Sources for a Biography of Princess Dashkova]* (Leipzig: E.L. Kasprowicz, 1876), pp. 158–61.

18 Martha Wilmot, Journal, 1805–7 (RIA: MS 12L20, pp. 210–13). For more on the Wilmots and their wider circle, see my 'Life after Emmet's Death: Sarah Curran's Literary and Friendship Circle', *Irish Studies Review* 30:2 (2022), 119–135 and my 'Anonymity, Irish Women's Writing, and a Tale of Contested Authorship: *Blue-Stocking Hall* (1827) and *Tales of my Time* (1829)', *Proceedings of the Royal Irish Academy* 119C (2019), 259–81; and Alexis Wolf, 'The 'Original' Journals of Katherine Wilmot: Women's Travel Writing in the Salon of Helen Maria Williams', *European Romantic Review* 30:5–6 (2019), 615–37.

19 The will is reproduced in Ekaterina Romanovna Dashkova, *Zapiski knyagini Dashkovoi*, ed. Nikolai D. Chechulin (St Petersburg: Izdatelstvo A.S. Suvorina, 1907), pp. 318–23.

20 Martha Wilmot, Journal, 1807–8 (RIA: MS 12L21, p. 219).

21 Martha Wilmot, Journal, 1808 (RIA: MS 12L22, pp. 119–20).

22 Ibid., p. 120.

23 Ibid., p. 160.

24 Ibid., pp. 90, 142.

25 Ibid., pp. 142, 149–50. Spelling has been modernized.

26 Diana Scarisbrick, 'Companion to a Russian Princess: Martha Wilmot's Green Book', *Country Life* 169 (1981), 76–8. See also Emma Gleadhill and Ekaterina Heath, 'Giving Women History: A History of Ekaterina Dashkova through Her Gifts to Catherine the Great and Others', *Women's History Review* 31:3 (2022), 361–86; Pamela Buck, 'From Russia with Love: Souvenirs and Political Alliance in Martha Wilmot's *The Russian Journals*' in Ileana Baird and Christina Ionescu (eds), *Eighteenth-Century Thing Theory in a Global Context: From Consumerism to Celebrity Culture* (Farnham: Ashgate, 2013), pp. 133–48.

27 Martha Wilmot, Journal, 1805 (RIA: MS 12L19, pp. 129–30).

28 Katherine Wilmot to Anna Maria Chetwood, 24 Sept. 1805 (RIA: MS 12L30, p. 41) – italics added.

29 Katherine Wilmot to Anna Maria Chetwood, 1 Oct. 1805 (RIA: MS 12L30, p. 44); Martha Wilmot, Journal, 1807–8 (RIA: MS 12L21, p. 165).

30 Martha Wilmot, Journal, 1807–8 (RIA: MS 12L21, p. 171) – italics added.

31 Harford Montgomery Hyde, *The Empress Catherine and Princess Dashkov* (London: Whitefriars Press, 1935), p. vii.

32 Simon Dixon, 'The Posthumous Reputation of Catherine II in Russia 1797–1837', *SEER* 77:4 (1999), 656.

33 Simon Vorontsov to Martha Bradford (*née* Wilmot), 26 Jan. 1813 (RIA: MS 12M18).

Notes 52–59

34 Dashkova, *Memoirs*, vol. I, pp. xxviii–xxix.

35 *The Literary Gazette and Journal of the Belles Lettres, Arts, Sciences, etc.* no. 1212 (11 Apr. 1840).

36 *The Monthly Review*, May–Aug. 1840.

37 Maria Edgeworth, Letter to Martha Bradford (*née* Wilmot), 27 July 1840 (British Museum, Add. MS 41295: NLI microfilm p1284, pp. 121–6).

38 Edgeworth to Bradford (*née* Wilmot), 27 July 1840, pp. 123–4.

39 Maria Edgeworth to Anna Ticknor, 19 Nov. 1840, in Helen Zimmern, *Maria Edgeworth* (London: W.H. Allen and Co., 1883), p. 204.

40 Dashkova, *Memoirs*, vol. II, p. 361.

41 Catherine Wilmot and Martha Wilmot, *The Russian Journals of Martha and Catherine Wilmot*, ed. Harford Montgomery Hyde and Edith Stewart (London: Macmillan, 1934), p. 79.

42 Toby W. Clyman and Judith Vowles (eds), *Russia Through Women's Eyes: Autobiographies from Tsarist Russia* (New Haven: Yale University Press, 1999), p. 18.

43 Dashkova, *Memoirs*, vol. I, p. xxi.

44 Ibid., p. 204.

45 Beth Holmgren, 'Introduction' in idem. (ed.) *The Russian Memoir: History and Literature* (Evanston: Northwestern University Press, 2003), p. xvii.

46 Martha Wilmot, Journal, 1805 (RIA: MS 12L19, p. 13).

CHAPTER 7

1 J.H. Adeane (ed.), *The Early Married Life of Maria Josepha, Lady Stanley, with Extracts from Sir John Stanley's 'Praeterita'* (London: Longmans, Green and Co., 1899), p. 332.

2 Morgan to Martha Wilmot, 19 Feb. 1810 (RIA: MS 12M18).

3 Dashkova, *Memoirs*, vol. II, pp. 324–32.

4 Eleanor Cavanagh to Henrietta Chetwood, 20 Aug. 1805 [copy made by Martha Wilmot] (RIA: MS 12L33, pp 12–16, and copy at RIA: MS 12L30, pp. 21–30); Eleanor Cavanagh to her father, 4 Oct. 1805 (RIA: MS 12L33, pp 25–29, and copy at RIA: MS 12L30, pp. 48–57). All quotes in this section are from these two letters, unless otherwise noted. Punctuation and spelling have been modernized where it aids the reader.

5 Michelle Lamarche Marrese, 'Liberty Postponed: Princess Dashkova and the Defense of Serfdom' in Sue Ann Prince (ed.), *The Princess and the Patriot: Ekaterina Dashkova, Benjamin Franklin, and the Age of Enlightenment* (Philadelphia: American Philosophical Society, 2006), pp. 23–38. On the treatment of serfs, see Michelle Lamarche Marrese, *A Woman's Kingdom: Noblewomen and the Control of Property in Russia, 1700–1861* (Ithaca: Cornell University Press, 2002), pp. 229–37.

6 Martha Wilmot, Journal, 1805–7 (RIA: MS 12L20, p. 25). For a detailed account of life in Moscow in the period, see Alexander M. Martin, *Enlightened Metropolis: Constructing Imperial Moscow, 1762–1855* (Oxford: Oxford University Press, 2013).

7 Martha Wilmot, Journal, 1805 (RIA: MS 12L19, p. 116).

8 Roosevelt, *Life on the Russian Country Estate*, p. 103.

9 Eleanor Cavanagh to her father, 4 Oct. 1805 (RIA: MS 12L33, p. 29).

10 Martha Wilmot to her family, 17 Nov. 1803 (RIA: MS 12L24, p. 126).

11 Katherine Wilmot to Alicia Wilmot, 2 Dec. 1805 (RIA: MS12L33, pp. 31–41).

12 Roosevelt, *Life on the Russian Country Estate*, p. 215.

SECTION III

1 John Ladeveze Adlercron, Journal of a Tour made ... in Russia by way of Denmark and Poland, 1805 (NLI: MS 3756); Adlercron Papers, including European passports issued to members of the family, 18th cent. (NLI: MS 8730); Arthur Pollock, Letters from Sweden and Russia to his Family, 1806–07 (Mountainstown House, Co. Meath: NLI microfilm p5308, Pollock Papers); A.P.W. Malcolmson, *Archbishop Charles Agar: Churchmanship and Politics in Ireland, 1760–1810* (Dublin: Four Courts Press, 2002), pp. 78–9, 85; Letter from 1st Earl to Viscount Somerton in Russia, 1806 (Hampshire Archives and Local Studies: 21M57/2A1/59 item 1); Lord Somerton to Agar, Moscow, introducing Mr Adlercron, 4–16 Mar. 1807 (PRONI: T3719/C/41/9).

2 Travel permit issued at St Petersburg to Corry Connellan, 13 Aug. 1845 (NAI: M.3730); Corry Connellan, 'A March to Palmyra', *New Monthly Magazine and Humorist* 74 (1845), 115–30.

3 John Ross Browne, *The Land of Thor* (New York: Harper and Brothers, 1867).

4 Ladeveze Adlercron, Journal of a Tour.

5 Anthony Swift, 'Russia and the Great Exhibition of 1851: Representations, Perceptions, and a Missed Opportunity', *Jahrbücher für Geschichte Osteuropas* 55:2 (2007), 242–63.

6 Daniel Wheeler to unknown recipient, 6 Dec. 1815 (Library of the Religious Society of Friends in Ireland: portfolio 9.36); William Patterson to unknown recipient, 15 Sept. 1815 (Library of the Religious Society of Friends in Ireland: portfolio 4.32); M.C. to her mother, 24 Nov. 1815 (Library of the Religious Society of Friends in Ireland: Fennell Collection, MSS Box 26, box ii g., letter 27); Robert Walsh, 'Reminiscences of Russia', *The Amulet: A Christian and Literary Remembrancer* 10 (1835), 145–76.

7 For a useful overview of this period and Alexander I's rule, see Alexander Polunov, *Russia in the Nineteenth Century: Autocracy, Reform, and Social Change, 1814–1914*, transl. Marshall S. Shatz (New York: M.E. Sharpe, 2005), pp. 27–50. See also Martin Malia, *Russia under Western Eyes: From the Bronze Horseman to the Lenin Mausoleum* (Cambridge MA: Harvard University Press, 1999).

CHAPTER 8

1 [Anon.], 'Pawnbroking in Ireland. Mr Barrington's Suggestions – Charitable Institution of Limerick', *The Dublin University Magazine: A Literary and Political Journal* 15 (1839), 675.

2 Heidi Hansson, 'The Gentleman's North: Lord Dufferin and the Beginnings of Arctic Tourism', *Studies in Travel Writing* 13:1 (2009), 61–73; Priti Joshi, 'Edwin Chadwick's

Notes 67–71

Self-Fashioning: Professionalism, Masculinity, and the Victorian Poor', *Victorian Literature and Culture* 32 (2004), 353–70.

3   Angela Byrne, 'A Gentlemanly Tour on the Fringes of Europe: William Hartigan Barrington in Scandinavia and Russia, 1837', *Irish Economic and Social History* 40 (2013), 31–47. DOI: https://doi.org/10.7227/IESH.40.1.2.

4   See Philip Carter, *Men and the Emergence of Polite Society* (London: Pearson Education, 2001); Michèle Cohen, '"Manners" Make the Man: Politeness, Chivalry, and the Construction of Masculinity, 1750–1830', *Journal of British Studies* 44:2 (2005), 312–29; Lee Davidoff and Catherine Hall, *Family Fortunes: Men and Women of the English Middle-Class, 1780–1850* (Chicago: University of Chicago Press, 1987); John Tosh, *Manliness and Masculinities in Nineteenth-Century Britain: Essays on Gender, Family, and Empire* (New York: Pearson Education, 2005).

5   Richard Lovell Edgeworth, *Essays on Professional Education* (London: J. Johnston, 1809), pp. 265–6.

6   W.H. Barrington, 'Journey to Moscow and Back', 1837 (NLI: MS 34,390/2), 27 June, 2 Sept., 14 Oct., 20 Oct., 10 Nov., 18 Nov.

7   Ibid., 21 Aug., 24 Aug.

8   Ibid., 6 July, 10 July.

9   Ibid., 21 July; Isabel de Madariaga, 'The Foundation of the Russian Educational System by Catherine II', *SEER* 57 (1979), 377.

10 Barrington, 'Journey to Moscow and Back', 25 July.

11 See Hubertus Jahn, 'Health Care and Poor Relief in Russia, 1700–1856' in Ole Peter Grell and Andrew Cunningham (eds), *Health Care and Poor Relief in Protestant Europe* (London: Routledge, 1997), pp. 157–71; Adele Lindenmeyr, 'The Ethos of Charity in Imperial Russia', *Journal of Social History* 23 (1990), 679–94; Adele Lindenmeyr, 'Public Life, Private Virtues: Women in Russian Charity, 1762–1914', *Signs* 18 (1993), 562–91; Wendy Rosslyn, 'Female Philanthropy in Early Nineteenth-Century Russia', *SEER* 84 (2006), 52–82.

12 Barrington, 'Journey to Moscow and Back', 17 July, 22 July.

13 This letter was copied into Barrington, 'Journey to Moscow and Back'.

14 Nini Rodgers, *Ireland, Slavery and Anti-Slavery: 1612–1865* (Houndmills: Palgrave Macmillan, 2007); Dom Mark Tierney, *Murroe and Boher: The History of an Irish Country Parish* (Dublin: Browne and Nolan, 1966), p. 151.

15 Marion McGarry, 'Creating a Noble Past: The Design of Glenstal Castle, 1836–61', *History Ireland* 18:2 (2010), 29; Helen Andrews, 'Barrington, Sir Matthew' in *DIB*.

16 Róisín Healy, *Poland in the Irish Nationalist Imagination, 1772–1922: Anti-Colonialism within Europe* (Basingstoke: Palgrave Macmillan, 2017), p. 100.

17 Barrington, 'Journey to Moscow and Back', 25 July.

18 Ibid., 28 Sept. On Norwegian poor relief, see Øivind Larsen, 'Ideology or Pragmatism? Health Care Provision and Poor Relief in Norway in the Nineteenth Century' in Ole Peter Grell and Andrew Cunningham (eds), *Health Care and Poor Relief in Protestant Europe* (London: Routledge, 1997), pp. 189–200.

71–78 *Notes*

19 Barrington, 'Journey to Moscow and Back', 25 July.

20 Barrington, 'Journey to Moscow and Back', 1 July.

21 See Cormac Ó Gráda, 'Poverty, Population, and Agriculture, 1801–45' in W.E. Vaughan (ed.), *A New History of Ireland v: Ireland Under the Union, 1801–70* (Oxford: Oxford University Press, 1989), pp. 109–10; Christopher Woods, *Travellers' Accounts as Source-Material for Irish Historians* (Dublin: Four Courts Press, 2010), pp. 26–8.

CHAPTER 9

1 All biographical information is from Sylvie Kleinman and Patrick M. Geoghegan, 'Kavanagh, Arthur Macmorrough' in *DIB*.

2 Sarah L. Steele, *The Right Honourable Arthur Macmurrough Kavanagh: A Biography* (London: Macmillan, 1891). Letter quoted in Donald McCormick, *The Incredible Mr Kavanagh* (London: Putnam, 1960), p. 79.

3 Janet M. Hartley, *The Volga: A History of Russia's Greatest River* (New Haven and London: Yale University Press, 2021), pp. 6–7.

4 Arthur Kavanagh to Mrs C. Doyne, 27 Aug. 1849, in Kavanagh Papers: Copies [by Lady Harriet Kavanagh] of letters from her son Arthur MacMurrough Kavanagh and from the Rev. David Wood describing a tour to Russia, 1 June–5 Oct. 1849 (NLI: microfilm p7156), pp. 28–30. Hereafter, Kavanagh Papers [1].

5 Arthur Kavanagh, *The Cruise of the R.Y.S. Eva* (Dublin: Hodges, Smith and Co., 1865), pp. v–vi. The *Eva* was said to have been named after Eva Gore-Booth (Thomas Kilgallon, 'Reminiscences', typescript (PRONI: D/4131/D/2/1, p. 36).

6 Maurice Moore, *An Irish Gentleman: George Henry Moore* (London: T. Werner Laurie Ltd, 1913), p. 33; Maurice Moore, 'George Henry Moore', *The Irish Review* 4:37 (1914), 34–45.

7 Moore, *An Irish Gentleman*, pp. 31–2.

8 Revd David Wood to Lady H. Kavanagh, 1 June 1849, Kavanagh Papers [1], p. 2.

9 Thomas Kavanagh to Lady H. Kavanagh, 29 July 1849, Kavanagh Papers [1], pp. 9–12.

10 Arthur Kavanagh to Lady H. Kavanagh, 8 Aug. 1849, Kavanagh Papers [1], pp. 13–17.

11 Arthur Kavanagh to his sister, 29 July 1849; Arthur Kavanagh to Lady H. Kavanagh, 12 Aug. 1849, Kavanagh Papers [1], pp. 12–13, pp. 22–5.

12 Quoted in Steele, *The Right Honourable Arthur Macmurrough Kavanagh*, pp. 31–2.

13 Christopher Ely, 'The Origins of Russian Scenery: Volga River Tourism and Russian Landscape Aesthetics', *Slavic Review* 62:4 (2003), *Tourism and Travel in Russia and the Soviet Union*, 666–82.

14 Rayford Ramble, *Travelling Opinions and Sketches, in Russia and Poland* (Dublin: John Cumming, 1836).

15 Quoted in Steele, *The Right Honourable Arthur Macmurrough Kavanagh*, pp. 34, 36.

16 Quoted in ibid., pp. 37–8.

17 Quoted in ibid., pp. 40–41.

18 Quoted in ibid., p. 42.

Notes 79–85

19 Diary extracts in ibid., pp. 45–9.

20 Quoted in McCormick, *The Incredible Mr Kavanagh*, p. 110.

21 Jeanne-Marie Warzeski, 'Mapping the Unknown: Gendered Spaces and the Oriental Other in Travelogues of Egypt by U.S. Women, 1854–1914', *History and Anthropology* 13:4 (2002), 310. See also Malek Alloula, *The Colonial Harem: Theory and History of Literature* (Minneapolis: University of Minnesota Press, 1986), and Inderpal Grewal, *Home and Harem: Nation, Gender, Empire, and the Cultures of Travel* (Durham NC: Duke University Press, 1996).

22 Quoted in Steele, *The Right Honourable Arthur Macmurrough Kavanagh*, p. 52. Emphasis added.

23 Arthur Kavanagh to Lady H. Kavanagh, 8 Aug. 1849, Kavanagh Papers [1].

24 Arthur Kavanagh to Lady H. Kavanagh, 12 Aug. 1849, Kavanagh Papers [1], pp. 22–5.

25 Thomas Kavanagh to Lady H. Kavanagh, 30 Aug. 1849, Kavanagh Papers: Letters to Lady Harriet Kavanagh mainly from her son Thomas, but also some letters from her son Arthur, during their tours in Russia, the Middle East and India, with some associated correspondence, *c.* 1845–1851 (NLI microfilm p7157).

26 Steele, *The Right Honourable Arthur Macmurrough Kavanagh*, pp. 125–6.

CHAPTER 10

1 Roderick McGrew, *Russia and the Cholera* (Madison WI: Wisconsin University Press, 1965), p. 5; Charlotte E. Henze, *Disease, Health Care and Government in Late Imperial Russia: Life and Death on the Volga, 1823–1914* (London: Routledge, 2011), p. 20; David Moon, *The Russian Peasantry 1600–1930: The World the Peasants Made* (London: Routledge, 1999), p. 29.

2 Martha Bradford to Viscountess Ennismore, 8 Dec. 1819, in Martha Bradford (*née* Wilmot), *More Letters from Martha Wilmot: Impressions of Vienna 1819–29*, ed. Harford Montgomery Hyde and Edith Stewart (London: Macmillan, 1935), p. 35.

3 Martha Bradford to Alicia Wilmot, 18 May 1821, in Bradford (*née* Wilmot), *More Letters from Martha Wilmot*, p. 107.

4 Martha Bradford to Alicia Wilmot, 27 Feb. 1823, in Bradford (*née* Wilmot), *More Letters from Martha Wilmot*, p. 187. William Bradford's sketch of John Bloomfield is reproduced in ibid., facing p. 196.

5 Ouseley's journey from Tbilisi to St Petersburg in 1814 is described in a personal account published in Gore Ouseley, *Biographical Notices of Persian Poets with Critical and Explanatory Remarks. To which is Prefixed a Memoir of Sir Gore Ouseley by J. Reynolds* (London: Oriental Translation Fund, 1846), pp. cxvii–ccxiv.

6 Mary Cahill and John Ó Néill, 'A Tortuous Tale – A New Twist on the Torcs from "Tara"', *Archaeology Ireland* 35:1 (2021), 32.

7 See Jean Lombard, *An Irish Woman in Czarist Russia* (Dublin: Ashfield Press, 2010).

8 E.M. Lloyd, rev. A.J. Heesom, 'Vane [formerly Stewart], Charles William, Third Marquess of Londonderry' in *ODNB*; Charles William Vane, *Recollections of a Tour*

220

86–95 *Notes*

in the North of Europe (2 vols, London: Richard Bentley, 1838); T.H. Sanderson, rev. H.C.G. Matthew, 'Plunkett, Sir Francis Richard' in *ODNB*; H.M. Stephens, rev. H.C.G. Matthew, 'Crampton, Sir John Fiennes Twisleton, Second Baronet' in *ODNB*; Patrick M. Geoghegan, 'O'Conor, Sir Nicholas Roderick' in *DIB*.

9 All biographical information is from H.M. Chichester, rev. Roger T. Stearn, 'Bloomfield, Benjamin, first Baron Bloomfield' in *ODNB*.

10 Georgiana Bloomfield (ed.), *Memoir of Benjamin, Lord Bloomfield* (2 vols, London: Chapman and Hall, 1884), vol. 2, p. 33.

11 Isabel de Madariaga, *Russia in the Age of Catherine the Great* (London: Phoenix Press, 2002), p. 516.

12 Personal recollections by Georgiana Bloomfield, in her introduction to *Memoir of Benjamin, Lord Bloomfield*, vol. I, pp. 8–10.

13 Excerpts from Benjamin's diary, in Bloomfield (ed.), *Memoir of Benjamin, Lord Bloomfield*, vol. II, pp. 89, 92, 94.

14 Georgiana Bloomfield, *Reminiscences of Court and Diplomatic Life* (2 vols, London: Kegan Paul, Trench and Co., 1883), vol. I, pp. 168–9; Richard McMahon, *A Violent Society? Homicide Rates in Ireland, 1831–1850* (Liverpool: Liverpool University Press, 2014); Christine Kinealy, *This Great Calamity: The Irish Famine 1845–52* (Dublin: Gill and Macmillan, 2006); Christine Kinealy, Gerard Moran and Jason King (eds), *'Fallen Leaves of Humanity': Famines in Ireland before and after the Great Famine* (London: Routledge, 2018).

15 Quotes from Georgiana's diaries and letters, in Bloomfield, *Reminiscences of Court and Diplomatic Life*, vol. I, pp. vii, 141, 168, 276, 292–3, 296–7.

CHAPTER 11

1 Clare Anderson, 'The Andaman Islands Penal Colony: Race, Class, Criminality, and the British Empire', *International Review of Social History* 63(S26) (2018), 25–43.

2 [Anon.], 'Russia', *The University Magazine: A Literary and Philosophic Review* 29:152 (Feb. 1847), 263.

3 Richard Southwell Bourke, *St Petersburg and Moscow: A Visit to the Court of the Czar* (2 vols, London: Henry Colburn, 1846) – all subsequent quotes in this section are from this edition of the book unless otherwise noted.

4 W.W. Hunter, *A Life of the Earl of Mayo, Fourth Viceroy of India* ([1875] 2nd ed., 2 vols, London: Smith, Elder and Co., 1876), vol. I, p. 56.

5 James Quinn, 'Bourke, Richard Southwell' in *DIB*; and Timothy G. McMahon, 'The Assassination and Apotheosis of the Earl of Mayo' in Timothy G. McMahon, Michael de Nie and Paul Townend (eds), *Ireland in an Imperial World: Citizenship, Opportunism, and Subversion* (London: Palgrave Macmillan, 2017), pp. 90–110.

6 Gerald Morgan, *Anglo-Russian Rivalry in Central Asia: 1810–1895* (Abingdon: Routledge, 1981); Alexander Morrison, 'Beyond the "Great Game": The Russian Origins of the Second Anglo-Afghan War', *Modern Asian Studies* 51:3 (2017), 686–735.

Notes 98–106

SECTION IV

1 Paul Huddie, *The Crimean War and Irish Society* (Liverpool: Liverpool University Press, 2015), pp. 70–74; David Murphy, *Ireland and the Crimean War* (Dublin: Four Courts Press, 2002).

2 Quoted in Róisín Healy, *Poland in the Irish Nationalist Imagination, 1722–1922: Anti-Colonialism within Europe* (Basingstoke: Palgrave Macmillan, 2017), p. 49.

3 *Irish Examiner*, 25 Sept. 1844. In *Poland in the Irish Nationalist Imagination*, Róisín Healy usefully summarizes some of the negative commentary directed against Russia in terms of the first and second partitions of Poland at pp. 33–5, 49, 55–7.

4 [Anon.], *Sketches of Travel in Russia, Turkey, Greece, &c, &c, in 1869* (Dublin: Webb and Jennings, 1870), pp. 105–6.

5 Joseph M. Hone and Page L. Dickinson, *Persia in Revolution: With Notes of Travel in the Caucasus* (London: T. Fisher Unwin, 1910), p. 185.

6 Charles Howard-Bury, *Mountains of Heaven: Travels in the Tian Shan Mountains, 1913*, ed. Marian Kearney (London: Hodder and Stoughton, 1990).

7 Samuel Gamble Bayne, *Quicksteps through Scandinavia, with a Retreat from Moscow* (London: Harper and Brothers, 1908).

8 Simon Sebag Montefiore, *The Romanovs: 1613–1918* (New York: Alfred A. Knopf, 2016), p. xxvii.

CHAPTER 12

1 Selina Bunbury, *Russia After the War. The Narrative of a Visit to That Country in 1856* (2 vols, London: Hurst and Blackett, 1857), vol. I, p. 41.

2 Biographical information on Bunbury is from Sinéad Sturgeon and Frances Clarke, 'Bunbury, Selina' in *DIB*; [Anon.], 'Irish Fiction', *The Irish Monthly* 44:517 (1916), 475–6; and Patrick Leary, 'Fraser's Magazine and the Literary Life, 1830–1847', *Victorian Periodicals Review* 27:2 (1994), 119.

3 Bunbury, *Russia After the War*, vol. I, p. 2.

4 Anthony G. Cross, *In the Lands of the Romanovs: An Annotated Bibliography of First-Hand English-Language Accounts of the Russian Empire (1613–1917)* (Cambridge: Open Book Publishers, 2014), p. 29.

5 Selina Bunbury, *Anecdotes of Peter the Great* (London: S. and J. Bentley, 1850), p. vi.

6 Bunbury, *Russia After the War*, vol. I, pp. 41–3, 45–6, 84, 89–90, 179.

7 Ibid., vol. I, pp. 13, 123–4.

8 Ibid., vol. I, pp. 307–8.

9 Ibid., vol. I, pp. 117–18, 308; vol. II, pp. 3–4.

10 Ibid., vol. I, pp. 24–5.

11 Ibid., vol. II, pp. 113–14.

12 Ibid., vol. II, pp. 116–17.

13 Ibid., vol. I, pp. 18, 37–8, 248, 321–2.

14 Ibid., vol. I, pp. 19, 38; vol. II, pp. 64–5.

15 Ibid., vol. I, pp. 26–7, 44–5, 111, 285.

16 Ibid., vol. I, pp. 228–9, 239, 319; vol. II, p. 98.

17 Ibid., vol. I, pp. 16–18, 62–3.

18 Ibid., vol. I, pp. 93–4.

19 Ibid., vol. I, pp. 10–11.

20 Ibid., vol. I, p. 77; vol. II, pp. 122, 150–2.

21 Ibid., vol. I, p. 6.

22 Ibid., vol. I, pp. 31–2.

23 Ibid., vol. I, pp. 50, 271, 276–7; vol. II, pp. 150–2.

CHAPTER 13

1 See Peter H. Hansen, *The Summits of Modern Man: Mountaineering after the Enlightenment* (Cambridge MA: Harvard University Press, 2013).

2 Information on Bryce's life and career is from James Quinn, 'Bryce, James' in *DIB*; and Christopher Harvie, 'Bryce, James, Viscount Bryce' in *ODNB*.

3 James Bryce, *Transcaucasia and Ararat: Being Notes of a Vacation Tour in the Autumn of 1876* ([1877] 4th ed., London: Macmillan and Co., 1896).

4 Ibid., pp. 49, 248–50.

5 Ibid., pp. 1, 2, 5, 70–71.

6 Ibid., p. 43.

7 Ibid., pp. 24–5, 130–31, 26, 37, 62, 132.

8 Ibid., pp. 257–8.

9 Ibid., pp. 279, 280–81, 294, 282; James Bryce, 'Armenia and Mount Ararat', *Proceedings of the Royal Geographical Society* 22:3 (1877–8), 183.

10 Bryce, *Transcaucasia and Ararat*, pp. 413, 443, 420.

11 Ibid., pp. 124, 416.

CHAPTER 14

1 All biographical information is from Helen Andrews, 'Higgins, Bryan' in *DIB*; Arnold Thackray, 'Higgins, Bryan' in Charles Coulston Gillespie (ed.), *Dictionary of Scientific Biography* vol. V (New York: Charles Scribner's Sons, 1972), pp. 382–4; and F.W. Gibbs, 'Bryan Higgins and His Circle' in A.E. Musson (ed.), *Science, Technology and Economic Growth in the Eighteenth Century* (London: Methuen, 1972), pp. 195–207. The claim that Higgins visited Russia seems to have originated in William K. Sullivan, 'Memoir of Bryan Higgins, M.D., and of William Higgins, Professor of Chemistry to the Royal Dublin Society', *Dublin Quarterly Journal of Medical Science* 8 (1849), 20.

2 Roderick E. McGrew, 'The First Russian Cholera Epidemic: Themes and Opportunities', *Bulletin of the History of Medicine* 36:3 (1962), 221.

3 See Janet M. Hartley, *The Volga: A History of Russia's Greatest River* (New Haven and London: Yale University Press), pp. 122–31.

Notes 120–126

4 'Dr Barry's First Letter', 1 July 1831, in *Official Reports Made to Government by Drs Russell and Barry on the Disease called Cholera Spasmodica, as Observed during their Mission to Russia in 1831* (London: Winchester and Varnham, 1832), p. 21.

5 'Letter from Drs Russell and Barry', 5 July 1831, in *Official Reports*, p. 22.

6 'Letter from Drs Russell and Barry', 6 July 1831, in *Official Reports*, p. 26.

7 'Second Report from Drs Russell and Barry', 16 July 1831, in *Official Reports*, p. 30.

8 'Letter from Drs Russell and Barry', 6 July 1831, in *Official Reports*, pp. 24–5, 28.

9 'Extract of a Private Letter from Dr Russell', 27 July 1831, in *Official Reports*, pp. 41–2.

10 McGrew, 'The First Russian Cholera Epidemic', 228.

11 'Further Report from Drs Russell and Barry', 20 Sept. 1831, in *Official Reports*, pp. 44–54.

12 'Report from Drs Russell and Barry', 22 Sept. 1831, in *Official Reports*, p. 82.

13 'Extract of a Private Letter from Dr Russell', 27 July 1831, in *Official Reports*, p. 41.

14 'Extract of a Letter from Dr. Barry', 30 July 1831, in *Official Reports*, pp. 107–8.

15 C.S. Breathnach, 'Barry, Sir David' in *ODNB*.

16 Biographical information is from Jeremy Williams, 'Turner, Richard' in *DIB*, and Edward Diestelkamp, rev. Mike Chrimes, 'Turner, Richard' in *ODNB*; Kew English Letters DC/26, f. 330: John C. Lyons to Sir William Hooker, 4 May 1848, quoted in E. Charles Nelson, 'Richard Turner: An Introductory Portrait', *Moorea: Journal of the Irish Garden Plant Society* 9 (1990), 3, available at https://irishgardenplantsociety.com/wp-content/uploads/2013/08/MOOREA-VOLUME-9-DECEMBER-1990-PDF-7725KB.pdf.

17 Neil Smith and Mervyn Busteed, 'A Diasporic Elite – The Emergence of an Irish Middle Class in Nineteenth-Century Manchester' in Ciaran O'Neill (ed.), *Irish Elites in the Nineteenth Century* (Dublin: Four Courts Press, 2013), pp. 197–208; 'Obituary', *Manchester Courier*, 14 Nov. 1894; 'The Irish National League of Great Britain', *The Nation*, 23 Apr. 1887.

18 Charles H. Moberly, 'An Account of the Conveyance of Light-Draught Steamers from England to the River Volga, with Remarks on the Inland Navigation of Russia', *Transactions of the Institution of Civil Engineers of Ireland* 7 (1864), 1–16; Obituary of Charles Henry Moberly, *Minutes of the Proceedings of the Institution of Civil Engineers* 151 (1903), 419–20.

19 David Murphy, 'Doyne, William Thomas' in *DIB*.

20 Information provided in this summary of Law's career is from Theodore Morison and G.T. Hutchinson (eds), *The Life of Sir Edward FitzGerald Law* (Edinburgh and London: William Blackwood and Sons, 1911), pp. 16–31; F.H. Brown, rev. H.G.C. Matthew, 'Law, Sir Edward Fitzgerald' in *ODNB*; and Patrick M. Geoghegan, 'Law, Sir Edward Fitzgerald' in *DIB*.

21 Morison and Hutchinson (eds), *The Life of Sir Edward FitzGerald Law*, pp. 2, 27, 16.

22 Biographical and career information is from Philip Schofield, 'Heron, Denis Caulfield' in *ODNB*; and Bridget Hourican, 'Heron, Denis Caulfield' in *DIB*.

23 Denis Caulfield Heron, 'A Visit to Russia', *Journal of the Statistical and Social Inquiry Society of Ireland* 6 (1873), 181–202.

128–133 *Notes*

CHAPTER 15

1 Thomas Kilgallon, 'Reminiscences', typescript (PRONI: D/4131/D/2/1, p. 36).

2 John Franklin, *Narrative of a Journey to the Shores of the Polar Sea, in the Years 1819, 20, 21, and 22* (London: John Murray, 1824). On the Arctic, see for example, Francis Spufford, *I May Be Some Time: Ice and the English Imagination* (London: Faber and Faber, 1996); Robert G. David, *The Arctic in the British Imagination, 1818–1914* (Manchester: Manchester University Press, 2000); Janice Cavell, *Tracing the Connected Narrative: Arctic Exploration in British Print Culture, 1818–1860* (Toronto: Toronto University Press, 2008); Huw Lewis-Jones, *Imagining the Arctic: Heroism, Spectacle and Polar Exploration* (London: I.B. Tauris, 2017).

3 Albert H. Markham, *A Polar Reconnaissance: Being the Voyage of the 'Isbjörn' to Novaya Zemlya in 1879* (London: C. Kegan Paul and Co., 1881), p. 7.

4 Albert H. Markham, 'The Arctic Campaign of 1879 in the Barents Sea', *Proceedings of the Royal Geographical Society and Monthly Record of Geography* 2:1 (1880), 35.

5 Markham, 'The Arctic Campaign of 1879'; Markham, *A Polar Reconnaissance.*

6 Markham, *A Polar Reconnaissance*, p. xii.

7 Ibid., p. 2.

8 Ibid., pp. xiii–xiv.

9 Markham, 'The Arctic Campaign of 1879', 37.

10 'Obituary: Sir Henry William Gore-Booth, Bart.', *Geographical Journal* 15:3 (Mar. 1900), 290.

11 Markham, *A Polar Reconnaissance*, p. 182.

12 *Illustrated London News*, 7 Jan. 1882, 10 June 1882.

13 Frank Nugent, 'Booth, Sir Henry William Gore-' in *DIB*.

14 Kilgallon, 'Reminiscences', p. 53.

15 Ibid., p. 54.

16 Nugent, 'Booth, Sir Henry William Gore-'.

17 Family information is from Irish Civil Records at www.irishgenealogy.ie; Death Notice: Thomas Kilgallon, *Sligo Champion*, 25 Jan. 1941.

18 Markham, 'The Arctic Campaign of 1879', 19, 27.

19 Markham, *A Polar Reconnaissance*, p. 248.

20 Markham, 'The Arctic Campaign of 1879', 19.

21 Ibid., 28.

22 Ibid., 17.

23 Pauric J. Dempsey, 'Hone, Joseph Maunsell' in *DIB*.

24 Hone and Dickinson, *Persia in Revolution*, pp. v–vi.

25 Ibid., p. 4.

26 Ibid., p. 185.

27 Ibid., p. 163.

28 Ibid., p. 179.

29 Hans Rogger, *Russia in the Age of Modernisation and Revolution 1881–1917* ([1983] London and New York: Routledge, 2014), p. 194.

Notes 133–144

30 Hone and Dickinson, *Persia in Revolution*, p. 185.

31 Ibid., p. 163.

32 Thomas McLean, *The Other East and Nineteenth-Century British Literature: Imagining Poland and the Russian Empire* (London: Palgrave Macmillan, 2012), pp. 135–53.

33 Hone and Dickinson, *Persia in Revolution*, pp. 161, 199, 208.

34 Ibid., pp. 159–62, 181, 215–17.

35 'Reviews', *The Geographical Journal* 36:3 (1910), 344; 'Persia in Revolution', *Bulletin of the American Geographical Society* 43:6 (1911), 462–3.

36 For example, *Belfast News Letter*, 26 Dec. 1907, referring to the deaths of a Scottish climber and his Swiss guide on the Wetterhorn in 1902.

37 *Irish Examiner*, 14 Apr. 1916; *Irish Independent*, 3 Oct. 1934; *Belfast News Letter*, 28 July 1934.

38 Mrs Aubrey le Blond, *True Tales of Mountain Adventure: For Non-Climbers Young and Old* (New York: E.P. Dutton and Co., 1903), p. 107.

39 See Clare Roche, 'Women Climbers 1850–1900: A Challenge to Male Hegemony?', *Sport in History* 33:3 (2013), 236–59; and Delphine Moraldo, 'Women and Excellence in Mountaineering from the Nineteenth Century to the Present', *International Journal of the History of Sport* 37:9 (2020), 727–47.

40 Mrs Aubrey le Blond, *Adventures on the Roof of the World* ([1904] 2nd ed., London: T. Fisher Unwin, 1907), pp. 51–64, 195–207; le Blond, *True Tales*, p. 194.

41 The assertion that le Blond was the most important woman of her age to write about mountaineering is made in Kathryn Walchester, '"A Fisherman Landing an Unwieldy Salmon": The Alpine Guide and Female Mountaineer', *Nineteenth-Century Contexts* 40:2 (2018), 183.

42 Mrs Aubrey le Blond, *Day In, Day Out* (London: J. Lane, 1928), pp. 165–177.

43 le Blond, *True Tales*, pp. ix, x.

44 Ibid., p. 87.

45 Ibid., pp. 5–6.

SECTION v

1 Review of *An Exile's Daughter* in *FJ*, 1 Apr. 1911.

2 Stephen A. Smith, *Russia in Revolution: An Empire in Crisis, 1890 to 1928* (Oxford: Oxford University Press, 2017).

3 See Niall Whelehan, *The Dynamiters: Irish Nationalism and Political Violence in the Wider World, 1867–1900* (Cambridge: Cambridge University Press, 2012).

4 Michael Newton, '"Nihilists of Castlebar!" Exporting Russian Nihilism in the 1880s and the Case of Oscar Wilde's *Vera; or, the Nihilists*' in Rebecca Beasley and Philip Ross Bullock (eds), *Russia in Britain, 1880 to 1940: From Melodrama to Modernism* (Oxford: Oxford University Press, 2013), pp. 35–52.

5 Michael Davitt, *Within the Pale: the True Story of Anti-Semitic Persecution in Russia* (New York: Barnes, 1903); Carla King, '"In a Humble Way, a Supporter of Russia":

Michael Davitt in Russia, 1903, 1904 and 1905' in Brian Heffernan (ed.), *Life on the Fringe?: Ireland and Europe, 1800–1922* (Dublin: Irish Academic Press, 2012), pp. 135–55.

6   E.B. Lanin [Emile Joseph Dillon], *Russian Characteristics, Reprinted, with Revisions, from the 'Fortnightly Review'* (London: Chapman and Hall, 1892), p. vii.

7   *Evansville Press*, 7 Oct. 1913; Mary Boyle O'Reilly, 'Parallel of Mendel Beilis and Leo Frank Cases: Both Jew Persecutions!', *The Day Book*, 24 Apr. 1915; Letters from Mary Boyle O'Reilly to Rev. Thomas Dawson OMI Regarding War Conditions in Belgium and Russia, 1913–15 (NLI: MS 13,997).

8   John Horgan, '"The Great War Correspondent": Francis McCullagh, 1874–1956', *Irish Historical Studies* 36:144 (2009), 542–63; Francis McCullagh, *With the Cossacks, Being the Story of an Irishman Who Rode with the Cossacks throughout the Russo-Japanese War* (London: Eveleigh Nash, 1906).

9   Alfred Comyn Lyall, *The Life of the Marquis of Dufferin and Ava* (2 vols, London: J. Murray, 1905), vol. I, pp. 322–3.

CHAPTER 16

1   Hariot G. Blackwood [Lady Dufferin], *My Russian and Turkish Journals* (New York: Charles Scribner's Sons, 1917), p. 80. For example, *Sheffield and Rotherham Independent*, 9 Apr. 1880; *The Dundee Courier and Argus and Northern Warder*, 9 Apr. 1880; *Jackson's Oxford Journal*, 10 Apr. 1880.

2   Richard Davenport-Hines, 'Blackwood, Hariot Georgina Hamilton-Temple-' in *ODNB*.

3   Lyall, *The Life of the Marquis*; the chapter relating to his time in Russia is at vol. I, pp. 288–324.

4   Amanda Andrews, 'The Great Ornamentals: New Vice-Regal Women and Their Imperial Work, 1884–1914', PhD Thesis, University of Western Sydney, 2004; Helen McCarthy, 'Women, Marriage and Work in the British Diplomatic Service', *Women's History Review* 23:6 (2014), 853–873.

5   Hariot G. Blackwood [Lady Dufferin], *Our Viceregal Life in India: Selections from my Journal* (2 vols, London: John Murray, 1889), vol. II, pp. 343–4, 346.

6   Ibid. vol. I, p. 233.

7   Ibid, vol. I, pp. 168–9.

8   Ibid., vol. I, pp. 229, 257–8.

9   Laura Kelly, *Irish Women in Medicine, c. 1880s–1920s: Origins, Education and Careers* (Manchester: Manchester University Press, 2012), p. 215.

10 Antoinette Burton, 'Contesting the Zenana: The Mission to Make "Lady Doctors for India", 1874–1885', *Journal of British Studies* 35:3 (1996), 368–97; [Anon.], 'The Countess of Dufferin's Fund', *The British Medical Journal*, 2:2062 (7 July 1900), 41; M.E. Staley, 'The Countess of Dufferin's Fund', *The British Medical Journal* 2:2071 (8 Sept. 1900), 695.

Notes 150–156

11 Maneesha Lal, 'The Politics of Gender and Medicine in Colonial India: The Countess of Dufferin's Fund, 1885–1888', *Bulletin of the History of Medicine* 68:1 (1994), 5–6.

12 Dufferin, *Our Viceregal Life*, vol. I, p. 172.

13 Melanie Oppenheimer, 'The "Imperial" Girl: Lady Helen Munro Ferguson, the Imperial Woman and her Imperial Childhood', *Journal of Australian Studies* 34:4 (2010), 513–25.

14 Neil Armstrong, '"I Insisted I was Myself": Clergy Wives and Authentic Selfhood in England, c. 1960–94', *Women's History Review* 22 (2013), 995–1013.

15 Sarah Richardson, *The Political Worlds of Women: Gender and Politics in Nineteenth Century Britain* (New York: Routledge, 2013), pp. 150–51.

16 Dufferin, *My Russian and Turkish Journals*, pp. 14–15.

17 Ibid., pp. 38, 53.

18 Ibid., pp. 88–9.

19 Ibid., p. 93.

20 Lyall, *The Life of the Marquis*, vol. I, p. 314.

21 Dufferin, *My Russian and Turkish Journals*, pp. 75–7, 94–5.

22 For detailed context on the period 1881–1905, see Dominick Lieven, *The End of Tsarist Russia: The March to World War I and Revolution* (New York: Penguin, 2015), pp. 46–90.

23 Dufferin, *My Russian and Turkish Journals*, pp. 30–31, 35, 66–7.

24 Ibid., pp. 109–114.

25 Ibid., p. v.

26 Lieven, *The End of Tsarist Russia*, p. 345.

27 Brian S. Faloon, 'Florence Barrington in Russia: 1917', *Old Limerick Journal* 24 (1988): 101–4.

28 Lieven, *The End of Tsarist Russia*, pp. 345–6.

29 Roger R. Reese, *The Imperial Russian Army in Peace, War, and Revolution, 1856–1917* (Lawrence KS: University Press of Kansas, 2019).

30 See Toby Thacker, *British Culture and the First World War: Experience, Representation and Memory* (London: Bloomsbury Academic, 2014).

31 Robert Holland, 'The British Empire and the Great War, 1914–1918' in *The Oxford History of the British Empire*, vol. IV: *The Twentieth Century* (Oxford: Oxford University Press, 1999), pp. 114–37.

CHAPTER 17

1 For biographical information, see Pamela Blevins, 'Ethel Voynich – "E.L.V.": Revolutionary, Novelist, Translator, Composer' (2005), available at http://www.musicweb-international.com/classrev/2005/feb05/voynich.htm; Arnold Kettle, 'E.L. Voynich: A Forgotten English Novelist', *Essays in Criticism* 7:2 (1957), 163–74; Anne Fremantle, 'The Russian Best-Seller', *History Today* 25:9 (1975), 629–37.

156–159 *Notes*

2   Ethel Lilian Voynich, 'Zametki o genezise *Ovoda*' [Notes on the Genesis of *The Gadfly*] in Evgeniya Taratuta, *Etel Lilian Voynich: sudba pisatelya i sudba knigi* [*Ethel Lilian Voynich: The Fate of the Writer and the Fate of the Book*] (Moscow: Gosudarstvennoe Izdatelstvo Khudozhestvennoy Literatury, 1960), p. 247.

3   Patrick Waddington, 'Voynich [*née* Boole], Ethel Lilian [Lily] [E.L.V.]' in *ODNB*.

4   Frederick J. Gregg, 'The Tzars and the People', *Dublin University Review* 1:6 (July 1885), 140–42; R.F. Foster, *Words Alone: Yeats and His Inheritances* (Oxford: Oxford University Press, 2011), pp. 136–7; John Millington Synge, *Letters to Molly: John Millington Sygne to Maire O'Neill 1906–1909*, ed. Ann Saddlemyer (Oxford: Oxford University Press, 1971), p. 190.

5   Iain Boyd Whyte and David Frisby, *Metropolis Berlin: 1880–1940* (Berkeley: University of California Press, 2012).

6   Todd H. Weir, *Secularism and Religion in Nineteenth-Century Germany* (Cambridge: Cambridge University Press, 2014), p. 25.

7   Evgeniya Taratuta, 'Nash drug Ethel Lilian Voynich', *Biblioteka ogonek* 42 (1957); transl. Séamus Ó Coigligh, *Our Friend Ethel Lilian Boole / Voynich* (Cork: University College Cork, 2008), p. 35, available at www.corkcitylibraries.ie.

8   Waddington, 'Voynich [*née* Boole], Ethel Lilian [Lily] [E.L.V.]'.

9   Susan Hinely, 'Charlotte Wilson, the "Woman Question", and the Meanings of Anarchist Socialism in Late Victorian Radicalism', *International Review of Social History* 57 (2012), 26.

10 Taratuta, 'Nash drug', transl. Ó Coigligh, p. 38.

11 Garnet Wolseley, *The Letters of Lord and Lady Wolseley, 1870–1911*, ed. George Arthur (London: Doubleday, 1922), pp. 95–106.

12 Voynich's time in Russia is detailed in Taratuta, *Etel Lilian Voynich*, pp. 27–54. This quote is from Gerry Kennedy, *The Booles and the Hintons: Two Dynasties That Helped Shape the Modern World* (Cork: Atrium, 2016), p. 130.

13 Taratuta, 'Nash drug', transl. Ó Coigligh, p. 40; Blevins, 'Ethel Voynich'.

14 Quoted in Taratuta, 'Nash drug', transl. Ó Coigligh, p. 8.

15 Sergey Mikhailovich Kravchinsky [Sergey Stepnyak], Diary, 4 June 1889 (RGALI: F. 1158, op. 1, d. 119, l. 16).

16 For more on the SFRF, see Barry Hollingsworth, 'The Society of Friends of Russian Freedom: English Liberals and Russian Socialists', *Oxford Slavonic Papers* 3 (1970), 46–64; Ron Grant, 'The Society of Friends of Russian Freedom (1890–1917): A Case Study in Internationalism', *Journal of Scottish Labour History Society* 3 (1970), 3–24; Luke Kelly, *British Humanitarian Activity in Russia, 1890–1923* (London: Palgrave Macmillan, 2018), pp. 113–57.

17 Rebecca Beasley, *Russomania: Russian Culture and the Creation of British Modernism, 1881–1922* (Oxford: Oxford University Press, 2020), p. 50.

18 *Belfast News Letter*, 8 Sept. 1891.

19 *Free Russia*, 5:6, 1 June 1894.

Notes 160–167

20 Hinely, 'Charlotte Wilson', 26.

21 *Free Russia*, 4:4, 1 Apr. 1893; *Free Russia*, 5:1, 1 Jan. 1894; *Free Russia*, 5:2, 1 Feb. 1894.

22 Robert Spence Watson, 'Preface' in [Sergey Stepnyak], *Nihilism As It Is: Being Stepniak's Pamphlets translated by E.L. Voynich, and Felix Volkhovsky's 'Claims of the Russian Liberals' with an Introduction by Dr R. Spence Watson* (London: T. Fisher Unwin, 1894), pp. x–xi.

23 Hinely, 'Charlotte Wilson', 26.

24 Taratuta, 'Nash drug', transl. Ó Coigligh, p. 4.

25 Waddington, 'Voynich [*née* Boole], Ethel Lilian [Lily] [E.L.V.]'; Taratuta, 'Nash drug', transl. Ó Coigligh, p. 6; Sergey Stepnyak, 'Introduction' in E.L. Voynich (transl., ed.), *The Humour of Russia* (London: Walter Scott, 1895), p. 15.

26 Sergey Stepnyak, 'Introduction' in Vsevolod Garshin, *Stories from Garshin*, transl. E.L. Voynich (London: T. Fisher Unwin, 1893), p. 4.

27 Kennedy, *The Booles and the Hintons*, p. 155.

28 Waddington, 'Voynich [*née* Boole], Ethel Lilian [Lily] [E.L.V.]'; Taratuta, transl. Ó Coigligh, p. 4.

29 Taratuta, 'Nash drug', transl. Ó Coigligh, p. 4.

30 Ibid., p. 4.

31 *Free Russia*, 3:12, 1 Dec. 1892; *Free Russia*, 4:12, 1 Dec. 1893.

32 John Slatter, 'The Russian Émigré Press in Britain, 1853–1917', *SEER* 73:4 (1995), 719.

33 Kennedy, *The Booles and the Hintons*, p. 166; *Free Russia*, 4:12, 1 Dec. 1893.

34 Kennedy, *The Booles and the Hintons*, p. 224.

35 Catherine Radziwill, *My Recollections* (New York: James Pott and Co., 1904), pp. 268–7. See also Margaret O'Callaghan and Caoimhe Nic Dháibhéid, 'MacBride, (Edith) Maud Gonne' in *DIB*.

36 Sigurd O. Shmidt, 'Great Works of Literature as a Source of Historical Knowledge', *Russian Studies in History* 47:1 (2008), 15.

37 Hinely, 'Charlotte Wilson', 26.

38 'The Gadfly and Its Author', *New York Times*, 20 Aug. 1898.

39 Andrew Cook, *Ace of Spies: The True Story of Sidney Reilly* (Stroud: The History Press, 2004); Blevins, 'Ethel Voynich'.

40 Peadar O'Donnell, *The Gates Flew Open* (Dublin: Mercier Press, 2013).

41 *Pravda*, 30 Aug. 1960. Author's translation.

42 E.L. Voynich, *Olive Latham* (Philadelphia: J.B. Lippincott, 1904), p. 278.

43 E.L. Voynich (transl., ed.), *Chopin's Letters* (New York: Alfred A. Knopf, 1931), p. vi.

44 Lara Vapnek, *Elizabeth Gurley Flynn: Modern American Revolutionary* (Philadelphia: Westview Press, 2015), pp. 122–37.

45 Correspondence between George Gavan Duffy and various individuals [including Voynich] relating to the settling of the affairs of Roger Casement, 1916–17 (NLI: MSS 10,763/21/28, 10,763/22/7, 10,763/26/40, 10,763/26/43, 10,763/28/10, 10,763/28/18, 10,763/28/25, 10,763/28/26).

CHAPTER 18

1 David Fitzpatrick, 'The Unimportance of Gender in Explaining Post-Famine Irish Emigration' in Eric Richards (ed.), *Visible Women: Female Immigrants in Colonial Australia* (Canberra: Australian National University, 1995), p. 148.

2 Hasia R. Diner, *Erin's Daughters in America: Irish Immigrant Women in the Nineteenth Century* (Baltimore and London: The John Hopkins University Press, 1983), p. 33.

3 Cormac Ó Grada, 'The Population of Ireland 1700–1900: A Survey', *Annales de démographie historique* (1979), 294.

4 Judith U. Poore, *The Memoirs of Emily Loch: Discretion in Waiting* (Kinloss: Librario, 2007).

5 Details of Eagar's family background and life prior to 1898 are from Sharon Slater, 'Margaret Eagar: The Czar's Nanny', *The Old Limerick Journal* 49 (2015), 8–10.

6 Olga Solodyankina, 'Cross-Cultural Closeness: Foreign Governesses in the Russian Empire, *c.* 1700–1850' in Johanna Ilmakunnas, Marjatta Rahikainen and Kirsi Vainio-Korhonen (eds), *Early Professional Women in Northern Europe, c. 1650–1850* (Oxon: Routledge, 2018), pp. 217–43.

7 *Kerry Evening Post*, 11 Apr. 1900.

8 Margaretta Eagar, *Six Years at the Russian Court* (New York: Charles L. Bowman, 1906), pp. 8–15, 90–91, 74.

9 Susan N. Bayley, 'The English Miss, German Fräulein and French Mademoiselle: Foreign Governesses and National Stereotyping in Nineteenth- and Early Twentieth-Century Europe', *History of Education* 43:2 (2014), 164; Deirdre Raftery, 'The Nineteenth-Century Governess: Image and Reality' in Bernadette Whelan (ed.), *Women and Paid Work in Ireland, 1500–1930* (Dublin: Four Courts Press, 2000), pp. 57–68.

10 Solodyankina, 'Cross-Cultural Closeness', pp. 217–43.

11 Bayley, 'The English Miss', 176.

12 Georgiana Bloomfield, *Reminiscences of Court and Diplomatic Life* (2 vols, K. Paul and Trench, 1883), vol. I, pp. 152–3.

13 Solodyankina, 'Cross-Cultural Closeness', pp. 217–43.

14 Anthony G. Cross, 'English – A Serious Challenge to French in the Reign of Alexander I?', *Russian Review* 74 (2015), 65.

15 Harvey Pitcher, *When Miss Emmie Was in Russia: English Governesses Before, During and After the October Revolution* ([1977] London: Eland, 2012), pp. xiii, 29–30.

16 Anthony G. Cross, 'Early Miss Emmies: British Nannies, Governesses and Companions in Pre-Emancipation Russia' in idem., *Anglo-Russica: Aspects of Cultural Relations between Great Britain and Russia in the Eighteenth and Early Nineteenth Centuries* (Oxford: Berg, 1993), p. 235; Ulrike Lentz, 'The Representation of Western European Governesses and Tutors on the Russian Country Estate in Historical Documents and Literary Texts', PhD thesis, University of Surrey, 2008.

Notes 171–176

17 *Kerry Evening Post*, 10 Jan. 1855.

18 *Ballinrobe Chronicle*, 17 Mar. 1877.

19 *Kerry Evening Post*, 17 Oct. 1899.

20 Joseph M. Hone and Page L. Dickinson, *Persia in Revolution: With Notes of Travel in the Caucasus* (London: T. Fisher Unwin, 1910), pp. 4–5.

21 Gunilla Budde, 'Als Erzieherinnen in Europa unterwegs: gouvernanten, governesses und gouvernantes' ['Travelling Teachers in Europe: Gouvernanten, Governesses, and Gouvernantes'] Europäische Geschichte Online (2011), available at: http://ieg-ego.eu/de/threads/europa-unterwegs/arbeitsmigration-wirtschaftsmigration/gunilla-budde-als-erzieherinnen-in-europa-unterwegs-gouvernanten-governesses-und-gouvernantes; Bayley, 'The English Miss', 164.

22 Margaret E. Lynch-Brennan, *The Irish Bridget: Irish Immigrant Women in Domestic Service in America, 1840–1930* (Syracuse: Syracuse University Press, 2009), pp. xvii, xxi–xxii.

23 Helen Rappaport, *Four Sisters: The Lost Lives of the Romanov Grand Duchesses* (London: Pan Macmillan, 2015).

24 Robert K. Massie, *Nicholas and Alexandra* ([1967] New York: Random House, 2000), p. 122.

25 Ermengarde Greville-Nugent, 'The Death of the Czarevitch (in 1865, translated from a private Ms., by the Hon. Mrs. Greville-Nugent)', *The Dublin University Review* 3:1 (Feb. 1887), pp. 11–15.

26 Eagar's articles include: 'Christmas at the Court of the Tsar', *The Quiver* (Jan. 1906), 26–30; 'Further Glimpses of the Tsaritsa's Little Girls', *The Girl's Own Paper and Woman's Magazine* 30 (1909), 366–7; 'More about the Little Grand Duchesses of Russia', *The Girl's Own Paper and Woman's Magazine* 30 (1909), 535; 'The Russian Court in Summer', *The Star* [Christchurch, New Zealand], 30 Sept. 1905. Her memoir was serialized in *Leisure Hour*, vol. 54 (1904–5): Apr. 1905, pp. 443–57; May 1905; June 1905, pp. 669–79; July 1905, pp. 755–61; Aug. 1905, pp. 867–74; Sept. 1905, pp. 935–42; and Oct. 1905, pp. 1005–15.

27 See Davitt, *Within the Pale*; King, '"In a Humble Way, a Supporter of Russia"', pp. 135–55.

28 Eagar, *Six Years*, pp. 245–8.

29 *The Times*, 2 Jan. 1905; Eagar, *Six Years*, p. 283.

30 See, for example, Eoin Butler, 'The Limerick Nurse Who Was Nanny to Children of the Last Tsar', *Irish Times*, 10 Mar. 2017; Mary Kenny, 'The Fascinating Story of the Belfast Nurse Who Became Nanny to Russia's Tragic Last Royal Family', *Belfast Telegraph*, 23 Oct. 2017; Mary Kenny, 'The Romanovs' Irish Nanny', *Irish Independent*, 22 Oct. 2017.

31 Kathy McKeon, *Jackie's Girl: My Life with the Kennedy Family* (New York: Gallery Books, 2017).

32 Massie, *Nicholas and Alexandra*, pp. 131–2.

CHAPTER 19

1 Lauren Arrington, *Revolutionary Lives: Constance and Casimir Markievicz* (Princeton: Princeton University Press, 2016), p. ix.

2 See Johannes Remy, *Brothers or Enemies: The Ukrainian National Movement and Russia from the 1840s to the 1870s* (Toronto: University of Toronto Press, 2016).

3 Arrington, *Revolutionary Lives*; Anne Haverty, *Constance Markievicz: Irish Revolutionary* ([1988] Dublin: Lilliput Press, 2016); Anne Marreco, *The Rebel Countess: The Life and Times of Constance Markievicz* (London: Phoenix, 2000); Lindie Naughton, *Markievicz: A Most Outrageous Rebel* (Newbridge: Merrion Press, 2016); Diana Norman, *Terrible Beauty: A Life of Constance Markievicz, 1868–1927* (Dublin: Poolbeg, 1988); Sean O'Faolain, *Constance Markievicz* (London: Sphere Books, 1934); Jacqueline Van Voris, *Constance de Markievicz: In the Cause of Ireland* (Amherst: University of Massachusetts Press, 1967).

4 Quoted in O'Faolain, *Constance Markievicz*, pp. 41–2.

5 Ibid., pp. 41–2.

6 Gail Baylis, 'What to Wear for a Revolution? Countess Constance Markievicz in Military Dress,' *Éire-Ireland* 54:3–4 (2019): 94–122.

7 Arrington, *Revolutionary Lives*, p. ix.

8 Ibid., pp. 111, 113, 156–7.

9 Ibid., p. 112.

10 Ibid., p. 115; Lindie Naughton (ed.), *Markievicz: Prison Letters and Rebel Writings* (Kildare: Merrion Press, 2018), p. 77.

11 Quoted in Arrington, *Revolutionary Lives*, p. 158.

12 Arrington, *Revolutionary Lives*, pp. 158–9.

13 Naughton (ed.), *Markievicz: Prison Letters*, pp. 142, 146.

14 Ibid., p. 142.

15 Ibid., pp. 72, 146.

16 Ibid., pp. 123, 173, 176–7, 148–9.

17 See Sonja Tiernan, '"Two Girls in Silk Kimonos": Constance and Eva Gore-Booth, Childhood and Political Development' in Siobhán Fitzpatrick and Mary O'Dowd (eds), *Sisters* (Dublin: RIA, 2022), pp. 125–46.

18 Biographical information is from Charles Lysaght, 'Leslie, John Randolph ('Shane')' in *DIB*.

19 Shane Leslie, *The Film of Memory* (London: Michael Joseph, 1938), pp. 291–2.

20 Ibid., p. 293.

21 Ibid., p. 295.

22 Ibid., p. 295.

23 Ibid., p. 291.

24 Ibid., p. 297.

25 Dushan Makovitsky, *U Tolstogo: Yasnopolyanskie zapiski* [*Tolstoy: The Yasnaya Polyana Notes*] (4 vols, Moscow: Nauka, 1979), 19 Nov. 1907. Transcript available at http://tolstoy-lit.ru/tolstoy/bio/makovickij-yasnopolyanskie-zapiski/1907-noyabr.htm.

Notes 185–192

26 Leslie, *The Film of Memory*, p. 296.

27 Ibid., p. 296.

28 The photograph is preserved as part of the Leslie Papers at Georgetown University Booth Family Center for Special Collections.

29 Leslie, *The Film of Memory*, p. 297.

30 Ibid., p. 297.

31 Ibid., p. 300.

32 Ibid., pp. 300–01.

33 Ibid., p. 301; Katarzyna Gmerek, 'Shane Leslie and the Irish Support for Language Struggle in Poland', *Studia Celtica Posnaniensia* 3:1 (2018), 89–108.

34 Leslie, *The Film of Memory*, p. 302.

35 Ibid., p. 300.

CONCLUSIONS

1 Brian S. Faloon, 'Florence Barrington in Russia: 1917', *Old Limerick Journal: Barringtons' Edition* 24 (1988), 101–04.

2 David Murphy, 'Crean, Thomas ('Tom')' in *DIB*.

3 Frederick O'Connor, *On the Frontier and Beyond: A Record of Thirty Years' Service* (London: John Murray, 1931), pp. 252–71.

4 Copies of the receipt signed by Martens in New York in 1920 are at NAI: DFA 2019/101/302 and NAI: AGO/1/454.

5 'T.D. Brought the Russian Jewels Here', *Irish Press*, 19 Jan. 1948.

6 *Irish Times*, 20 Jan. 1948.

7 *Dáil Debates*, vol. 113, no. 12 (15 Dec. 1948), available at https://www.oireachtas.ie/en/debates/.

8 *Dáil Debates*, vol. 110, no. 3 (9 Mar. 1948), available at https://www.oireachtas.ie/en/debates/.

9 Valuation by Christie's of London, 6 Jan. 1949 (NAI: DFA/10/2/169).

10 NAI: DFA/10/2/169; Barry Whelan, 'Éamon de Valera: A Republican Loan and the Secret of the Lost Russian Jewels', *Scoláire Staire* 3:1 (2013), 24–28.

11 Maria Luddy, 'Convent Archives' in Rosemary Raughter (ed.), *Religious Women and Their History: Breaking the Silence* (Dublin: Irish Academic Press, 2005), pp. 98–115.

12 Mother Mary Theophane, 'The Educational Work of the Sisters of Saint Columban', *The Capuchin Annual* (1955), 298; Mother Mary Theophane, 'From Sancta Sophia, Shanghai', *The Eastern Star: Bulletin of The Missionary Sisters of Saint Columban* 1:2 (1947), 4.

13 Jean Lombard, *An Irish Woman in Czarist Russia* (Dublin: Ashfield Press, 2010).

14 Rebecca Wills, *The Jacobites in Russia* (East Linton: Tuckwell Press, 2002), pp. 189–90.

15 Andrew James Blumbergs, *The Nationalization of Latvians and the Issue of Serfdom: The Baltic German Literary Contribution in the 1780s and 1790s* (Amherst NY: Cambria Press, 2008), pp. 96, 99–100.

INDEX

1798 rebellion (Ireland) 14–15, 108

Act of Union (1801) 14–15
Adair, William 16–17
Adlercron, John Ladeveze xxxiv, 47, 63–4
Afghanistan 95–6
Agar, Welbore Ellis (Viscount Somerton) 47, 63
Albania 74–5
Alexander, tsarevich 173
Alexander I 65, 171
Alexander II xxiv, 101, 122, 126, 139
    assassination 124, 139, 145, 147, 151–2, 157, 192
Alexander III 133, 157–8, 163, 176
Alexandra, Empress 168–9, 172–3
Alexei Nikolaevich, tsarevich 173, 175
Alfred, Prince xxiv
All Russia Industrial and Art Exhibitions (1829–33) 85
Allison, Thomas xxix
Alpine Club 112, 137
Alps, the 111–12, 137
Alsace-Lorraine 162–3
American Bureau of Information 166
American Communist Party 166–7
American War of Independence 19–21
Amu Darya River 127
Anglo-Afghan War, Second 96
Anna, Empress 3, 6–7, 9, 24
Ararat, Mount 114, 116
Arctic, Russian 129–32
Arkhangelsk xxi, 2, 27, 181
Armenia xxviii, 87, 113, 115, 118

Army Works Corps 123
Arrington, Lauren 180
Astrabad 78
Augustus III of Poland 12
Austro-Hungarian Empire 178
Avril, Philip xxix
Azov 7, 192

Bagwell, William 16
Baku 132–5
Ball, John 112
Banks, Sir Joseph 119
Bantysh-Kamenskii, Dmitri 52
Barents Sea 129
Barrington, Florence 153, 188
Barrington, Sir Matthew 66–7
Barrington, William Hartigan xxiii, 63–4, 66–71, 188
Barrington's Hospital, Limerick 67
Barrow, John xxxi, 34
Barry, Sir David 100, 120–2
Batumi 132, 135
Batyushkov, Konstantin xxxviii
Baylis, Gail 179
Bayne, Samuel Gamble 100
Beilis, Menahem Mendel 144–5
Belarus 7–8, 10, 12
Bell, Robert xxxi
Benevento Insurrection (1878) 164
Berehaven, Lord (Richard White) xxiv
Berlin 9, 18, 21, 88, 156
Bismarck, Otto von 163
Blackwood, Hariot Georgina Hamilton-Temple *see* Dufferin, Lady

Index

Blackwood, Frederick Temple Hamilton-Temple *see* Dufferin, Lord
Blevins, Pamela 165
Bloody Sunday, Russia (1905) 144
Bloomfield, Benjamin 85–7
Bloomfield, Georgiana 85, 87–8, 170
Bloomfield, John Arthur Douglas 63–4, 83–4, 86–8
Bloomfield family 83
Boland, Frederick 190
Boland, Harry 189
Bolsheviks 181–2, 188–9
Boole, Charles 155–6
Boole, Ethel Lilian *see* Voynich, Ethel Lilian Boole
Boole, Lucy 157
Boole, George 155
Bourke, Lt-Gen. John Jocelyn 90
Bourke, Richard Southwell (Lord Mayo) 62–4, 89–96
Bowring, Sir John xxxix
Boyle (*née* de Lacy), Catherine 8
Boyle O'Reilly, John 144
Boyle O'Reilly, Mary 144–5
Bradford, Blanche Elizabeth 55
Bradford, Catherine Dashkov 55
Bradford, Martha *see* Wilmot, Martha
Bradford, Wilmot Henry 55
Bradford, Revd William 55, 84
British Empire xxii, xxv, xxxiv, 63, 89, 95, 118, 154, 174, 191
British Factory 23–4
Brotherhood of Saints Cyril and Methodius 178
Browne, Frances xl
Browne, George 7
Browne, George, the younger 8–9, 192
Browne (*née* de Lacy), Helen 8
Browne, John Ross xxxii, 63
Bruce, Peter Henry xxix
Bryce, 1st Viscount, James xxviii, 99, 112–18
Bryce, Mount 113
Bunbury, Revd Henry 101
Bunbury, Selina xxiv, 97, 99, 101–10, 116

Burnaby, Colonel Fred 138
Burnaby, Mrs Fred *see* le Blond, Lizzie
Burrough, Stephen xxvii
Butler, Lady (Elizabeth Thompson) xl–xli
Butler, James, 2nd Duke of Ormond 6

Campbell, Thomas xxii
Casement, Sir Roger 167
Casway, Jerrold 10
Catherine I 8
Catherine II (the Great) xxiii, xxxiii, xxxv–xxxvi, 9, 14, 22, 28, 32–3, 44, 53, 69, 98, 119, 192
Catholics xxii, xxxiii, 1–2, 6, 8, 10–11, 15, 17, 18–19, 31–2, 61, 88, 118 *see also* Roman Catholic Church
Caucasus xxxiii, xl, 75, 84, 99, 113–18, 134–3, 136 *see also* Transcaucasia
Cavanagh, Eleanor xxiii, 36–7, 56–61
Chancellor, Richard xxi
Charles VI 9
Charter of the Nobility (1785) 14
Chetwood, Henrietta 57
Chişinău (Kishinev) pogrom 144, 174–5
cholera outbreaks 64, 83, 88, 100, 120–1
Chopin, Frédéric xxxvii, 166, 192
Christian Bible Society 65
Circassians xiii, xxxiv, xl, 84, 98, 127, 132–4 *see also* Russo-Circassian Wars
Civil Engineer Corps 123
Clementi, Muzio xxxvi
Colburn, Henry 90
Collie, J. Norman 113
Collins, Samuel xxix
communism 166–7, 182, 186, 189–91
Communist Party 182
Congress of Vienna (1815) 65, 98
Connellan, Corry 63
Connolly, Nora 182
Connor, Bernard xxx
Constantine, Grand Duke 125
Cook, Andrew 165
Coxe, William xxix, 68–9
Crampton, Sir John Fiennes Twisleton 85
Creagh, James 98–9, 113

Crean, Tom 188
Crimean War xxiv, xxvi, xxxiv, xli, 90,
    97–8, 100, 115, 120, 122–3, 171, 192
Cromarty, Jacqueline xxv
Cross, Anthony xxv, 171
Culloden, Battle of 13
Cunningham, Lord 19

Dashkov, Mikhail Ivanovich 48
Dashkov, Pavel 49
Dashkova, Anastasiya 49
Dashkova, Princess Ekaterina Romanovna
    xxxvi, xxxviii, 9, 36–7, 44, 46–55, 59, 192
Davitt, Michael 144, 174, 184
de Custine, Marquis 92
de Lacy (Stuart), Annabella 8
de Lacy (Boyle), Catherine 8
de Lacy, Franz Moritz 20
de Lacy (Browne), Helen 8
de Lacy (*née* von Loeser), Martha
    Phillippina 8
de Lacy, Maurice 7
de Lacy, Patrick O'Brien 7
de Lacy, Peter 3, 5, 7–9, 11–12, 192
de Lacy family 6–8, 10
de Valera, Éamon 189–91
Dease, Francis 5
Decembrist movement 43
Denny, Lady Arabella 47
Despard, Charlotte 189
Dickinson, Page Lawrence xxxiv, 99, 132–6
Dickinson, Sara xxxi
Diderot, Denis 49
Dillon, Emile (E.B. Lanin) 144
Dixon, Simon 52
Dobson, David xxv
Dostoyevsky, Fyodor 160
Doyne, William Thomas 123
Drury (Kilgallon), Isabella 131
Dublin Statistical Society 125
Dufferin, Lady (Hariot Georgina
    Hamilton-Temple-Blackwood) 145–6,
    147–54, 192–3
Dufferin, Lord (Frederick Georgina
    Hamilton-Temple-Blackwood) 124,
    147–8, 151

Dufferin Fund 148–50
Dulanty, John 190
duma 143

Eagar, Margaretta xxiv, 145–6, 168–76
East India Company 74, 82
Easter Rising xxvi, 167, 180
Edgeworth, Maria 53–4
Edgeworth, Richard Lovell 67–8
Eger, Elizabeth 49
Egger, Sabine xxvi
Elizabeth I, Empress xxiii, 3, 8–9, 94
Ems Ukaz 162, 178
Engels, Friedrich 161
Epstein, Anna Mikhailovna 158
Everest, Mary 155

Fanin, Sasha 158–9
Fedorovna, Evdokia 30
Fenians xxxiii, 91, 125, 143–4
Feodorovna, Empress Dowager Maria 43, 49
Ffolliott, Agnes 169
Ffrench, Kathleen 85, 191
Ffrench, Robert 85, 191
Ffrench (*née* Kindyakova), Sofia
    Alexandrovna 85, 191
Field, John xxiii, xxxvi–xxxvii, 192
Finland 12
Fly Sheets (*Letuchie Listki*) 161
Forbes, George, 3rd Earl of Granard xxxv,
    22–5, 27, 31–4
Fox, Stephen, 1st Baron Holland 25
Franco-Prussian War 162
Franklin, John 129
Frederick II (the Great) 9, 18
Free Russia 159–62
Free Russian Press 161
French Revolution 35, 182

Gadfly, The (Ethel Voynich) 157, 162–7
Gaelic League 183
Gannibal, Abram Petrovich 5
Gavan Duffy, George 167
George I, King 6
George III, King 20
Georgia 99, 115, 118, 127, 132–5
Gerald of Wales xxii

237

Index

Glinka, Mikhail xxxvi–xxxvii
Godkin, Edward 98
Goethe, Johann Wolfgang von 17
Gogol, Nikolay 93
Goldsmith, Oliver xxxvii
Gonne, Maud 162–3
Gordon, General Patrick xxv, 6
Gore-Booth, Constance *see* Markievicz, Constance
Gore-Booth, Henry 74, 128–32
Grachevsky, Mikhail 94
Granard, 3rd Earl of *see* Forbes, George
Great Andaman penal colony 89–90, 96
Great Exhibition, London (1851) 65
Great Famine 64, 87–8, 91, 98
Great Northern War (1700–21) xii, 7, 24, 33
Green, William Spotsford 112
Gregg, Frederick James 156
Greville-Nugent (*née* Ogilvy), Ermengarde 173
Gunning, Sir Robert 22
Gurley Flynn, Elizabeth 167

Hakluyt, Richard xxvii–xxviii
Hamilton (*née* Ryder), Catherine 47–9, 52
Hamilton, Mary 48
Hannan, Mary Josephine 149
Hartley, Janet M. 73
Hawkins-Whitshead, Elizabeth *see* le Blond, Lizzie
Hayes, Matthew Horace 99
Healy, Róisín xxvi, xxxii, 71
Herbert, Amanda 49
Heron, Denis Caulfield 125–7
Higgins, Bryan 119
Himalayas 112, 114
Hinely, Susan 159–60
Holland, 1st Baron (Stephen Fox) 25
Holroyd, Sarah ('Serena') 56–7
Hone, Joseph Maunsell xxxiv, 99, 132–6
Hooker, Sir Joseph Dalton 129
Howard-Berry, Charles 99
Hrodna province, Belarus 7–8
Huddie, Paul xxvi
Hunter, W.W. 91
Hyde, H. Montgomery 52

Imboden, Joseph 136
Imlay, Gilbert 36
Imperial Russian Army 153, 180
Indian Mutiny 89–90
Ireland, Republic of 191
Irish Free State 189
Irish Friends of Soviet Russia 189
Irvine, Frances 73
Isbjörn expedition 129–32
Ivan I 27
Ivan II 27
Ivan IV 3, 94
Ivan VI 9

Jacob, Rosamond 189
Jacobites xxxiii, 1–3, 4–7, 11, 13, 15–17, 21, 41, 44–5, 192
Jefferies, James xxxv, 22–3, 25, 29–31
Jenkinson, Anthony xxvii
Jordan, John xxv
Joseph II, Emperor 20

Kantemir, Antiochus 27
Kantemirs 5
Kara Sea 129, 132
Karageorgia, Julia 123
Karamzin, Nikolay xxxviii–xxxix, 42
Karaulov, Vasily 158, 161
Karaulova, Praskovya 158, 161
Kavanagh, Lady Harriet 72–3, 75
Keith, General James 8–9
Kennedy, Sarah 171
Kent, Rockwell xli
Kiely, Mr (visitor to St Petersburg) 16
Kilgallon (*née* Drury), Isabella 131
Kilgallon, Thomas 128, 131
Kilmaine, Baron *see* Tyrawley, 2nd Baron
Kindyakova (Ffrench), Sofia Alexandrovna 85
King, John Glen 23, 27
King, Margaret (Lady Mount Cashell) 37, 45
Kipling, Rudyard 149
Kirkwood, Harriet xli
Kirwan, Charles 75
Kishinev (Chişinău) pogrom 144, 174–5

238

Index

Knights of Malta 14, 16
Korsakovs 5
Koslov, Ivan xxxviii
Kravchinsky, Sergey *see* Stepnyak, Sergey
Kražiai massacre (1893) 160
Kremlin 103–4, 107, 139
Kropotkin, Petr xl, 157
Kurdistan 74, 116
Kyiv xxiii, 144, 178, 182
Kyivan Rus' 93

Ladies' Alpine Club 136–7
Lal, Maneesha 150
Lanin, E.B. (Emile Dillon) 144
Law, Edward Fitzgerald 123–5
le Blond, Aubrey 138–9
le Blond (Hawkins-Whitshead), Lizzie
    xxiv–xxv, xxxiv, 100, 112, 136–41
League of Book Carriers 162
Leoniv, Leon Ivanovich xxxvi
Leonowens, Anna 169
Lermontov, Mikhail xxxiii, xxxviii, 5
Leslie, Norman 183
Leslie, Shane (John Randolph) xl, 177,
    183–6
Letuchie Listki (Fly Sheets) 161
Levesque, Pierre Charles xxviii
Lithuania xxx, 98, 160, 185–6
Litvinov, Maxim 182
Loch, Emily 169
Lockhart, Robin Bruce 164
Londonderry, Marquess of *see* Vane,
    Charles William
Louis XV, King of France 18
Lviv 162, 182
Lynch, George 100
Lynch-Brennan, Margaret 172

Macartney, George, Earl Macartney xxxi,
    1, 3, 22–3, 25–34, 36
McClean, Thomas 134
McCullagh, Francis 145
McDonagh, John xxvi
MacGeoghegan, James 17
McGilligan, Patrick 190
Mackay, Aeneas 116

McKeon, Kathy 175
McLean, Thomas xxvi
McLoughlin, Barry xxvi
MacMurrough Kavanagh, Arthur xxiii,
    63–4, 72–82, 128
MacMurrough Kavanagh, Thomas 64,
    72–6, 80–2
Macpherson, James xxxvii
Main, Mrs *see* le Blond, Lizzie
Makitovitsky, Dushan 184
Malik Qasim Mirza 78–80
Malta 16
Malvina, Miss (Bunbury's companion) 107
Maria Alexandrovna, Grand Duchess xxiv
Marjanishvili, Kote 165
Markham, Albert Hastings 129–32
Markham, Clements 129
Markievicz, Casimir Dunin 177–8, 180–2
Markievicz (Gore-Booth), Constance 145,
    177–82, 186
Markievicz, Stanislas 181
Marsh, Narcissus xxix
Martens, Ludwig Karlovich 189
Marx, Eleanor 161
Mashkov, Ilya xli
Massie, Robert 176
Matochkin Strait 129
Matterhorn 112
Matweitsch family xxxix
Mauritius (monk) xxiii
Mayo, Lord *see* Bourke, Richard
    Southwell
Mayo (*née* Wyndham), Lady Blanche
    89, 91–2
Mazzini, Giuseppe 156
Mentzel, John-Daniel xxix
Menzikoff, Prince xxix
Merezhkovsky, Dmitri xl
Mezentsov, General Nikolai 157
Mezzeroff, Professor 143
Mickiewicz, Adam 166
Millevoye, Lucien 162
Moberly, Charles H. 123
Mont Blanc 112, 137
Montefiore, Simon Sebag 100
Moore, Arthur 144

Index

Moore, George Henry 75
Moore, Maurice 75
Moore, Thomas xxxviii
Morgan, Elizabeth 48–9, 57
Morris, William 159, 161
Moscow 2, 69, 84, 87, 106, 151
Mottley, John xxix
Mount Cashell, Lady (Margaret King) 37, 45
Mount Cashell, Earl, Stephen 37
Muravyev, Count 85
Murdoch, Steve xxv, 6
Murphy, David xxvi, 123
Murphy, Mary 144

Napoleonic Wars xxiii, xxxiv, 5, 7, 10, 16, 35, 60, 63, 98
Neva, River 29, 65, 90, 97, 109
Newman, Agnes 167
Nicholas I 11, 65, 93, 110, 171
Nicholas II xl, 143, 168, 172, 180
    daughters, see OTMA
Nill, Annie 167
Nizhny Novgorod xxii, 73–4, 86–7, 114–15, 123, 158
Novaya Zemlya 129, 131
Nunan, Seán 189

O'Brien, Admiral 9
O'Brien, Daniel 6
O'Brien, William xl
O'Connell, Daniel 70–1
O'Connor, Emmet xxvi, 189
O'Connor, Sir Frederick 188
O'Conor, Sir Nicholas Roderick 85
O'Donnell, Peadar 165
O'Donovan, Edmond 99
O'Dwyer, Sir Michael Francis 99
O'Faolain, Sean 178–9
O'Flaherty, Roderick 17
Ogilvy (Greville-Nugent), Ermengarde 173
O'Halloran, Sylvester 17
O'Hara, Anthony 9, 13–17, 21, 43–4, 192
O'Hara, Charles 14–15
O'Hara, Charles Hubert 13
O'Hara, James *see* Tyrawley, 2nd Baron
O'Neill, Charles 122

Oppenheimer, Melanie 150
O'Reilly, Alexander 41
O'Reilly, Jenny (Jenny Quin; Evgeniya Ivanovna Vyazemskaya) xxxviii, 36–7, 39–45, 192
O'Reilly family (Breifne) 41, 45
Ó Rinn, Liam xl
Orlov, Count Alexei Grigoryevich 53–4
Ormond, 2nd Duke of (James Butler) 6
O'Rourke, Count Cornelius 8, 12
O'Rourke, Archbishop Edward 10
O'Rourke, Count John 9, 18–21
O'Rourke, Count Joseph 7, 11–12
O'Rourke (*née* Stuart), Martha 8
O'Rourke, Count Nicholas 12
O'Rourke family 6–8, 10
Orr, James xxxix–xl
O'Shea, Major 64
Ossian xxxvi
Ostafyevo 41–2
OTMA (Olga, Tatiana, Maria, Anastasiya), daughters of Nicholas II and Alexandra 168, 172–3, 176
Ottoman Empire 12, 22, 113–14, 118, 133–4, 151, 163
Ouseley, Sir Gore xxxvi, 84

Panin, Nikita 29
Panjdeh Incident 124
Paul I 171
Percheron, Adelaide Victoria xxxvi
Persia 132–3
Persian Empire 114, 133–4
Persian Revolution (1909) 133
Peter I (the Great) xxii–xxiii, xxxiii, xxxv, 1, 4, 6, 30, 58
Peter III 33, 53–4
Petrograd 181, 188 *see also* St Petersburg
Pitcher, Harvey 171
Plunket, Frederica 112
Plunkett, Francis Richard 85
Pobedonostsev, Konstantin 163
Poe, Marshall xxvii
Poland xxvi–xxvii, xxx, xxxii, xl, 43, 71, 98, 117, 126, 144, 167, 180–1, 192
    partition xxxiv, 12, 65, 70, 185
Polish Relief Fund 162

240

Polish revolution (1831) 108
Polish Succession, War of 12, 192
Pollock, Arthur 47, 63
Ponsonby, John Brabazon 84–5
Poor Law (1838) 67
Poyning's Law 32
Pravda 165
Prior, James 5
Protestants xxii, 32, 35, 71, 86, 88, 114, 172
Pugachev revolt 60
Pushkin, Alexander xxxiii, xxxviii, 5, 42

Quin, Henry xxxvi
Quin, Jenny *see* O'Reilly, Jenny
Quinlan, James 5

Rada, Central 181
Radziwill, Princess Catherine 163
Raffalovich, Sophie xl
Randolph, Sir Thomas xxi
Rasputin 175, 188
'Rayford Ramble' 77
Red Army 182
Red Terror 182
Reese, Roger 153
Reilly, Sidney (Sigmund Rosenblum) 164–5
Riga 8–10, 192
Risorgimento 164
Roman Catholic Church 189–91
Roosevelt, Priscilla 59–60
Rosenblum, Sigmund (Sidney Reilly) 164–5
Rosier, Madame xxxix
Rou, Alexander Arturovich 123
Rowe, Arthur 122–3
Russell, William Howard xxiv, 98, 120–2
Russia Company 2, 23–4
Russian Empire 2, 4, 63, 86, 98–100, 115–16, 118, 122–3, 127, 128, 132–3, 135–6, 141, 143–4, 160, 173–4, 177–8, 180–1, 185–6, 191–2
Russian Free Press Fund 161
Russian Orthodox Church xxxiii, 32, 65, 71, 92
Russian Revolution (1905) 143
Russian Revolutions (1917) xxvi, 143, 153, 177, 181

Russian Volunteer Fleet 181
Russo-Circassian Wars 98
Russo-Japanese War (1904–5) 143–5, 173–4
Russo-Swedish War 12
Russo-Turkish Wars xxxiii, 5, 7, 12, 113
Ryall, John 156
Ryder (Hamilton), Catherine 47

St Petersburg xxiii, 4, 28–30, 58, 86–7, 99, 102, 106, 109, 120, 151, 153–4, 158, 170
   Winter Palace 9, 152, 170
Saltykov-Shchedrin, Mikhail 158
Savage, John xxx
Scott, Hamish 28
Scutari 99
Serbia 12
Seven Years War 33
Shanghai 191
Shaw, George Bernard 159, 161, 165
Sheehy-Skeffington, Hanna 189
Sher Ali Afridi 89–90, 96 [I *think* the references to 'Afridi' on pp. 90, 96 should be 'Sher Ali'?]
Sher Ali Khan 96
Sheridan, Richard Brinsley xxxvii
Shlisselburg Prison 90, 94, 96
Shostakovich, Dmitryridi 165
Siberia xxxiii, 69, 81, 87, 92–4, 98, 145, 158, 161, 188
Simbirsk (Ulyanovsk) 85, 191
Simonov Monastery, Moscow 71
Smith, Henry 5
Smith, Leigh 130
Society of Friends of Russian Freedom (SFRF) 159–60, 162
Solodyankina, Olga 170
Somerton, Viscount (Welbore Ellis Agar) 47, 63
Sophia of Achaea 27
Sosnovka 183–4
Spa, Belgium 35–6, 39–40, 47–9
Spenser, Edmund xxi
Stanislaus, King of Poland 18
Stanley, Lady Maria Josepha 56–7
Steele, Sarah 73

241

Index

Stepnyak, Sergey (Sergey Kravchinsky) 157–62, 164
Sterne, Laurence xxxvii
Stoker, Bram xl
Stuart (*née* de Lacy), Annabella 8
Stuart, Lady Jane 28
Stuart (O'Rourke), Martha 8
Stuart, James 6
Sveaborg Fortress, Finland 105, 107

Tajikistan 95
Taratuta, Evgeniya 157, 167
Tassie, James xxxv–xxxvi
Tbilisi 78, 84, 113, 127, 135, 171
Thompson, Elizabeth (Lady Butler) xl–xli
Tighe, Elizabeth xxvii
Tighe, William xxvii
Tolstoy, Leo xxxvi–xxxvii, xl, 144, 184–5
Tolstoy, Sophia 185
Townsend, Horatio 35–6
Transcaucasia 113–16, 118, 132 *see also* Caucasus
Trans-Siberian Railway 100, 138–9
Treaty of Amiens (1802) 16
Treaty of Limerick (1691) 1, 4
Treaty of Ryswick (1697) 4
Trench, Herbert xl
Trirogoff, Mr 126
Troitskoe 47, 59–60
Tsarskoe Selo 105, 151, 170, 172, 176
Tsebrikova, Maria 158
Turberville, George xxi
Turgenev, Ivan xxxviii, xl, 42–3
Turner, Richard 122
Tyndall, John 112
Tyrawley, 2nd Baron (and Baron Kilmaine) (James O'Hara) 22–3, 25, 27, 30–1

Ukraine 145, 162, 178–9, 181
Ulyanovsk (Simbirsk) 85, 191
Ural Mountains xxxiii
Urmia, Lake 80–1
USSR 143, 189

Valuev Circular 162, 178
Vane, Charles William (Marquess of Londonderry) xxxi, 85, 195
Varvarin, Battle of 12
Victoria, Queen xxiv, 147, 174
Vienna 83–4
Vikings xxii
Vilnius 185
Volga, River xxvii–xxviii, 73–4, 77, 86, 113, 115, 120, 158
von Benckendorff, Count Alexander Konstantinovich 183
von Loeser (de Lacy), Martha Phillippina 8
Vorontsov, Count Simon 52
Voynich, Ethel Lilian Boole (Lily) xxiv, xxxvii, 145–6, 155–67, 192
Voynich, Mikhail Wilfrid 157, 161, 164, 166
Voynich manuscript 162
Vyazemsky, Aleksandr Alekseyevich 44
Vyazemsky, Prince Andrey Ivanovich 39–42
Vyazemskaya, Evgeniya Ivanovna *see* O'Reilly, Jenny
Vyazemsky, Petr Andreyevich xxxviii, 41–3

Wakhan Corridor, Afghanistan 96
Wall, Richard 22
Walpole, Robert xxxiii, 98
Walsh, Revd Robert 65
Warsaw 12, 126–7, 133, 157, 171
Watson, Robert Spence 160
Wheatley, Francis 47
White, Richard, Lord Berehaven xxiv
White, Thomas 64
White Army 182
White Russians 191
Wilde, Oscar 143–4
Williamite War 1
Wills, Rebecca xxv, 6
Wilmot, Edward 47
Wilmot, Katherine xxiii, xxviii, xxxv, xxxviii, 36–7, 46–7, 49–50, 51, 53–5, 56–7, 60, 192

Index

Wilmot (Bradford), Martha xxiii, xxxv–xxxvi, xxxviii–xxxiv, 35–8, 46–7, 49–55, 56–8, 60, 84, 174, 192
Wilson, Charlotte 157
Wilson, Tim xxvi
Wogan, Charles 6
Wolff, Larry xxxiv
Wollstonecraft, Mary 36–7
Wolseley, Viscount Garnet 157–8
Wood, Revd David 64, 73, 75–82
World War I 153–4, 180, 188
World War II 166
Wortley Montagu, Lady Mary 28

Wylie, Richard 171
Wyndham, Blanche (Lady Mayo) 89, 91–2
Wyse, Sir Thomas xxxiv

Young Ireland xxxiii
Youvatshev, Ivan 94
Ystridde-Orshanski, Ilya Grigoryevich 142
Yuryevets 122
Yusopovs 5

Zaroubin, Georgy 190
Zhukovsky, Vasily xxxviii, 93
Zhyvotivka (Zywotowka) 178–82